How to Do *Everything* with

GarageBand™

Emile Menasché

McGraw-Hill/Osborne

New York Chicago San Francisco Lisbon
London Madrid Mexico City Milan New Delhi
San Juan Seoul Singapore Sydney Toronto

The McGraw·Hill Companies

McGraw-Hill/Osborne
2100 Powell Street, 10th Floor
Emeryville, California 94608
U.S.A.

To arrange bulk purchase discounts for sales promotions, premiums, or fund-raisers, please contact **McGraw-Hill**/Osborne at the above address. For information on translations or book distributors outside the U.S.A., please see the International Contact Information page immediately following the index of this book.

How to Do Everything with GarageBand™

1234567890 CUS CUS 01987654

ISBN 0-07-225676-1

Publisher	Brandon A. Nordin
Vice President &	
Associate Publisher	Scott Rogers
Acquisitions Editor	Marjorie McAneny
Project Editor	Jennifer Malnick
Acquisitions Coordinator	Agatha Kim
Technical Editor	Mike Levine
Copy Editor	Dennis Weaver
Proofreader	Claire Splan
Indexer	Claire Splan
Composition	ITC, Melinda Moore Lytle
Illustrator	ITC, Melinda Moore Lytle

This book was composed with Corel VENTURA™ Publisher.

Dedication

For Bridget, Annie, and Rebecca—with love, Dad.

About the Author

Emile Menasché has been using computers to make music—and writing about it—for fifteen years; his work has appeared in *Men's Health, PC Magazine, Guitar World, Musician, Keyboard, Electronic Musician, Home Recording,* and many others. He's the author of *The Desktop Studio* (Hal Leonard) and is Editor-in-Chief of *In Tune Monthly,* a music magazine for teenage music students and their teachers.

Emile's composing credits include the feature film *Parallel Sons*, the television program *B. Smith with Style,* and the upcoming documentary *American Farm*. As a guitarist and producer, he's worked with artists such as Dean Friedman, David Amram, New Middle Class, Monica Zane, The Significant Others, and his own band, Speak the Language. You can come say hi at www.speakthelanguage.net and www.menaschemedia.com.

Contents

Foreword

Not that long ago, the idea of using a computer as a recording studio or musical instrument was unthinkable to most musicians. Computers were for working, not playing, and the complex musical programs on the market were inscrutable to all but the most tech-savvy engineers.

Even today, while there are some fabulous professional recording and sequencing programs available for musicians, most of them are expensive, come with a manual the size of a phonebook and are just was well-written, and seem like they were created to scare away the majority of musicians.

Enter GarageBand. When Apple bought Emagic, maker of the recording program Logic, I suspected they would deliver an easy-to-use recording tool for *musicians*—not engineers. Mission accomplished. GarageBand was created for musicians and hobbyists who want to compose, create, and record with the ease of use of their 1980s-style multitrack cassette recorder, combined with the tools and effects of today's modern digital recording studio.

When I first tried GarageBand, the colorful audio tracks reminded me of Legos and the countless hours I spent playing with my kids showing them the creative possibilities inside of those buckets of colored plastic. Building your song in GarageBand is as simple as putting Lego pieces together. Start with one of the built-in drum loops, add some chords, some bass, some vocals, and with a little imagination thrown into the mix you've got a composition you can preserve and enjoy for years to come.

While GarageBand cannot replace the higher-end programs like Logic for professional applications, it does let you create a remarkably great-sounding recording, mix it, and burn it to a CD or export to iTunes to be shared via the Internet or enjoyed on an iPod.

A special note to the 60 million+ guitarists around the globe: You *must* read this book. A guitarist himself, Emile shows you the ins and outs of GarageBand's many fantastic built-in guitar effects—including reverb, echo, chorus, and the program's surprisingly rich guitar sounds for gain and distortion. He'll also show you how to use "technology-equipped guitars" to play all of the built-in software instruments like piano, strings, and lush synth sounds.

Most folks are absolutely stunned when they hear just how good GarageBand sounds. The simplicity of the program lets musicians spend less time on the technical details and more on the part they love—creating music. Let Emile be your guide to understanding the features of this powerful program and begin using GarageBand to make your *own* music!

Enjoy.

—Patrick Cummings, president, Brian Moore Guitars
and iGuitar designer

Acknowledgments

Many people were instrumental in the creation of this book, and all of them went way beyond the call of duty to make this happen. The first shout-out has to go to the entire team at McGraw Hill/Osborne. To Margie McAneny, who jumped on the idea of doing a GarageBand book and championed me as its author, very special thanks. Your encouragement, patience, and wisdom made the impossible possible.

To Jennifer Malnick, I bow very low: You actually made the arduous process of turning my manuscript into publishable material fun, even if you didn't know it at the time. Also, thanks to Agatha Kim, copyeditor Dennis Weaver, and proofreader Claire Splan, who kept the project moving forward smoothly.

Tech editor, friend, and *Electronic Musician* stalwart (and fellow Mets sufferer) Mike Levine's insight and good humor were both a help and comfort throughout this book. Mike, an accomplished composer, also provided an insightful entry into the Voices of the Community collection.

Jon Chappell (author of *Build Your Own PC Recording Studio* among many books) generously introduced me to the folks at McGraw-Hill/Osborne and also took time out of his busy schedule to add his voice to the community.

Thanks to the other people who took the time to share their ideas in Voices of the Community pieces: Will Edwards, Brian Culbertson, Ken Micalef, Dave Simons, Danny Miles, Randy Fuchs, Kirk McElhearn, Marc Schonbrun, and Pat Cummings of Brian Moore custom Guitars, whose GarageBand-friendly iGuitar is bringing a traditionalist instrument into the 21st Century. Thanks to Guy Hart-Davis (author of *How to Do Everything with iLife '04*), whose insight into using iTunes and troubleshooting OS X was especially valuable.

I'm grateful to the folks at Apple who answered questions, provided tips, and helped secure software and images, especially Xander Soren, Quincy Carroll, and Christine Wilhelmy. Thanks also to the people at Marshall Amplifiers, Pro Co cables, M-Audio, Edirol, and Yamaha for letting us use images of their products. A special tip of the cap to my colleagues at *Guitar World* and, especially, to the crew at *In Tune Monthly,* who provided contacts, ideas, and encouragement. Their commitment to developing musicians extends beyond the confines of their own publications.

Finally, thanks to my family—Amy, Bridget, Annie, and Rebecca—for your patience, support, and endless cups of tea.

Introduction

Welcome to GarageBand. If you've tried the program, you may already know that it boasts that rare combination in the world of software: it's user friendly *and* powerful. To put it in very technical terms, it's a lot of fun to use.

The concept of creating music on a computer is not all that new: Commercial recording studios and professional producers, composers, and engineers have been using computers since the 1980s; today they're standard equipment for composers, home recordists, remixers, teachers, and more. With its ability to record and edit music in a variety of ways, the computer has revolutionized the way music is made and distributed.

But for most of its time as a music-making tool, computer software has been a bit of a boondoggle for the musician who didn't consider him or herself a computer person: The software can be expensive and the features, though powerful and seductive, can also be a little overwhelming. Musicians who are used to the simple pleasure of playing their instrument, or even the basic technology of using a tape recorder, often find professional programs to be overkill. I've known more than a few people who've bought a whole computer-music system only to put it away within weeks and go back to their old tape recorder, hoping the next software release will be a comfortable fit. It can be an expensive dream.

In all fairness, most manufacturers have tried to reach the emerging computer musician with "lite" versions of their software. Unfortunately, these generally are as complicated as the professional programs from which they're derived, but lack their best features. It's like going to the trouble of learning a new language, but not being allowed to use any verbs or adjectives.

GarageBand is just the opposite. It has the sexiest features—sweet-sounding Software Instruments, elastic Real Instrument loops, and the ability to record multitrack audio—and does away with the most complex editing routines that only the real hardcore computer musician needs. The program is all about action—the verbs, and expression, the adjectives. It may not do everything, but like a sporty two-seat roadster, what it does, it does with style.

Who Should Read This Book

This book is intended for musicians, composers, producers, teachers, and anyone else who wants to make music with GarageBand. No previous experience with a computer as a musical tool is necessary, though you will need to have a basic knowledge about how to use Mac OS X. But this book isn't only for the complete beginner: If you've worked with other music software and are interested in learning which of your favorite routines you can do with GarageBand, you'll learn it here too.

GarageBand can be a bridge between the new and the veteran computer musician. I had a recent experience that brought this out. I was holed in my office with my PowerBook, going over parts of the book, when my nine-year-old daughter, Annie, popped in for a visit. I'd done most of my work in GarageBand in my music studio, and this was really my first opportunity to sit down and show her the program.

We booted up and started with a blank slate, then opened the GarageBand's loop browser—where you can search for and audition Apple Loops—and did some listening together. She picked out a very basic funk drumbeat and, being a beginning cellist, immediately wanted to hear some classical strings with it. We grabbed a lively loop and then started adding more parts. Finally, I opened the keyboard window and we played in a simple melody with the mouse. A drag here, a copy and paste there, and in about 10 minutes we had the beginnings of a real song.

But the cool thing about the experience wasn't what we ended up with; it was how we got there. Annie and I were able to work on this song together, and because we weren't playing instruments, we were equals (my guitar and my experience as a musician can sometimes be a barrier when I want to "jam" with my kids; it's easy for them to just listen, get lost, or get bored). Here there was no prize for technical expertise or theoretical knowledge. She picked the loops and decided where to put them, and I showed her how to stretch and transpose and otherwise make them her own. I learned that she likes classical music but also enjoys some of the "world" music flavors, that she prefers lively rhythms (she insisted we go back to the original sprightly tempo at which we started), and that she has an ear for putting the pieces together. She did more than just pick the parts—she told me why she had chosen them.

Soon I had to get back to work, Mom was calling, and Riley the dog had decided to see if he could use me (and the PowerBook) for a landing strip (he's practicing to become a projectile). And so we saved the song and closed up shop, and Annie took Riley for a timeout.

But the story didn't quite end there. I popped into the kitchen a while later and mentioned to my wife what Annie and I had done together. "I know," she said. "She told us. She was all excited." And I think that says it all about the potential of a program like GarageBand. It is an opportunity to explore and to share, to play and to ponder, to listen and to be heard. If you've used more professional music products, you'll be amazed by how quickly GarageBand cuts through the red tape and gets you making music. And if you've never made music with a computer before—or never made music at all before—you'll be amazed by how easy it really is.

How This Book Is Organized

How to Do Everything with GarageBand is organized into four basic parts. Part I, "Get to Know GarageBand," shows you a quick overview of GarageBand's basic features and concepts, and helps you install and configure your computer. Even if you're an experienced computer musician, you may want to check this section out to get "the lay of the land." Part II, "Make Music with GarageBand," is where we start making music. If you already have GarageBand on your system, you might want to jump to these chapters and go through some of the exercises outlined in them. These are meant to be a jumping off point for your own work, as opposed to a step-by-step tutorial. Part III, "Create a Finished Master," takes you a little deeper into the program and also into the general concepts of computer-based music production. Here you'll learn how to edit, mix, add effects, and export your songs to iTunes. Many of the ideas discussed in Part III are as creative as they are technical. You'll find some stuff that's definitely not available in a typical owner's manual or help screen. Part IV, "Take GarageBand Beyond Its Horizons," offers a look at ways you can expand on your studio by adding peripheral hardware and additional software. It also outlines ways to share your songs with the world at large—and how to solve problems—or eliminate them *before* they occur.

Finally, the Appendixes offer a glossary and a list of resources. Online, you can also find "Missing Appendix C," which includes setup diagrams to show you how you might configure your studio.

Conventions Used in This Book

Throughout the book you'll find references to menus, switches, controls, and commands. When we refer to a menu command, we detail it like so: Menu | Command. For example, File | Save means open the File menu and use the Save command. If you see that vertical line, you know it's a menu. For keyboard commands, we use small caps to indicate any keys you must press to execute the routine. For example, press COMMAND-S for Save. Many of GarageBand's features have keyboard equivalents, and they're real timesavers (see the inside back cover of this book for more details).

You'll also find some special callouts sprinkled throughout the book:

 *Tips* alert you to timesaving features or give you ways to go beyond the basics.

Notes let you know what to look out for in the book, and offer some essential background information about a feature or action.

 *Cautions* *let you know to be wary about what you're doing. Cautions aren't necessarily a sign of danger, just a note to pay special attention.*

 As we were finishing this book, Apple released version 1.1 of GarageBand, which offered some important enhancements and improvements to the program. Many of these are highlighted with a special icon, and should be of particular interest to people who started with an earlier version of the program.

You'll also find a variety of different sidebars throughout the book. *Did You Know?* sections give you some special insight into GarageBand and computer music in general. *How to* sidebars teach you specific procedures, often with a step-by-step rundown of how it's done. *Voices from the Community* sidebars let you hear from other people in the computer music community, including recording artists, producers, composers, critics, and more. Finally, the special section in the middle of the book, "Cooking with GarageBand," gives you some hands-on ways to create your own sounds and perform some interesting tricks that take GarageBand beyond the fundamentals. Guitarists and sound designers take special note: Here you can learn how to put your own imprint on the sounds you create with GarageBand's power amp simulation and Software Instruments.

Have Fun

GarageBand is a hands-on, fun musical experience. It's time to turn on the computer, get some sounds happening, and start making some music. I hope this book will be a worthy companion on your journey.

Part I

Get to Know GarageBand

Chapter 1

Get Started with GarageBand

How to…

- Differentiate between Real Instrument, Software Instrument, and loop-based tracks
- Identify an audio (Real Instrument) waveform
- Identify sequencer (Software Instrument) data
- Learn the user interface
- Understand the timeline
- Identify the basic tools
- Use the Transport
- Navigate the menus
- Understand tempo and time signature
- Open the built-in keyboard

GarageBand, like the other elements of Apple's iLife suite, offers an interesting paradox. In some ways, it's an entry-level program: With its simple interface and "instant gratification" vibe, it's sure to appeal to you nonmusicians who've always felt excluded by the music-making process—or to musicians who have felt intimidated by recording technology. But GarageBand also boasts some powerful high-tech features under the hood—tools like Software Instruments and time- and pitch-stretching. These make it appealing to professionals who want to get an idea or two down without going through the hassle of booting up a more elaborate piece of software, or who want to use GarageBand to augment an application such as Apple's Logic Pro 6.

In this chapter, we'll take a stroll around GarageBand's user interface and learn a few key terms that will come up again and again throughout the book. Before we open the garage door, however, let's take a look at the technological developments that have paved the way to GarageBand.

First, A Little Background

In the mid 1980s, computers began to revolutionize music. Although multitrack audio recorders had been around for decades, and the sequencer—a data recording device that allows musicians to program a musical performance instead of having to play it real time—had become an accepted part of the electronic musician's arsenal, it wasn't until the late 1980s that the two technologies would begin to meet and take shape within the confines of the personal computer.

Over the course of the 1990s, software that combined audio and MIDI ("Musical Instrument Digital Interface," a data standard that's widely used in sequencers) proliferated. Pretty soon, the software began to include audio effects and sophisticated mixing capabilities, thus reducing the need for expensive hardware. The final piece of the puzzle came only in the last few years: thanks to their sophisticated processors, modern computers are capable of providing the instruments themselves.

Nowadays, computers are at the heart of almost every recording studio, from the plushest pro facility to the most streamlined laptop-based studio-in-a-backpack.

> NOTE   *A program that combines audio and MIDI recording is called a digital audio workstation (DAW), or a digital audio sequencer. Not all DAWs include MIDI, but the term is commonly used to describe digital audio sequencers.*

Why the history lesson? GarageBand is an amalgamation of all of this high technology. It offers multitrack audio recording, multitrack MIDI recording, built-in effects, and software-based instruments. Not only that, GarageBand uses technology (which Apple first provided in its application Soundtrack) that allows you to change the tempo of a prerecorded audio file without changing its pitch, and change pitch without changing tempo. This feature—called time stretching and pitch shifting—gives you, the *maestro,* enormous flexibility. You can use and reuse the same segments of audio—called loops—at a number of different tempos and keys. Now that's power!

Did you know?   Acid Reign

Real-time time/pitch stretching of audio files was pioneered by Sonic Foundry's software package for Windows called Acid (Sonic Foundry is now owned by Sony). Acid became so popular in music production circles, that "Acidized" audio files became a standard in loop-based audio production. Apple Soundtrack directly imports Acidized files, but at this writing, you'll need to use the free Loop Utility (see Chapter 13) to convert the file.

Say Hello to GarageBand

Although GarageBand can tackle some complex tasks, it's also designed to be accessible for first-time computer musicians. As a veteran of music software and hardware, I've seen the technology get more powerful—and more complex. Typically, pro computer musicians, audio engineers, and producers must contend with multiple windows, phonebook-sized owners' manuals, and menus and command structures that are as dense and scary as a *Lord of the Rings* battle scene. For the demands of professional recording, these esoteric commands make or break a project. But for musicians, they can get in the way of the music.

GarageBand (see Figure 1-1) keeps things to a reasonable minimum. It provides you with the tools you need to make music, without burdening you with the complex setup and configuration routines required by a so-called "professional" audio workstation program. Can it do everything that a reasonably equipped audio workstation can do? No. In fact, there are a few features that would enhance the program without making it overly complicated (see the "Wish List" section later in the chapter). But if you're looking for a quick and easy way to write, record, edit, and mix a song, GarageBand is hard to beat.

FIGURE 1-1   Say "hello" to GarageBand. Its combination of audio, MIDI, and loop-based production makes music fast and fun—no matter your previous experience.

Understand the Basic Features

As I mentioned above, GarageBand helps you produce music in a number of different ways. It works as a multitrack audio recorder, a sequencer, and a loop-based production tool. Before we dig into these features, let's take a look at how each one works and complements the others. We'll learn about a few key elements of the typical music-production workstations (computer music veterans can feel free to skip to the next section).

Real Instruments: Multitrack Audio Recording and Playback

A multitrack recorder is a device that can record and play back more than one audio track at a time. This technology was first developed with analog tape, and later made its way to the digital domain. It's been at the heart of modern music production for nearly 50 years.

The cool thing about a multitrack is that it lets you record tracks one at a time and combine them into an arrangement. With a traditional two-track tape recorder, when you record over the same section of tape a second time, you erase whatever material previously existed. With a multitrack, you not only keep the original material, but you can hear it play back as you record the new stuff. This practice is called overdubbing. Figure 1-2 shows how a multitrack works.

NOTE   *A linear multitrack tape deck is a powerful tool, but when you substitute a hard disk for tape, the medium becomes even mightier. With a hard disk, you can record many versions of the same track without erasing the original. Even more important, you can edit the material you record without changing the original in any way. This type of editing has revolutionized the music business in recent years. We'll cover editing throughout the book, but it will receive special attention in Chapter 7.*

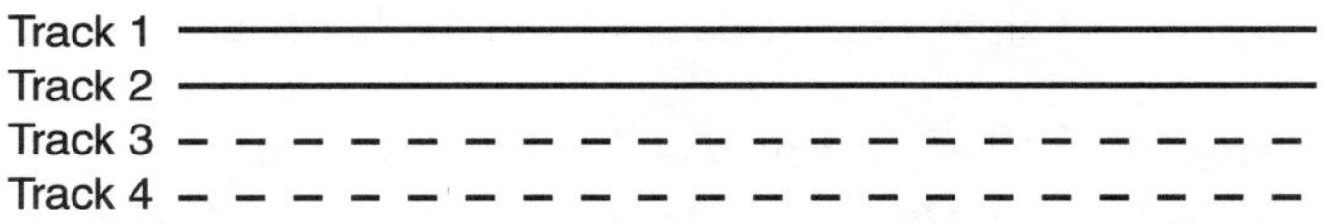

FIGURE 1-2   In this illustration of a multitrack recording, the solid tracks were recorded first. The tracks depicted by a dashed line were recorded later, without erasing the first.

Digital Audio (Real Instruments)

GarageBand's Real Instrument tracks are an example of random-access multitrack audio recording. With the aid of an audio interface (you can use your computer's internal audio inputs or a third-party device), GarageBand converts an analog audio signal (such as the output of a microphone or guitar) into digital data and stores it on your hard disk in a special file format called AIFF. Once it's on disk, the file is represented by a digital waveform, as shown here. This is what you'll see when you work with one of GarageBand's Real Instrument regions:

NOTE *In GarageBand, you work with segments called* regions, *which point to the original file. But while these regions represent an audio file, the edits you make on them do not affect the original data in the file. You can cut up and move regions around the arrangement, while the original file remains intact.*

We'll learn how to read and work with digital waveforms starting in Chapter 3, but for now it's important to note how audio files, which represent actual audio recordings, differ from MIDI data, which consists of commands that trigger a device so that it makes sounds.

Sequencing (Software Instruments)

The concept of sequencing can be a little confusing when you're new to it, but in practice it's not that intimidating. Here's the story: A sequencer is used in audio production, but it doesn't actually record or play back audio. Instead, a sequencer records commands, played by a device called a *controller,* and then feeds those commands to a separate device (sometimes known as a *slave*), which produces the actual sound. Figure 1-3 shows how this works in the hardware realm.

NOTE *The controller and the sound module can be the same device. This is commonly the case when a keyboard synthesizer acts as both controller and sound source.*

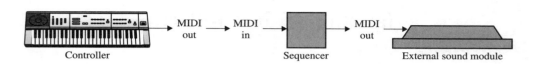

| FIGURE 1-3 | The controller sends commands to the sequencer, which stores them in memory and uses them to trigger the sound module. |

NOTE

Although not referred to specifically by the name "MIDI sequencer," GarageBand's Software Instrument tracks behave much like the tracks found in any MIDI sequencer (such as Apple/Emagic's Logic series). We'll cover MIDI in more depth in Chapters 6 and 8, but for now you should know that MIDI messages are used to tell GarageBand's Software Instruments what notes to play, and also controls other aspects of their sound and performance.

Sequencer Data

GarageBand's Software Instrument tracks record sequencer data, as shown here. Each horizontal bar represents a note.

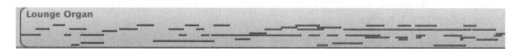

TIP

GarageBand lets you alter the pitch, placement in time, duration, and other qualities of individual notes (or groups of notes). This is a powerful feature for composing, arranging—and for fixing mistakes.

Loop-Based Production

Linear audio tracks—the kind you'd record on a tape recorder—are all well and good when you know what you want to play, but loop-based production—the assembly of audio tracks from prerecorded loops—has become a powerful alternative for composers and producers who want to go beyond the limitations of their own ability to play and record performances in real time.

In loop-based audio production, you incorporate small, prerecorded snippets of audio into your songs. Usually, these loops are rhythmic sections of music—drum loops are probably most common—but they can also be riffs, chord progressions,

Did you know?

Jammin' with Jam Pack

On its own, GarageBand is a fun and capable program, and comes with enough loops and effects to get you started. But Apple's Jam Pack, which includes a ton of cool loops and great effects, is a valuable enhancement. We'll include exercises and procedures for both standard and Jam Pack–enhanced GarageBand sessions, but if you're planning to get beyond the basics of what GarageBand can do, I highly recommend that you add Jam Pack to your wish list.

and even short melodies. When working with loops, the challenge is in getting them all to fit together and play back at the same tempo and key. With a conventional DAW, it can be very difficult to integrate these loops without diminishing their sound quality.

Fortunately, GarageBand saves you from this tedious task. It automatically matches any Apple Loop to the song's current tempo and key signature, even if the original was recorded at a completely different speed and pitch. We'll cover loops in more depth in Chapter 5.

 *Real Instrument tracks that you record yourself are not encoded with loop information.*

Learn the User Interface

GarageBand's user interface is designed to give you direct access to the tools you need to make music. One way it does this is by keeping the tools themselves to a minimum. Another is by making just about every feature and command available from the main window, shown in Figure 1-4.

Timeline

The timeline (see Figure 1-5) is where most of the action takes place. Like most music software, GarageBand lets you arrange the elements of your song in a grid. Each track is displayed in its own row. At the top of the timeline is the beat ruler, which displays the song's time duration in bars and beats (for more on bars and beats, see the sidebar "Music 101"). The playhead shows the current song position; you can drag it to move through the song.

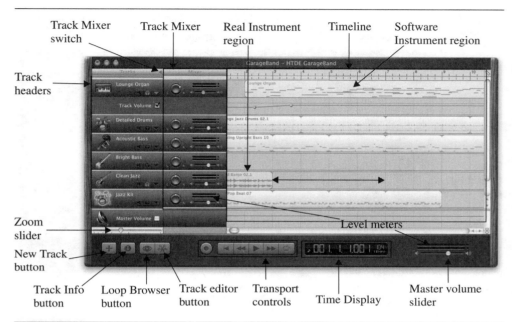

Track Mixer switch · Track Mixer · Real Instrument region · Timeline · Software Instrument region · Track headers · Zoom slider · New Track button · Track Info button · Loop Browser button · Track editor button · Transport controls · Time Display · Master volume slider · Level meters

FIGURE 1-4   Most of the action in GarageBand takes places in the main "GarageBand" window.

 GarageBand's beat ruler does not show absolute time—that is, hours, minutes, and seconds. However, you can see the absolute duration of your song in the Time Display.

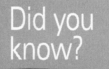

Love Triangles

Whenever you see a triangle in the GarageBand windows, take a second to click on it. These are switches that can be used to reveal more information or parameters in a window or section of a window. Examples include the Track Mixer switch in the main window, the Details switch in the Track Info Inspectors, and the Advanced switch in the Editors.

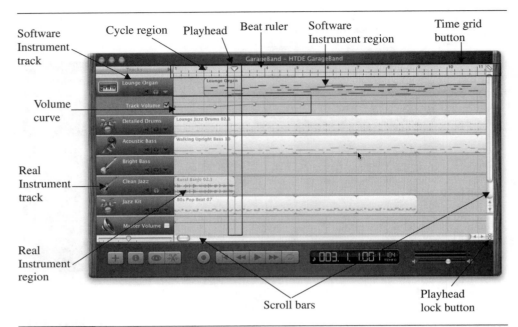

Software Instrument track — Cycle region — Playhead — Beat ruler — Software Instrument region — Time grid button

Volume curve

Real Instrument track

Real Instrument region

Scroll bars

Playhead lock button

FIGURE 1-5   The GarageBand timeline shows all the elements of each project, including Software Instrument tracks and regions, loop tracks and regions, audio tracks and regions, and volume curves.

Track Headers

Track headers (see Figure 1-6) show names and icons of the various instrument tracks, and let you set the playback status of the tracks with Mute and Solo buttons. You can expand a track header to show the track's volume curve.

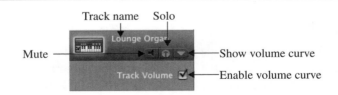

Track name — Solo

Mute — Show volume curve — Enable volume curve

FIGURE 1-6   The track header

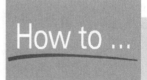

Playhead Lock, Stock, and Barrel

The Playhead is probably the most important control in GarageBand. Not only does it let you locate to different parts of your song, it also serves as an editing tool (for example, you use it to set the position at which you can split and paste regions in the timeline), and as an indicator of your system's resources (when the Playhead starts to glow red, GarageBand is reaching its processing limits).

The Playhead Lock button (located at the bottom-right corner of the timeline) changes the way GarageBand displays the song as it is playing. When Playhead lock is active (the two triangles are aligned), the Playhead stays in the middle of the window, and it appears that the regions are moving past the Playhead—the Playhead always remains in view. When the Playhead lock is off (the triangles are offset), the regions stay static, and the Playhead moves across them; once the Playhead leaves the window, it leaves your view.

Zoom In and Out

Most likely, your work in GarageBand will range from big picture activities (such as recording, building a song with Apple Loops, and mixing your tracks to create a master) and detailed activities (such as editing regions). GarageBand's visual display lets you configure your view to suit the task at hand.

The zoom sliders are basically self-explanatory: slide to the left (CONTROL-LEFT ARROW) to zoom out and see the big picture; slide to the right (CONTROL-RIGHT ARROW) to zoom in for a more detailed look.

 *When the Automatic setting is active in the Grid pop-ups, the current zoom setting will affect the grid settings.*

The track headers also provide a gateway to the Track Info Inspectors, shown next, which display the track's basic parameters and allow you to add effects. Double-click the track header to open the inspector.

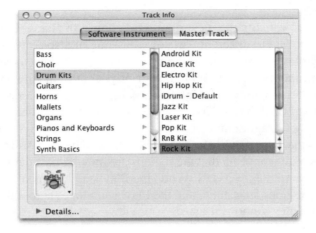

Select Tracks in the Track Header

To select a track in the track header, click on it. You can also use the UP and DOWN arrow keys to move from track to track. If a Track Info Inspector (shown above) is open, it will show the settings for each track you select—no need to reopen the window every time you switch tracks.

Controls

The lower part of the GarageBand window (see Figure 1-7) offers a number of important controls. Here's where you'll add tracks, open editors, navigate through the project, and set the project's master volume level.

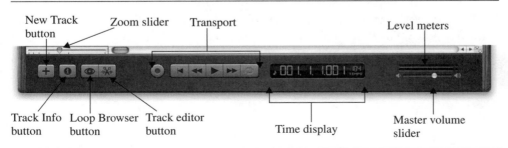

FIGURE 1-7   At the bottom of the GarageBand window is a group of controls; it's not officially called a control panel, but we'll use the term for the sake of simplicity.

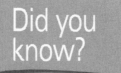

Inspector Clues

In official GarageBand lingo, the Track Info and New Track windows are known as "inspectors." An inspector is a window that's always on top and cannot be hidden by another window.

New Track and Track Info Inspectors

The New Track button is used to add a track to the project. When you click it, you'll see the New Track Inspector, which gives you some choices for both Real Instrument and Software Instrument tracks (see Figure 1-8).

The Track Info button opens the Track Info Inspector (see Figure 1-9), which lets you set various parameters for the track.

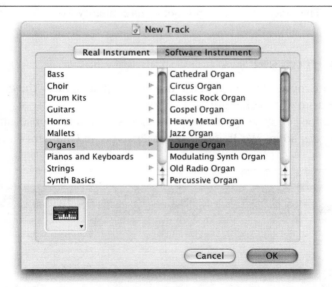

FIGURE 1-8   The New Track Inspector appears when you click on the New Track button, or when you create a track in the Track menu.

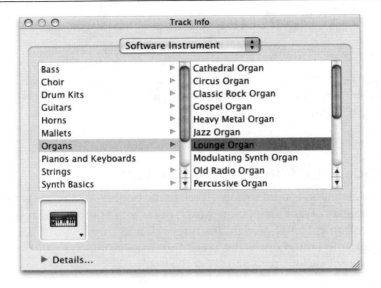

FIGURE 1-9 The Track Info Inspector: notice its similarity to the New Track Inspector

The Loop Browser

Click the Loop Browser button, and the browser appears below the control panel at the bottom of the GarageBand window.

You use the loop browser (see Figure 1-10) to search for, choose, and add Apple Loops files to your song. We'll cover this extensively in Chapters 4 and 5.

FIGURE 1-10 The loop browser lets you sort through all the loop files in your system.

Track Editors

The track editor shows a detailed view of the currently selected track. The content of the track editor depends on whether the track is a Real Instrument (see Figure 1-11a) or a Software Instrument (see Figure 1-11b). We'll be spending a lot of time in this window throughout the book.

Transport

The transport is used to shuttle through the project. Its individual controls are shown in Figure 1-12.

Transport Key Equivalents

All of the transport controls have key equivalents, and these can speed up your work considerably. Table 1-1 shows the how you can use your computer keyboard to run GarageBand.

Time Display

The time display shows the song position in either bars and beats, or in absolute time (hours, minutes, seconds, and fractions of seconds). You toggle between the two displays by clicking on the button inside the window (see Figure 1-13).

Use the Time Display to Navigate Your Song

In addition to showing you where you are in the song, the time display can also be used to move the Playhead. Double-click in the any section of the display to enter a new song position. You can also click and drag the mouse up or down in any area of the time display to move the Playhead by a specific subdivision of time. For example, if you want to locate to Bar 10, double-click the bar display

(a)   (b)

FIGURE 1-11   The track editor can display a detailed look at (a) audio (Real Instrument) and (b) MIDI (Software Instrument) tracks.

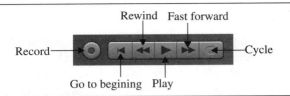

FIGURE 1-12   The transport

and type **10**; to move the Playhead by milliseconds, set the time display to real
time and click and drag in the milliseconds (right-most) section of the display or
type the value of the appropriate field of the time display.

Master Volume and Level Meters

The master volume control lets you set the overall level of the project. It changes
the output for *all* the tracks at the same time. To raise the volume, move the slider
to the right; movement to the left lowers the volume. The level meters let you see
whether your project's audio level is approaching *clipping*—an overload that can
cause a nasty-sounding distortion.

> TIP   *If you need more overall volume and your meters are getting close to clipping,
> turn up the volume on your Mac audio system or speakers rather than in
> GarageBand.*

Action	Button
Play/pause	SPACEBAR
Go to beginning	HOME or Z
Go to end	END or OPTION-Z
Move Playhead forward 1 measure	RIGHT ARROW
Move Playhead back 1 measure	LEFT ARROW
Record start/stop	R
Turn cycle on or off	C
Turn metronome on or off	COMMAND-U

TABLE 1-1   Key Equivalents for GarageBand's Transport Controls

(a)   (b)

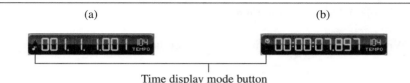

Time display mode button

FIGURE 1-13   The time display shows bars and beats (a) or absolute time (b). You can toggle between the two by clicking on the Display Mode button.

Volume Key Equivalents

Like the transport, the master volume can be controlled by your computer's keyboard. COMMAND-UP ARROW raises the volume; COMMAND-DOWN ARROW lowers it.

Track Mixer

The track mixer (see Figure 1-14) lets you set the level and stereo position (or pan) of each track. Unlike the master volume slider, the track mixer's controls work on individual tracks, and are used to set each track's parameters relative to the other tracks in the song. Like the master output, each track has a level meter that lets you monitor against clipping.

NOTE   *GarageBand's audio tracks can be either mono or stereo.*

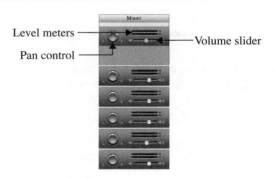

Level meters ———
Volume slider
Pan control ———

FIGURE 1-14   The track mixer is used to set the level of individual tracks.

You can open and close the track mixer:

- With the Track Mixer switch in the track header
- By selecting it in the Track menu
- By pressing COMMAND-Y

Menus

Although most of GarageBand's commands are accessible directly from the main window, it's sometimes easier in the early going to find them in the menus—which also clue you into some of the keyboard shortcuts.

File Menu

The File menu lets you do typical File menu stuff like open, close, and save files. It also has a handy Open Recent... command and lets you export your music to iTunes—your avenue to sharing music with the world at large.

    GarageBand's new Save as Archive command lets you store all of the elements in your song in one file. This is ideal for backup and for transporting your song to a different computer.

Edit Menu

The Edit menu includes Cut, Copy, and Paste commands, but also offers the important Split command (COMMAND-T), which lets you divide regions into separate segments—an important part of the random-access arranging process—and the Join Selected command (COMMAND-J), which lets you join two regions into one. It also includes

1

the all important Undo (COMMAND-Z) and Redo (SHIFT-COMMAND-Z) commands. We'll explore GarageBand's editing features extensively in Chapter 8.

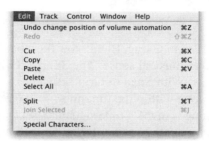

Track Menu

The Track menu lets you create or delete tracks, and determine whether to hide or show the track mixer, Track Info, and master track.

 GarageBand's new Duplicate Track command (COMMAND-D) lets you make a copy of all the settings of any track. It's very handy when you want to build a multitrack arrangement.

Control Menu

The Control menu lets you activate the metronome (which provides a time reference as you play), enable count in, show and hide the loop browser and editor panes, and determine whether the audio regions snap to a grid when editing.

Snap Judgment

When you arrange regions in GarageBand, you'll probably want to position them in a way that makes musical sense. The Snap to Grid (COMMAND-G) feature helps you do this. With Snap to Grid activated, any regions you place into the timeline—or move within the timeline—will land on a predetermined musical value. If your song is in a 4/4 time signature, set the grid to 1/1 Note to move or place a region by a full measure. If you want to move the region in increments of one beat, set the grid to 1/4. You can change the grid value with the Timeline Grid button (shown here). Generally, it's best to leave Snap to Grid active.

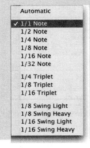

NEW IN 1.1 The Window menu's new Zoom command lets you instantly fill your computer screen with your GarageBand window.

Window Menu

The Window menu lets you minimize GarageBand (so that you can look like you're working when the boss walks by) and open the Keyboard window, which lets you play GarageBand software instruments directly from your computer without the need for an external MIDI controller. (The Bring All to Front command has no effect on GarageBand. If the program is open, all windows are automatically in the front.)

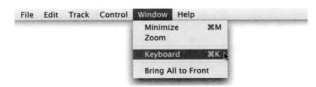

Time Signature

The time signature tells you what's going on inside each measure. A time signature looks like a fraction, but it's not really a division problem. Its numbers show two things in relation to the measure: the top value indicates number of beats in each measure, and the bottom value tells you what type of note receives one beat.

Figure 1-15 shows a measure in 4/4 time. There are four beats in the measure (top number); a quarter note receives one beat. In 6/8 time, there are six beats in a measure, and an 8th note receives one beat. In that measure, a quarter note would receive *two* beats.

Musical note values are relative: the quarter note's duration is measured in relation to other note values, such as eighth notes (quarter note is twice as long), half notes (quarter note is half as long), whole note, and so on. Table 1-2 shows how various note values relate to one another.

> **TIP**   *Changes in tempo and time signature affect the actual duration and speed of each note, but they* don't *affect how one type of note relates to another. A quarter note is* always *twice as long as an eighth note and half as long as a half note.*

Tempo

As you may have noticed, a time signature might tell us about the structure of a song, but says nothing about the absolute speed or duration of individual notes or measures. For that, we need to know a song's tempo. Tempo is measured in beats-per-minute (BPM) and is traditionally indicated by ♩ = X, where X is the number of beats per minute.

If a song has a tempo of 120 BPM and a time signature of 4/4, there are 120 quarter notes in one minute. (We could also turn the equation on its head and say that, at 120 BPM, each quarter note is a half-second long.)

FIGURE 1-15   One measure in a 4/4 time signature. This measure contains four quarter notes, and each one receives one beat.

4	×	Quarter	=	Whole
2	×	Quarter	=	Half
2	×	Eighth	=	Quarter
4	×	Eighth	=	Half
8	×	Eighth	=	Whole
2	×	Sixteenth	=	Eighth
4	×	Sixteenth	=	Quarter
8	×	Sixteenth	=	Half
16	×	Sixteenth	=	Whole
3	×	Eighth-note Triplet	=	Quarter

TABLE 1-2 Note Values and How They Relate to One Another

NOTE *Electronic musicians usually divide seconds into milliseconds—thousandths of a second. In the 120-BPM example, a quarter note would last 500 milliseconds, while an eighth note would be 250 milliseconds long. GarageBand can show milliseconds in its time display.*

Wish List

GarageBand is a great program, but there are some things it doesn't do—at least not yet. If you're an experienced sequencer user, you might want to note these "missing" features. Here are a few from our own personal wish list—and a few ideas for working around these "limitations."

Did you know?

A Sign of the Times

Not all time signatures use even numbers: 3/4, or waltz time, is very common, yet has three quarter-note beats in each measure. More esoteric "odd" time signatures include 9/8, 5/4, 7/8 and 7/4—Pink Floyd's '70s megahit song "Money" is an example of a song in 7/4. GarageBand can work with 3/4, 4/4, 5/4, 6/8, and 7/8 time signatures.

Music 101: A Short Course

GarageBand is a nontraditional composing tool designed for musicians and nonmusicians alike, but it still uses some traditional musical concepts. The most important of these have to do with how GarageBand relates to time.

Every piece of music, no matter the style or tempo, is divided into units called measures (the measure is sometimes known as a "bar"—ironic, since so many of us musicians have measured some time in bars).

Multiple Tempos

Unlike Apple's Soundtrack, GarageBand does not support more than one tempo per song. If you want your piece of music to speed up and slow down over the course of a single song, you're pretty much out of luck.

 *You* can *play at different tempos by disabling the metronome and playing freely. However, you won't be able to use the grid to edit your music. Another option is to record one piece of music in two or more song files, each with its own tempo. Later, you can export the mix of each song file and edit them together.*

Multiple Time Signatures

As with tempos, GarageBand does not support multiple time signatures. If you're an experienced musician, you can probably work around this with some careful counting and creative use of the grid settings (if you're not an experienced musician, you probably don't care about multiple time signatures yet). For example, if you want to add a bar of 3/4 to a 4/4 song, you can—it's just that the following bar will start on "beat 4" instead of beat 1, as it would if there was a time signature change.

 *Use GarageBand's Split command to create a new region for each track in the section that's in the new time signature. This will serve as a visual reference for the time signature change.*

"Merge" Recording on Software Instrument Tracks

When you record a MIDI track or on a typical sequencer, you can go back after the fact, put the track into record, and record again: the original data will not be erased (unless you explicitly tell the sequencer to do so). Instead, the new data is "merged" with the existing data, and the track plays both. This is very handy when you want to build, say, a drum part, because it lets you play one sound at a time.

GarageBand *can* merge record if the cycle is active when you first start recording a region; as the region cycles, you can layer on top of what you recorded in the previous pass. But once you turn the cycle off or stop recording, *you can no longer layer data to the region*—not in standard mode, and not by reactivating the cycle. Any new recording will erase the existing data.

Instead of layering to the same track, use GarageBand's Duplicate Track command to create, well, duplicate tracks. Record each fresh part to its own track.

Time-Stamp Recordings You Make Yourself

Unlike the Apple Loops that come with GarageBand, the Real Instrument recordings you make yourself are not time stamped. If you record a part in GarageBand and then change the song's tempo after the fact, the part you recorded will be out of sync with the rest of the song.

You can convert your own recordings to Apple Loops by downloading the free Apple Loop utility, See Chapter 13 for details on how to so this.

Markers

GarageBand does not have a marker feature. On a typical sequencer, markers are used for both visual reference and to locate quickly to different parts of a song.

You can create visual landmarks by creating a region (or regions) for each important part of the song. Name each new region to indicate where it occurs in the song, as shown here. In this example, we created empty regions by erasing all the data inside an Apple Loop and copying the empty region to each location, then renaming each region appropriately.

Digital Signal Processing and Other Editing Features

GarageBand lets you chop up audio files—be they Apple Loops of files you've recorded yourself or Real Instrument tracks—but it doesn't offer the kind of editing

Voices from the Community

Strike Up the (Garage)Band!

When Steve Jobs first introduced GarageBand at the Macworld Expo in San Francisco in January 2004, I was stunned. Here was a program I had never expected, never even imagined: a sort of iMovie for music. At first, it looked superficial, but as the presentation went on, I realized how much of a quantum leap this was. And at the right price!

I watched this presentation via Apple's webcast with my 13-year old son by my side. He was totally blown away by the ability to create music like this, and told me that he wanted a copy as soon as possible.

When we got the program, I was again amazed by its simplicity. Sure, even the simplest program hides some pretty powerful features, but it was so easy— even for my son—to start mixing loops and making music. Of course, this isn't true creation; pasting loops together is pretty simplistic, but it's a start. And for a kid his age to be able to have this much control over music is a good way to start discovering not only what it means to be creative, but to get a feel of the tiny details that make a difference in a song.

It got better, though. I have a Yamaha P-80 digital piano, with a MIDI output, and bought a cheap MIDI-to-USB interface so I could feed input from the keyboard into my Mac. That's when things got interesting. Now I could play guitar, drums, or brass instruments with my keyboard. No longer was it a mere keyboard; now it was a full-fledged synthesizer, thanks to GarageBand.

My only regret is that it took so long for such an intuitive program to be designed. I have a fair amount of experience playing music—I played a lot when I was a teenager—and had tried demo versions of some of the standard music software. But these programs were more complex than the pilot's cabin in a 747, and I never got anywhere. Now, with GarageBand, I can make music on my own, mixing it as I want, working at my own speed. And the results are surprising (at least in sound quality).

If the program itself is powerful and interesting, it's the concept that's a real groundbreaker. Putting such tools in the hands of amateurs and hobbyists makes it much more likely that some of these kids who start fiddling with GarageBand today will become the musicians of tomorrow. If that happens, it will show that all this technology is truly worthwhile.

—Kirk McElhearn writes books and articles about Macintosh
computers and software. He lives in a village in the French Alps.
His latest book is How To Do Everything with Mac OS X Panther,
published by McGraw-Hill/Osborne.

power that's available on a typical digital audio sequencer. Important DSP functions like normalize, change gain, and D.C. offset removal are not part of the program.

TIP *You can use a third-part audio editor to perform these functions. See Chapter 13 for more information.*

Moving On

In Chapter 2, we'll install and configure GarageBand, make audio connections, and test the system. We'll also go over system requirements and discuss how the components of your computer affect the performance of GarageBand (and other audio software). Even if you already have the software up and running on your system, you can use this chapter as a checklist to help you get the best possible performance from GarageBand.

Chapter 2

Get Started with GarageBand

How to...

- Determine the system requirements
- Install GarageBand
- Install GarageBand content and tutorials
- Configure your audio system
- Make audio connections
- Test your system

We live in an age of ever more powerful computers, and for an author, this fact presents a bit of a challenge. What do you say when the high-end specs of today are likely to have the cutting edge of day-old spaghetti by tomorrow?

Quite frankly, the minimum system requirements for GarageBand seem a bit optimistic on first glance. It might be an entry-level program, but it is power hungry; the bare minimum system requirements will get you the bare minimum in performance.

Fortunately, Apple has updated its line from top to bottom, and even their entry-level machines boast enough CPU power to run GarageBand with software instruments. And this is important, because the installer scans your system to check that it meets its minimum requirements. If your computer doesn't pass muster, GarageBand will not install.

System Requirements

GarageBand requires a powerful computer on which to run, and like a lot of music applications, the more horsepower (both in terms of processor speed and RAM) you have at your disposal, the more you'll be able to do with the software. Here's a list of the basic requirements: we'll follow it up with a few words about each component.

- Macintosh G3, G4, or G5 computer
- 600-Mhz G3 processor or better (G4 or G5 needed for software instruments)
- 256MB of physical RAM (1GB recommended for consistent performance)
- A DVD-ROM drive
- 4.3GB of free hard drive space*

---

*when installed with the complete iLife package

- ■ OS X 10.2.6 or later (10.2.8 recommended)

- ■ QuickTime 6.4 or later (QuickTime 6.5 included)

Additional Requirements for Jam Pack

Jam Pack adds a great deal of power to GarageBand by providing more than 2,000 additional loops, as well as a range of software instruments, effects, and guitar amp simulations. In order to install it, GarageBand must be already installed on your computer. In addition, you'll need 3GB of free disk space. The other system requirements are the same as for GarageBand, so you won't need to upgrade your computer to take advantage of Jam Pack.

The Processor

The CPU, or central processing unit, is at the heart of every computer, and while it's not the sole measure of performance, it's an important benchmark in determining a computer's suitability for processor-intensive work such as multitrack audio.

For three years, the G4 was Apple's flagship processor. These days, the G5 has supplanted it as the king of Apple's desktop models. However, on the laptop front, the G4 still graces both the top-of-the-line PowerBooks and entry-level iBooks. For potential GarageBand users, this is both good news and bad news. The good news: you don't need a G5 to run GarageBand, The bad news: if you have an older machine, such as a G3 iBook or an early G4, you may have to endure sluggish and inconsistent performance.

RAM

It has become a truism in all computer circles: *You can never have too much random access memory, or RAM* (not to be confused with hard disk storage). In audio applications, RAM is especially important because it's often used as a buffer for audio as it plays back on your hard disk. RAM affects the number of tracks you can reliably play back at one time. So if there's no such thing as "too much," how much is enough? I recommend at least 512MB; some technicians I've spoken with insist on 1GB as a safe baseline.

NOTE   *RAM is one of the easiest parts for the do-it-yourselfer to upgrade, but it's absolutely essential that you use the exact type of RAM your specific model requires. Various Apple computers require different types of RAM. Most retailers offer low-cost RAM upgrades—among other perks—to new computer buyers.*

Did you know?

Punch the Clock

CPU speed obviously affects overall computer performance, but in music applications an increase in CPU speed has its greatest impact on the number of software instruments and real-time audio effects, or plug-ins, you can run, and, indirectly, the number of audio tracks you can have open. There's no set rule on the number of plug-ins to the number of megahertz: Some plug-ins, such as complex reverb effects, tax the processor more than others.

Hard Drive

The hard drive is the heart of any computer-based recording system, and for good reason: it is to audio software as tape is to the tape recorder—the recording medium. The size and speed of your hard drive will have a direct impact on your work. Fortunately, fast, speedy drives are commonplace, and the internal drive on a typical desktop computer should be more than enough for all but the most demanding audio project. If you plan on sticking to GarageBand's prerecorded loops, you can probably get by without adding a second drive.

However, if you intend to record audio of your own, you may want to add a second hard drive and dedicate it exclusively to audio. First, unlike a prerecorded disk library—which by definition has a fixed size—the recordings you make yourself can take up lots of disk space before you know it. That's especially true if you're taking several passes at the same song, or section of music, and want to choose from among the takes at a later time.

Second, the operating system will often use the system drive in the background, and this can slow the performance of some audio applications. Finally, a dedicated audio drive is easier to maintain, back up, and copy.

CAUTION *Laptop users may find that their computer's internal drive, with a rotation speed of under 5,000 rpm, is too slow for audio.*

In terms of audio, hard disks have two important specs: rotation speed, and seek time. The faster the rotation speed, and the shorter the seek time, the better. For multitrack audio, look for a drive with a rotation speed of at least 7200 rpm and a seek time under 8 milliseconds—and a large cache, if possible.

2

Did you know?   **Driving Ambition**

Apple computers offer several options for adding a second drive that's suitable for audio. With a desktop machine, you can add an internal drive at a relatively modest cost (on most models, another relatively easy one for the do-it-yourselfer). External drives can be connected to Firewire and—on some models—the new USB 2.0 ports. An external drive costs more, but it's portable, and is easier to replace once full (yes, they do get full). Hardcore desktop audio types sometimes opt for expensive high-speed SCSI drives, but for those, you'll need to install an optional card in your computer, which seems like overkill for GarageBand.

DVD Drive

The GarageBand program itself would be small enough to install from a CD-ROM, so why the DVD? It's the content that takes up most of the space. All those audio loops require disk space. Hence, you need a DVD reader in order to install the program. Since DVD readers are generally standard issue on computers with a CPU capable of handling GarageBand, this isn't an overly rigorous requirement. But if

Did you know?   **Get on the Bus**

A hard drive is connected to a signal path called a bus, and the bus throughput—the amount of data it can process in one second—is another important factor in overall audio performance. At one time, expensive Ultra and Super SCSI drives, running on special buses, were the only disks that were considered fast enough for professional audio. And while SCSI is still in use, most modern drives—including the internal ATA drives in your Mac and Firewire 400 and 800 devices—boast throughput that is more than up to the task of multitrack audio. Although USB 1.0—the type found on all but the latest Macs—is too slow for hard drives used in audio applications, USB 2.0 does get the job done. But remember, it's the bus, and not just the drive, that's important here: connect a USB 2.0 drive to a USB 1.0 bus, and your performance will be limited by the slower bus throughput.

you have an older computer with an upgraded CPU (but an old CD-ROM drive), you may need to upgrade your optical drive as well.

A DVD-RW drive, such as Apple's Superdrive, is a valuable option. A DVD-RW lets you write, or "burn" data to a DVD disc, and is an outstanding tool for backing up your projects. Thanks to a storage capacity of 4.7GB, a DVD-RW can hold more than six-and-a-half times as much data as a typical CD. Even a modest project that includes high-resolution audio and video files can exceed the capacity of a 700MB CD-R.

Even better, if you're using GarageBand to create background music for your iMovie projects, you can use iDVD to burn them to disc and share with the world at large.

CAUTION *If you're considering upgrading to DVD-R by adding a third-party drive, beware: Apple's iDVD software is not compatible with all third-party drives. As of this writing, the Superdrive is actually a Pioneer DVR-106, which can be purchased from some vendors and installed as a replacement to the internal DVD/CD-R Combo Drive. DVD-R drives from other manufacturers—which are available as external Firewire devices—may require a separate DVD burning application such as Roxio Toast.*

The Operating System

Apple's UNIX-based OS X took a while to find its legs in audio applications, but as it has matured, the OS has become an outstanding platform for desktop media of all kinds. GarageBand requires at least version 10.2.6, or Jaguar; as of this writing, Panther, aka OS X 10.3.4, is most current; 10.4 (Tiger) should be available soon.

No matter what operating system you are using, however, it's *almost* always best to keep your computer current by updating any subreleases that may be available. Before installing GarageBand, I recommend that you log onto the Internet and run Apple's Software Update application; it's a great tool for keeping current with all your software—including your operating system.

CAUTION *If you're using third-party audio or MIDI software or hardware, check with the manufacturer before upgrading your operating system. Sometimes, changes in the OS can cause conflicts or incompatibilities with third-party hardware. If a new driver is in the offing, you may want to wait until it's available before upgrading your Mac's operating system. I've experienced a few of these issues when moving from Jaguar to Panther, especially when running non-Apple applications.*

Voices from the Community

Get Isolated

When setting up your computer for music production, try to put the computer itself as far away from your ears as possible. This will ensure that the computer's fans don't contribute to the ambient noise level when you're closely monitoring your recorded sound. So as a start, take that computer off the desktop! Try sliding it underneath the tabletop and as far off to the side as you can, putting as many barriers and surfaces in the "line of hearing" (between your ears and the CPU) as possible. Isolating the computer case from the floor helps keep the floor from amplifying the fans' vibrations, too. When moving your computer around and placing barriers, be sure not to block the computer's fan ports, which ensure healthy airflow. Blockage could cause the computer to overheat, which can damage the internal components.

—*Jon Chappell, author of* Build Your Own PC Recording Studio
(McGraw-Hill/Osborne) and Rock Guitar for Dummies
(John Wiley & Sons)

Install GarageBand

Okay, enough system talk; it's time to rip open the iLife package, pull out the discs, and install the software.

Log on to your computer as administrator, and insert the GarageBand disc. After perusing the Readme file for late-breaking news (you do that with all your software, right?), you can double-click the installer and follow the onscreen instructions. You'll be asked to accept the licensing agreement and enter your name.

Choose a destination disc; remember, your install disc will need at least OS X 10.2.6. GarageBand will be placed in the /Applications folder of your hard drive; a GarageBand icon automatically appears in the dock.

NOTE   *Apple calls for the "latest version" of OS X, but you don't need to upgrade to OS X 10.3 to run GarageBand.*

In addition to the program itself, the installer places the GarageBand loops on your hard drive in /Library/Application Support/GarageBand/Apple Loops/.

 *This folder will also contain the Jam Pack loops and any other audio you use with GarageBand.*

Software instruments are stored in the folder in /Library/Application Support/ GarageBand/Instrument Library/.

Open and Register GarageBand

The first time you launch GarageBand, you'll be confronted by a registration screen. You might as well fill it out now and get it over with—otherwise, the screen will keep popping up every few days to remind you of what you already know: it's important to register your software. To complete the registration, you'll need to be logged on to the Internet.

Once you're registered, you're done with the preliminaries. Before we start going through the software, let's set some preferences for our audio system.

GarageBand and OS X Audio Settings

GarageBand, as a Core Audio–compatible application, uses your system's audio settings as a basis for its own signal routing. This is in contrast to audio applications such as Pro Tools and Cubase SX, which address audio hardware independently. For basic audio I/O (the short way to say "ins and outs"), we'll be using your system's internal audio for both input and output signal paths. You can check

 **Install Jam Pack**

Once you have GarageBand installed, you can install Jam Pack, which adds a wide array of loops, effects, and instruments to your creative palette. All you have to do is pop the disc into the DVD drive, double-click the GarageBand_ Jam_Pack.pkg, and follow the instructions: the installer checks your system to make sure that Jam Pack can be installed correctly, asks for a destination disc, then places the loops, instruments, and effects into the appropriate folders.

NOTE *Once the Jam Pack is installed, GarageBand sees its contents automatically. There's no need to do anything else to gain access to the additional loops, instruments, and effects.*

your computer's basic audio settings in the Sound preference panel, found within the System Preferences, shown here:

Apple computers have always been very flexible as far as system audio routing is concerned. The system can address any Core Audio–compatible external hardware.

In addition to the Sound control panel, OS X offers the AudioMidi Setup utility, which gives you a detailed look at all the Core Audio interfaces available on your system and lets you make advanced settings. If you already have a third-party interface and want to use it with GarageBand, you may need to access the Audio MIDI Setup utility to set it up.

Make Basic Audio Connections

Although GarageBand utilizes prerecorded loops, it is also capable of recording audio in real time, something we'll be doing as we work through the book. Later we'll address the use of advanced third-party interfaces, but for now, let's create a simple input and output system using your Mac's internal audio.

Input Routing

Input routing is probably the most important factor in audio recording: if the source material sounds horrible going in, there's little chance that the final mix will sound good. Most—though not all—Apple models sport a minijack mic/line input. This jack can be used for a condenser microphone (provided the mic has a minijack), but it's pretty limited compared to the mic and line inputs found in a hardware mixer, or even in a moderately priced third-party interface.

In addition to analog ins and outs, the G5 models also offer digital inputs and outputs. These offer superior sound quality, but in order to take advantage of them, you'll need an analog-to-digital converter, or A/D, to convert the analog signals generated by a microphone into the digital format the computer requires.

Connect the Input Source to the Computer

For now, let's assume we're using a condenser mic and the stereo analog input:

- Plug the mic's output cable into the Mac's analog mic input.

- Launch System Preferences, and open the Sound preference pane (see Figure 2-1).

- Select the Input tab.

- Select Built-in audio controller as the input device.

> NOTE   *The G5, with its digital inputs, offers a slightly different set of options. The Input pane of Sound Preferences lets you select between Line-In and Digital-In. For this illustration, use the analog line-in.*

- Set the Input Volume slider to about halfway

Speak or sing into the microphone at a level close to what you'll want to record. The Input Level meters should be firing, indicating that signal is coming into the computer. Adjust the Input Volume slider so that the average signal is about 75 percent of the meter reading. This will provide a healthy signal, but should prevent louder signals from overloading the inputs and causing unwanted distortion.

Monitoring

The monitoring system—the speakers and amplifiers used to listen to the audio—plays a crucial role in a professional studio environment. Without accurate monitors, an engineer is flying blind. In fact, most engineers like to listen to their mixes on several

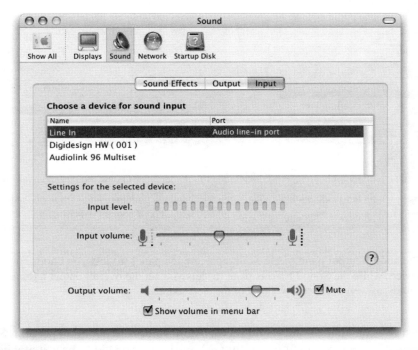

FIGURE 2-1   The Sound preference panel's Input pane

different systems to make sure they sound good on all of them, insurance against the inevitable coloration offered by a particular set of speakers in a particular room.

So while you *could* use GarageBand with your computer's internal speakers, you'll get better results by connecting a stereo monitoring system. This can consist of a pair of headphones, a pair of powered monitors (speakers with the power amplifier built in), or your home stereo system. Invest in the best monitors you can afford.

A monitor's position has a great impact on its sound. The ideal listening environment is to have the speakers at ear level, three to five feet in front of you.

Set the Output and Volume

Since we're still in the Sound preference pane, let's select the Output tab. Set the output device to your built-in audio controller (see Figure 2-2a). (The name of the output may vary depending on your model Mac: in this case, it's Headphones.) Next, select the Sound Effects tab (see Figure 2-2b). Let's set the Output Volume to maximum

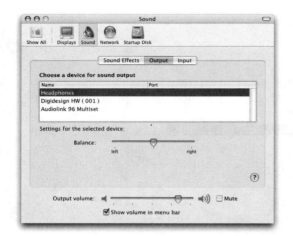 

FIGURE 2-2 The audio Output pane of the Sound preference panel (a) lets you choose an output device, while the Sound Effects pane (b) lets you set the overall output level for system sounds, as well as the relative level of the alert sounds.

for now (you can adjust it later) and set the Alert Volume to about 30 percent. Select an alert and listen through your monitors. You should be able to hear it at a healthy volume, but it shouldn't overpower you.

Finally, check the option Show Volume In Menu Bar, so that we won't need to return to the preference panel every time we want to adjust the system volume.

CAUTION *When we start working with GarageBand, you'll be happy that you lowered the alert volume. There's nothing worse than cranking up a song, only to be startled out of your chair by a loud system alert! You might also want to keep your speakers turned down when you start the computer—you can get a very loud "bong" when you start up.*

Moving On

Congratulations: You have installed and registered GarageBand. The fun is about to start. In the next chapter, we're going to open our first project, set up the preferences, and start making some music. If you want to learn more about audio signal flow, and see some advanced setups, you might want to check out the illustrations in Appendix C, at www.osborne.com, *before* moving on to our next chapter.

Part II

Make Music with GarageBand

Chapter 3

Open Your First Project

How to...

- Launch GarageBand
- Create a song file
- Save a song file
- Create an archive file
- Set a song's tempo
- Set a song's pitch
- Set the song's time signature
- Set preferences

By now, you've installed GarageBand and made and tested MIDI and audio connections. You're probably itching to get going (you may even have skipped ahead and made music). Well, you can rest easy, because we're almost there.

Unlike some music software—which requires extensive setup and configuration before you can start making music—GarageBand is mostly about instant gratification. But there are still a few things you'll need to do at the outset of each project. First, let's launch the program.

Launch GarageBand

When you start the program, GarageBand gives you an "initializing" message while it looks for the last open song, which it loads automatically. Because we don't have a previous song, we're going to get the New Song dialog box (see Figure 3-1).

Here's where you set important project parameters, such as key, or base pitch, time signature, tempo, and the location of the project file.

Name and Save the Song

This job is basically self-explanatory. If you're familiar with OS X file navigation, it should be pretty easy to name and locate your file. However, there are a couple of things to keep in mind. First, when you create a new song in GarageBand, the program stores all the accompanying data, including all track information, in one large package file. In addition to the basic performance information—the actual music in the

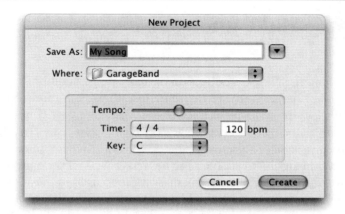

FIGURE 3-1   The New Project dialog box lets you name your project, and set its key, time signature, tempo, and file location.

timeline—the package will contain any individual audio files that you record as part of the song. These files can get quite large, so be sure to allow enough disk space before saving.

> **TIP**   *If your song will include your own original audio tracks, save it to your dedicated audio hard drive. This will improve performance.*

A descriptive name is always a good thing, but you can always rename the song by doing a Save As as the project takes shape.

NEW IN 1.1   In earlier versions of GarageBand, when you closed a song, you quit the program. With version 1.1, you can now close a song without quitting. Press COMMAND-W, choose Close IN the File menu, or close the window by clicking the Close button with your mouse. GarageBand will prompt you to save if you have any unsaved changes to the song.

Set Project Tempo, Time Signature, and Key

Before you start a song, GarageBand asks you to establish the basic parameters of tempo, time signature, and key. It needs this information in order to set up the grid—which is the framework upon which GarageBand's editing is based—and to take advantage of the metadata that's included with the Apple Loops. Metadata is a cool way to say *embedded information,* which allows these audio files to automatically play back at the correct tempo and key.

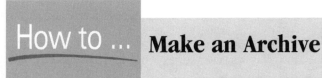 **Make an Archive**

A complete song file can be a collection of many parts: audio files you record yourself, Apple Loops, Software Instrument settings, and more. Normally, GarageBand's loop browser keeps track of the whereabouts of your loops so that it knows where to find them every time you open your song. However, if you plan to take the song to another person's computer, you may find that some of the loops in your collection are not available. The new Save as Archive option (available in the File menu) lets you save a copy of every loop used in the song into the package file (in addition to the audio files you record yourself). This way, all the elements of the song are together, ensuring that if you open the file on a different machine, the loops will be available.

 *When you're finished with a project, use Save as Archive and copy the resulting file onto CD or other backup medium.*

 Although you can make changes to parameters such as the song's tempo and base-key after you've already started working on the song, it's important to finalize these settings before you begin recording your own audio tracks. Unlike Apple Loops, the tracks you record yourself are not elastic—they can't be transposed, and they won't play in sync if you change tempo after the fact.

Tempo

The tempo controls the speed at which a song plays back, and is measured in beats per minute (BPM). GarageBand has a range of 60–240 BPM. You can set the tempo by using the tempo slider, or by typing a number in the Tempo field. If you enter a value that's outside of GarageBand's tempo range, the software will automatically adjust it to either 60 or 240.

Time Signature

Every piece of music—from the most rigid electronic dance number to the loosest minimalist soundscape—has a time signature. A song's time signature forms its rhythmic structure by determining a) how many beats there are in each measure, and b) what type of note gets one beat.

> NOTE   *See Chapter 1, "Music 101, A Short Course," for more about time signature.*

The default time signature is 4/4—four beats per measure, with a quarter note getting one beat. This will probably be the choice for 90 percent of your songs. If you need to change time signature, do so with the Time pop-up menu, as shown in Figure 3-2.

> NOTE   *GarageBand supports the following time signatures: 2/2, 2/4, 3/4, 4/4, 5/4, 6/8, 7/8, 9/8, and 12/8.*

Key

In standard musical notation, a song's key determines not only which pitch is the tonal center of the song, but also which scales will be used throughout the song. In GarageBand, the key is more concerned with the former—establishing a root note for the song. This is essential because GarageBand uses this information—along with the metadata embedded in the Apple Loops—to match the prerecorded audio files to one another and to the song in general. Figure 3-3 shows the Key pop-up menu. Note that GarageBand does not make a distinction between major and minor keys.

> NOTE   *Just because a song is in a particular key, you don't have to play software instruments in that key. You can play anything you like. However, the key is more important when working with GarageBand loops.*

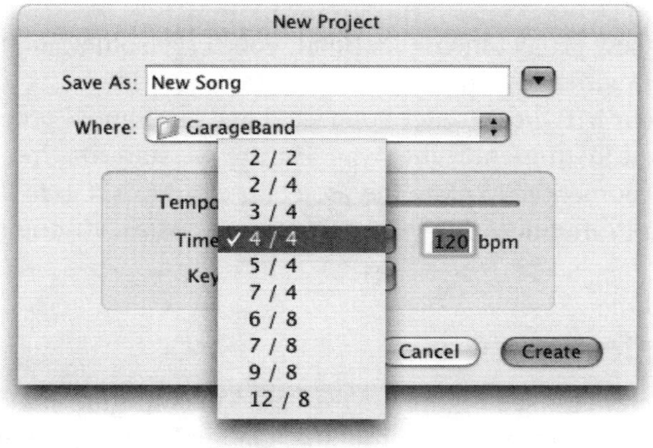

FIGURE 3-2   The Time pop-up menu

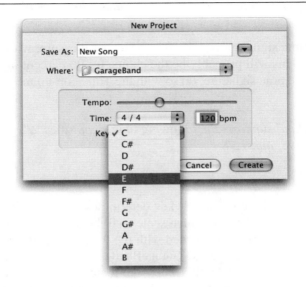

FIGURE 3-3 The Key pop-up menu

Once key, time signature, and tempo are set, you're ready to click the Create button and start your song. You'll see a blank slate—well almost.

Set Preferences

When you start a new project in GarageBand, you'll see something like Figure 3-4—an empty timeline with only one track in the Tracks column.

If you have your MIDI controller connected and configured properly, you should be able to play that instrument right away. Before we start making music, however, we should take a moment to explore the project preferences. Go to the GarageBand menu and choose Preferences (you can also press COMMAND-comma to access this menu).

General Preferences

The General preferences (see Figure 3-5) are used to configure some miscellaneous GarageBand features, such as the metronome, GarageBand's behavior when closing an effects preset, and the way the loop browser works with keywords.

3

FIGURE 3-4   A New GarageBand project is like a blank canvas. The Grand Piano software
instrument track (left) opens by default.

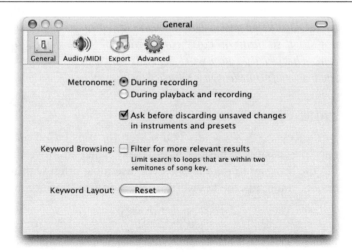

FIGURE 3-5   General preferences screen

Metronome

The metronome provides a time reference as you play and record your piece. If you want to hear a time reference as you're practicing a part, select the option During Playback and Recording. If you just need the metronome while recording, but want to hear playback without it, select During Recording.

TIP *You can toggle the metronome on and off, regardless of the preference setting, by selecting it in the Control menu, or by pressing COMMAND-U.*

Ask Before Discarding Unsaved Changes...

This option is self-explanatory: when checked, GarageBand will warn you if you're about to lose any edits you've made to a software instrument or to a real instrument's effects. Leave it on unless the constant reminders become annoying. When they do, you know where to go to get rid of 'em.

Keyword Browsing

One of GarageBand's coolest features is its ability to sort through lots of Apple Loops and organize them by genre, tempo, and key. When you search for a file using the loop browser, you can restrict the results so that only files within two semitones of the root key will come up.

CAUTION *When you pitch-shift an audio file by more than a few semitones, the playback can sound unnatural. Filtering the search so that it returns files that are close to the root key prevents this. However, you may want to uncheck this option to start, so that you can hear a wider selection of audio files and determine whether they can work for you—despite being more than two semitones away from the song's base key.*

Keyword Layout

The loop browser's Keywords view lets you search for files based on a descriptive keyword, such as "percussion," "bass," "world," etc. You can move the keyword buttons around in the browser to put the ones you use most often within easy reach. The Reset button lets you return the keywords to their original position in the browser.

NOTE *We'll discuss the loop browser and keyword searches in depth in Chapter 5.*

3

Audio and MIDI Preferences

The Audio/MIDI preferences pane (see Figure 3-6) lets you determine how the pieces of hardware connected to your system will work with GarageBand.

Audio Output

This pop-up menu determines which piece of audio hardware will be used to play GarageBand's audio. The default is Built-in Audio, but you can use any compatible Core Audio device that's connected to your system.

NOTE   *We'll discuss third-party audio interfaces in more depth in Chapter 12.*

Audio Input

This pop-up menu determines which piece of audio hardware will be used to record audio into GarageBand. The default is Built-in Audio, but you can use any Core Audio device that's connected to your system.

NOTE   *Although GarageBand is compatible with multichannel audio interfaces, it can only record up to two channels at a time.*

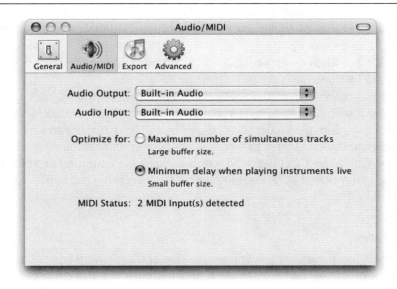

FIGURE 3-6   The Audio/MIDI preferences pane

What's the Delay?

Apple's Core Audio is what is known as a *native* audio system—so called because the audio processing is done by the computer's internal central processing unit (CPU), not by any processors that are mounted on external hardware. This is true whether you are using the computer's built-in audio connections or an external, third-party Core Audio–compatible audio interface.

NOTE *Non-native audio devices do exist—the best known is the Digidesign Pro Tools HD system—but most of the audio interfaces available to consumers and home and project studio owners are of the native variety.*

Latency

When an audio signal passes through a native audio system's inputs, the computer processes it before routing it back to the outputs. This processing causes a slight delay, called *latency*, of the output signal. With early native audio systems, the latency was quite severe—delay of 750 milliseconds (or 3/4 of a second) was not uncommon. It was almost impossible to play and monitor your signal at the same time. Today, thanks to faster processors and more sophisticated audio driver software, latency can be so slight as to be barely perceptible. Low latency is not only important when recording audio tracks; it also affects the responsiveness of software instruments.

When software such as GarageBand is working at its lowest latency, it just *feels* better under your fingers. It's more responsive. However, the more tracks and effects you add, the harder your computer will have to work to keep up, and the sound quality can suffer as a result. It's important to remember that any distortion caused by CPU overload won't damage the computer or your tracks. If the computer seems to be bogging down, try increasing the buffer size.

Buffer Size

The Optimize for: parameter lets you set the size of the memory buffer GarageBand uses when it processes audio. A larger buffer will give you more tracks and more reliable performance, but also creates a longer latency (see the above sidebar, "What's the Delay"). Smaller buffers yield better latency—but fewer tracks. This can also put more of a load on the computer's processor and cause the software to slow down or distort playback.

You can change the buffer size to meet your current requirements at any time. Use a smaller buffer when recording audio and software instrument tracks. Increase buffer size when mixing, especially if you plan to use lots of effects.

MIDI Status

The MIDI Status field tells you how many MIDI inputs are connected to your system, but does not let you change them. If you want to add or configure a MIDI controller or (other MIDI device), go to the Audio/MIDI setup application.

OSX's Audio MIDI setup application is found in the /Applications/ Utilities folder.

Export Preferences

The Export preferences pane (see Figure 3-7) is used to create song information for any GarageBand songs you export to iTunes. Parameters include iTunes Playlist, Composer Name, and Album Name. Simply type the information into the appropriate field.

FIGURE 3-7   The Export preferences pane

Advanced Preferences

The Advanced preferences pane lets you fine-tune GarageBand's performance to suit your computer and compositional style. Here, you can determine the maximum number of Real and Software Instrument tracks, the number of voices per software instrument, and the default way in which Apple Loops will be rendered when you drag them into the timeline.

Real Instrument Tracks

You set the number of Real Instrument tracks via the pop-up menu (see Figure 3-8). Settings include Automatic (the default), 8, 16, 32, 64, and 255. If you're running into CPU problems, try restricting the project to a lower number of tracks.

 GarageBand bases the Automatic setting on its assessment of your computer's processing power. This setting should be adequate for most users; I'd leave it alone unless you begin to experience problems.

Software Instrument Tracks

As with Real Instruments, settings here are made via a pop-up menu. They include Automatic, 8, 16, 32, and 64.

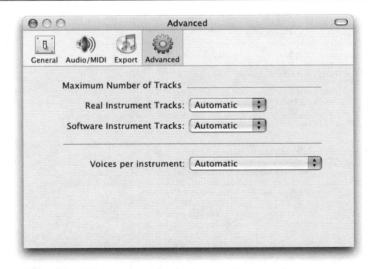

FIGURE 3-8   The Real Instrument Tracks pop-up menu in the Advanced preferences pane

Voices per Instrument

The Voices per Instrument parameter determines the maximum number of notes each instrument will be able to play. The more notes that GarageBand plays back at a time, the greater the strain on the CPU. By restricting the maximum number of notes, you can improve performance. The pop-up is shown here:

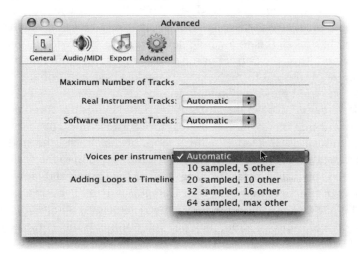

 With version 1.1, GarageBand gives you more flexibility in how you add Apple Loops to the timeline. When Convert to Real Instrument is checked, both Software and Real Instrument Apple Loops can be played as Real Instruments when dragged into the timeline. This can save system resources.

> NOTE *When this option is selected, you can still drag a Software Instrument loop into the timeline in its original form by holding the OPTION key as you drag the file from the loop browser.*

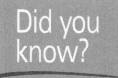

Real Softies

Software Instruments offer you the most editing flexibility, but they also use more system resources than Real Instrument loops. But the files used to create the Software Instruments also contain the data GarageBand needs to play them as audio files—which is what Real Instrument loops are.

Use GarageBand to Inspire Your Students

As a guitar teacher, improvisation is a subject that every student can't wait to start. Over the years, I relied on ready-made "backing" tracks for students to take home and practice improvising with. While these tracks served the purpose, GarageBand has taken this to a whole new level. We start with a simple drum loop and extend it for the correct number of bars—something that makes the students aware of musical form. Next up, we add a bass line from the loop library or we write one and I play my iGuitar to trigger a software bass instrument. Using the transpose feature, we get the loops in the right key for the chord progression that we are working on—which is a great tool for teaching music theory and interval relationships. Instead of using a loop for the chords, the student plugs into GarageBand and lays down a chord track that we loop to the correct length. We export to iTunes and burn a CD for them to take home and jam with. After a few weeks of practice, they plug into GarageBand and lay down a great solo. At the end of the day, not only have they learned something about form, harmony, transposition and improvisation, they had fun doing it—this is the key to happy, successful students.

—Musician and educator Marc Schonbrun is the author of
The Everything Home Recording, The Everything Rock and
Blues Guitar *and* The Everything Reading Music Books

Moving On

Now that we've gotten the basic setup in order, we're ready to make some noise. In the next chapter, we'll finally start making tracks.

Chapter 4

Create Tracks and Add Loops

How to...

- Create a Software Instrument track
- Create a Real Instrument track
- Find loops in the loop browser
- Place a Software Instrument loop on a track
- Place a Real Instrument loop on a track
- Understand the difference between Software Instrument and Real Instrument regions
- Loop a region
- Resize a region
- Move a region
- Change the display order of the tracks

Now that we've navigated the preferences, we're ready to make some music. We'll start where we left off in Chapter 3—with a new, blank project (see Figure 4-1). Note that we've opened the loop browser. If you have not done so already, do it now by clicking the Loop Browser button, by pressing COMMAND-L, or by selecting Show Loop Browser from the Control menu.

When you make music in GarageBand, you don't need to do things in an orderly fashion—that's one of the best parts of computer-aided composition. However, we're going to start with software instruments and loops, and move from there. But if you really want to work with your own original audio tracks, or are most interested in recording your performances via MIDI, feel free to skip ahead to those sections.

Create a New Track

Actually, when you first launch GarageBand, this step has been done already. As you see, there's a grand piano waiting. If you have your MIDI controller connected, play the keys: you should be able to hear the grand piano plinking away.

However, unless you're an ardent disciple of Liberace, you may not want to start every project with a piano. You have the option of replacing the piano with a new instrument, or creating a new track with its own instrument, and ignoring the piano track.

FIGURE 4-1   This new project won't be blank for long.

   Although the tracks are displayed in sequence onscreen, there's no rule that says you have to start with track 1 and move from there. You can record in any order.

There are three ways to create a new track:

■ Click the New Track button (shown here) in the GarageBand window.

■ Select New Track from the Track menu.

■ Press the shortcut keys OPTION-COMMAND-N.

Laying a Foundation

Most of my tracks start with a drum groove or beat. That's an especially cool way to work with GarageBand—because there are so many loops to work with, you can instantly get a groove going. The right groove can be very inspiring for the rest of the track.

Once I get an eight-bar pattern that really works, I start adding a bass line or chord changes (usually with a piano or electric piano). Initially, these are just basic sounds to help the song's structure and give it a feel. Later I might go back and replace these sounds with different instruments.

Often, I will entirely fill out an eight-bar piece and completely produce it so that it sounds close to what the final CD version might be *before* moving on to the next section. For me, I get excited if I have an incredibly slamming eight bars. If that first section seems like a hit, then it's worthwhile to continue the rest of the song. If I'm not feeling those eight bars, I might not even go on with the idea.

At this point, I still haven't started the melody. I'll typically leave that until the entire track is done. I might be hearing ideas, but I'll save the final creation of the melody for last.

I often work with a partner, and we work with [backing] tracks, building them up so that the song is completely produced. Then we'll send the track to another songwriter, who might add lyrics and melody on top of the background we created. A lot of R&B tracks are done that way.

The important thing is to follow your inspiration and go where the music leads you.

—Keyboardist, writer, and producer Brian Culbertson has composed music for commercials and soundtracks, and has collaborated with a long list of A-level artists, such as Dave Koz, Donny Osmond, Bob James, and others. His latest solo album is Come on Up *(Warner Brothers). You can learn more about him at www.brainculbertson.com.*

When you create a new track, the New Track Inspector appears (see Figure 4-2). Here, you can select whether the new track will be a Software or Real Instrument, and make settings that will affect its sound.

TIP *You can use the arrow keys to move up and down through the choices in the New Track Inspector.*

FIGURE 4-2 The New Track Inspector with Software Instrument selected

Create a Software Instrument Track

With the New Track window open, select the Software Instrument tab. You'll see two columns. The left one lets you choose an instrument category; the right lets you choose a specific instrument within that category. In this case, we'll choose Drum Kits | Rock Kit. As you can see, a new track appears, with a drum icon, in the track header (see Figure 4-3).

You can hear the individual drum sounds by playing your MIDI controller. Each drum sound is assigned to its own key: C1 is the bass drum; D1 is the snare, F#1 is the closed hi-hat, etc. For a complete list of drum sounds and their key assignments, see Chapter 6.

Create a Real Instrument Track

You can create a Real Instrument track in much the same way that you create a Software Instrument track, but this time when you open the New Track window, click the Real Instrument tab. You'll see the same two-column approach we just described—categories to the left, individual settings to the right (see Figure 4-4).

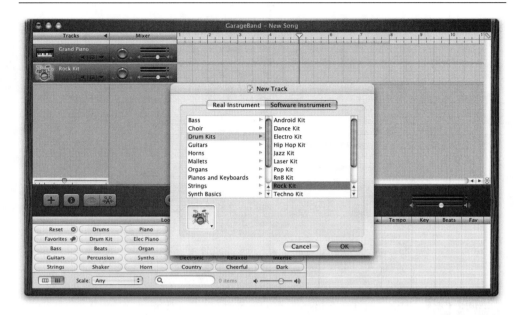

FIGURE 4-3 The GarageBand window now has a new track—Rock Kit.

FIGURE 4-4 The New Track Inspector with Real Instruments selected

CAUTION   *You cannot play a Real Instrument track with your MIDI controller. These tracks are used for prerecorded audio files, or for the audio files you record through your computer's inputs.*

As you can see in Figure 4-4, a Real Instrument track offers a couple of extra parameters. The Format option lets you choose whether the track will be stereo (two channel) or mono (one channel). GarageBand can handle both types of audio files, and will automatically adapt the file to fit the track. The Monitor radio button lets you set whether any sound you feed through your Mac's inputs will be audible through the track (Monitor on).

NOTE   *The Monitor option applies to recordings you make yourself, and has no bearing on the playback of Apple loops.*

Create a New Basic Track

GarageBand's instrument-specific tracks give you a jump start when creating sounds that are appropriate for various instruments, but sometimes it's best to start with a blank slate. The command New Basic Track (found in the Track menu) creates a new Real Instrument track with no effects enabled. You can use this to build a preset of your own.

Did you know?

Vive la Différence

There are some significant differences between Real and Software Instrument tracks. When you create a Software Instrument, you're actually activating a synthesized or sampled sound that you can play, and at the same time, you're making audio settings that will help enhance the sound of that synth or sampler. A Real Instrument track does not include any synthesizers or samplers, but does give you a bunch of tools so that you can adjust the track's sound for a specific application. These include EQ (which changes the tone) and effects like reverb (which creates a room-like ambience to the sound), echo, and others.

Place a Loop in a Track

Now that we have created a couple of tracks, we're ready to hear what they sound like. Although you could play the Software Instrument without a MIDI controller, let's instead start by loading up a few Apple Loops. To open the loop browser:

■ Click the Loop Browser button in the GarageBand window.

■ Select Show Loop Browser in the Control menu.

■ Press the key combination COMMAND-L.

The loop browser is part musical collaborator, part database. With it, you can search and audition the audio and MIDI files in the GarageBand library.

The left side of the loop browser's display is populated by Keyword buttons, which are used to search for loops. To the right is the results list, which displays the loops and offers some important information about each loop, such as its length, key, tempo, whether it consists of audio or MIDI data, and whether it is part of your favorites list.

 For a more detailed view of the loop browser, see Chapter 5.

Select the keyword Drum Kit, and the display should look something like Figure 4-5.

FIGURE 4-5 The loop browser shows a selection of drum loops.

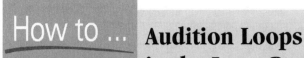

Audition Loops in the Loop Browser

GarageBand comes with several gigabytes worth of loops—even more if you have Jam Pack. Blindly adding these to your song would be a bit of a pain in the neck. Fortunately, you can audition each loop, at the current song tempo, by double-clicking on it in the results list. (If the loop has already been selected, you only have to click on it once.) To stop the loop's audition, click on it once again, or select another loop, or initiate playback of the song.

As you scroll through the results list, you'll notice that some entries are green and have a musical note icon next to them. These are primarily designed to work with Software Instruments.

	Classic Rock Beat 04	140	-
	Classic Rock Beat 05	140	-

Blue entries have a waveform icon. These are designed for Real Instrument tracks.

	Effected Drum Kit 01	120	-
	Effected Drum Kit 02	110	-

Real Instrument regions come in two colors: blue *for Apple Loops (audio files with special metadata that lets GarageBand manipulate their tempo and pitch); and* purple *for Real Instrument recordings (which are standard audio files that are not encoded as Apple Loops). The big difference? GarageBand can time-stretch and transpose the blue regions, but not the purple.*

Add a Software Instrument Loop to the Timeline

To insert a loop into your song, select it in the results list and drag it onto the timeline. As you drag the loop, you will see the loop's name displayed with a + sign; a vertical line shows you where in the song the loop will end up, as shown in Figure 4-6. You can add a loop to an existing track or drag the loop to a blank space to create a new track for it.

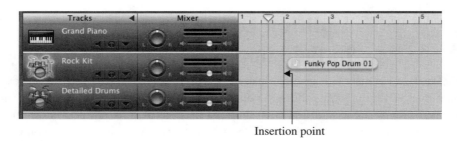

Insertion point

FIGURE 4-6   Here we're dragging the loop Funky Pop Drum 01 to the track Rock Kit. Note the vertical line, which indicates the insertion point.

Remember, GarageBand can convert a Software Instrument loop into a Real Instrument loop when you add it to the timeline. Refer to Chapter 3 for more information.

In this example, we've placed the loop at the start of the song by dragging it to the very beginning of the timeline. Feel free to put the loop right up against the edge of the track's start point—GarageBand will place it at the start of the song for you. Once you insert the loop into the timeline, it becomes a *region,* which you can move and edit without affecting the data inside the original loop. This technique is known as *nondestructive* editing.

When you first insert a loop into the timeline, you can place it at the start of any measure, but you cannot put it "inside" a measure—for example, at the measure's second beat—even if Snap to Grid is turned off, or the grid is set to a fraction such as 1/4 note, 1/8 note, etc. However, once the loop is in place, you can *move around the timeline by the current grid value.*

Figure 4-7 shows our song with the drum region in place. Note that its right outside edge is rounded. In a moment, we'll see how we can drag this right boundary to make the region repeat in the timeline.

At this stage, it helps to see the big picture. Use the zoom slider to zoom out and get a good overview of the song. For maximum visibility, maximize the GarageBand window by clicking the window's Zoom button (or choosing Zoom in the Window menu).

FIGURE 4-7   Our first loop is in place and we're ready to build our song.

Because it's a Software Instrument loop, the region contains MIDI data—information that tells the Software Instrument what to play. It shows a series of bars, which indicate the notes contained in the part.

 *For an in-depth look at Software Instrument tracks, see Chapters 6 and 8.*

Play the Region

Before we do anything else, let's take a listen to the region in the timeline. Start playback. As the Playhead passes over the region, you should hear some drums coming through your sound system. (If you don't, you may be experiencing audio problems; see Chapter 14 for troubleshooting tips.) Once the Playhead passes the outside boundary of the region, the sound stops, although the Playhead keeps moving merrily forward through the silence. Stop playback. We're going to remedy this in a second, but first let's add a Real Instrument loop to the timeline.

 *You can play the same section of music over and over again by activating the cycle region. The cycle automatically repeats a specified part of the song over and over.*

Add an Audio Loop to the Timeline

You add an audio, or Real Instrument, loop to the timeline the same way you do a Software Instrument loop. Select a blue region in the results list and drag it onto the appropriate track. Let's add a second drum track, but let's make this one a Real Instrument loop. Funky Latin Drums 15 seems to do the trick. Figure 4-8 shows the song with the new region in place.

A Real Instrument region looks and behaves differently from its Software Instrument counterpart. First, instead of note commands, it contains actual audio data. You can edit this data (we'll do a lot of that in Chapter 8), but not with the same precision that you can MIDI data. However, you *can* stretch these Real Instrument regions, just as you can Software Instruments.

Change a Region's Duration

Even with today's short attention spans, a two-bar drum loop like Funky Pop Drum 01 probably isn't going to be enough to make you a songwriting sensation. With a traditional sequencer program, the only way to extend a region such as this would be to copy and paste it in the timeline. While you could do that with GarageBand (and there are some situations where that's the right move), it's much easier to take advantage of GarageBand's loop and resize functions, which let you drag a region's boundaries to suit your musical goals.

FIGURE 4-8 We've now added an audio region to the arrangement. Note the differences in the display of Real Instrument regions and Software Instrument regions.

CAUTION *Edits (and most other actions) can be undone and redone with the Edit |
Undo (COMMAND-Z) and Edit | Redo (SHIFT-COMMAND-Z) commands.
GarageBand has multiple undo steps, but once you save a file, "undo
history" is reset—edits made before the save cannot be undone or redone.*

4

Drag the Region's Boundaries

To change a region's duration, click and hold its right boundary. Drag the cursor to
the right to extend the region; drag to the left to shorten it.

You can alter a region's boundaries two ways:

- Loop the region, so that it repeats continuously.

- Resize the region to reveal move of the content within it.

CAUTION *As with other timeline operations, the grid setting will affect how you stretch
a region. For example, if you want to stretch by a full measure or more, set
the grid to 1/1 note. For finer resolution—say one or two beats—set the grid
to 1/4 or 1/2, etc. (Obviously, you can still stretch the loop by a full measure
at these settings as well.) The grid setting will only affect your edits if the
Snap to Grid option is active.*

Loop a Region

Most of the time, you'll probably want to stretch the region's boundaries
so that it "loops," or repeats continuously. When you click in a region's
upper right-hand corner, the cursor turns into the loop pointer.

Now, when you drag the region's boundary to the right, the contents of the region
will repeat, or "loop," to form a continuous part. Release the cursor at the point where
you want the region to stop. Figure 4-9 shows the original Funky Pop Drum 01 region,
which has been stretched to be eight bars long.

TIP *Two visual clues show you that you've successfully stretched a region in
loop mode: the region has segments, which indicate the start and end of
the original loop, and the music inside the region appears to be repeating
over the region's entire duration (see Figure 4-10).*

Resize a Region

Although GarageBand is designed as a loop-construction program, it does allow you
to alter a region's boundaries *without* looping its contents. Why would you want to

The region Funky Pop Drum 01, after we've stretched it with the loop pointer

do that? Several reasons: You may, for example, want to let the final note of a region decay at the end of a song. Or, you may want to shorten a two-measure region so that it's only one measure long. Or, you may need to fine-tune the boundaries of a region you've recorded yourself. We'll look at these applications in depth in Chapters 7 and 8, but for now it's important to see the different ways that the loop and resize functions affect the music you're hearing.

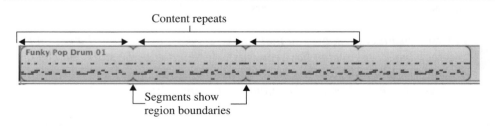

FIGURE 4-10 In this close-up of Funky Pop Drum 01, we can see segments, which indicate the loop's original start and end points. Note how the music contained in the loop is duplicated within each segment.

To resize a region, click on its *lower* right- or left-hand boundaries. The resize pointer appears. Note that it doesn't have the circular arrow of the loop pointer.

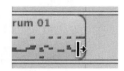

4

To extend a region from the end, drag its lower-right corner, as shown in Figure 4-11. As you'll see, when we do this with Funky Pop Drum 01, the region opens up into empty space, and there are no segment boundaries to indicate the loop points.

You can also resize a region at its beginning. Simply drag the lower-right boundary, as shown in Figure 4-12.

CAUTION   *You cannot shorten a Software Instrument region by moving its boundaries to later than the source loop's original start point.*

NOTE   *In order to better illustrate this technique, we moved the region later in the timeline.*

TIP   *Although Figures 4-11 and 4-12 show that we ended up with blank space when we extended the region, this isn't always the case. Resizing is an effective editing tool, especially when working with regions you've recorded yourself.*

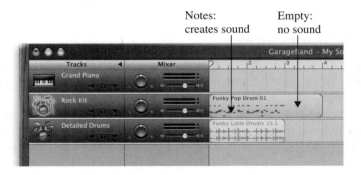

FIGURE 4-11   Funky Pop Drum 01, after being resized. Note the blank space to the right; the loop only contains two measures worth of music, so stretching it beyond that point results in silence.

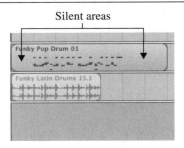

Silent areas

FIGURE 4-12   We've extended Funky Pop Drum 01 by dragging its left boundary further left. As in Figure 4-11, this extension resulted in silence.

Resize Real Instrument Regions

Real Instrument regions behave in much the same way as Software Instrument regions—that's one of GarageBand's greatest charms—but there are some differences when resizing. With a Real Instrument region:

- You *can* resize the beginning of the region so that it starts later than the source loop file.

- You *cannot* resize the end of the region so that it decays longer than the source loop file.

 *Save your work! As soon as your song begins to take shape, save the file. If your computer or GarageBand crashes, you'll lose any unsaved changes!*

Move a Region

Once you place a region in the timeline, it's not stuck there. You can move it forward or backward in the song by dragging it horizontally in the timeline. As with resizing, the Snap to Grid setting will help determine where the region lands.

You can also move a region to a different track by dragging it vertically in the timeline. The destination track must be of the same type as the region. For example, you can only move a Software Instrument region to a Software Instrument track, and you can only move a Real Instrument region to a Real Instrument track. The tracks themselves need not be the same instrument, however; you can, for example, move a region from a strings Software Instrument track to a piano Software Instrument track.

> TIP   *You can move regions diagonally—that is, to a different track and a different time position.*

 GarageBand added a handy new feature in version 1.1—the ability to drag tracks up and down in the track header. At first, this might seem like a minor addition. But as your song expands and your screen gets more cluttered, it may be useful to be able to move some tracks in and out of view. You might, for example, want to place two related tracks—such as two percussion parts—together for easier editing. To move a track, select it in the track header and drag it up or down with the mouse. The other track politely makes way for one you're moving. This has no effect on playback.

4

Moving On

Now that we know the basics of how to create tracks, find and audition loops, and place them in the timeline, we can let our creativity take over. In Chapter 5, we'll start building an arrangement with Apple Loops.

Chapter 5

Create a Song with Apple Loops

How to...

- Search for Apple Loops
- Use the loop browser's Button view
- Use the loop browser's Columns view
- Create a list of favorite loops
- Audition loops in the loop browser
- Add loops to the song from the loop browser
- Create a rhythmic bed
- Create and refine a bass track
- Create additional tracks

GarageBand lets you make music three different ways. You can construct a song using the provided Apple Loops, record tracks that trigger Software Instruments via MIDI, and record original audio through your computer's audio inputs. You can mix and match all three techniques, but there is a major distinction between the first two and the last one. When you work with Apple Loops and Software Instruments, you can change the song's tempo after you've recorded your tracks. But once you record your own audio into GarageBand, the tempo must stay fixed or your audio will be out of sync.

In this chapter, we'll expand on what we started in Chapter 4 and build a song with Apple Loops. As we work through GarageBand's features, keep in mind that we're not talking about a linear process with a concrete beginning and end. Some people like to start a song by establishing a rhythmic bed, while others prefer to come up with a melody first, and flesh out the background later. If you're feeling inspired, you might want to just roll the metronome and start playing; if you feel stuck, you might want to audition a bunch of loops for inspiration. As you get more comfortable with GarageBand, you'll find your own way of working.

Before we start building the song, let's take a closer look at the loop browser, which acts as GarageBand's central nervous system.

Open the Loop Browser

The loop browser is one of GarageBand's most powerful features. It lets you search for and audition Apple Loops, add them to your song, and view vital information about them, such as their original tempo, key, and duration. Apple Loops aren't just time- and pitch-stretchable; they also contain keyword information that allows the loop browser to search for them. To open the loop browser, click the loop browser button in the GarageBand window (shown here), select Show loop browser from the Control menu, or use the keyboard shortcut COMMAND-L.

 The loop browser offers two views. (Button view is on the right; column view is on the left.) You can switch between them with the view buttons, shown here.

Use the Button View

The Button view (see Figure 5-1) shows the Apple Loops' keywords as buttons. Click a button to search for loops that are tagged with keywords. Once you've clicked a keyword button, you'll notice that some keywords are grayed out, while others remain bold. The bold keywords help you search through subcategories—categories within a main group. For example, under Guitar, you have choices like Acoustic, Electric, Distorted, and so on. Conversely, if you were to start with the Distorted keyword, you'd find choices like Guitars, Bass, Organ, Electric, Acoustic, etc. This works well because it gives you a choice on how to search: by mood, genre, instrument, or a combination of all three.

> TIP   *The Button view is ideal when you're not sure what you want, and want to browse through lots of options. It's great when you need a specific instrument in a specific genre with a specific mood—for example, "Bass" in the "Rock/ Blues" genre that's a "Single" instrument "Electric," "Clean," and "Intense."*

Let's hunt for a bass track with the Button view. Start by clicking the keyword button Bass. A number of loops appear in the results list. We can narrow the search further by clicking on one of the 14 remaining keywords. Let's choose Rock/Blues. By now, the results list will have fewer options, but they'll be closer to what we want.

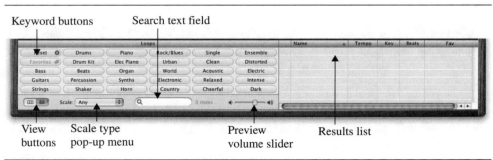

FIGURE 5-1   The loop browser's Button view

We can narrow the search further by clicking the Electric button. The result list looks something like this:

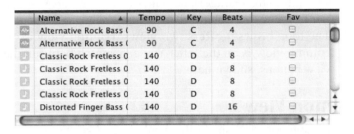

Click a button a second time to deactivate its keyword and return to a broader view.

Use the Column View

The Column view (see Figure 5-2) shows the keywords in a set of Finder-like columns. This gives you a more hierarchical look at the Apple Loops on your system. You start by choosing Keyword type, then a subcategory, and finally, a keyword.

The Column view is useful if you want to focus on one particular category. You can look at loops by instrument, musical genre, or mood. Figure 5-3 shows a search-by-instrument for "electric piano."

Use the Search Field

Although it's fun to browse through loops and get ideas, you may not want to wade through a long list every time you need a sound. The Search field lets you type in a name or part of a name, as shown in Figure 5-4. You can search all loops

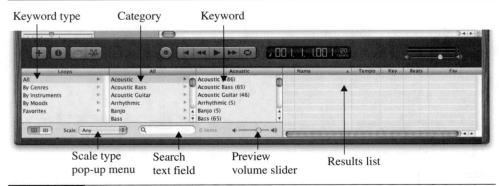

FIGURE 5-2   The loop browser's Column view

FIGURE 5-3	The loop browser's Column view shows the results of a search for "electric piano."

(set keywords to All), or just those matching a specific keyword. In the example shown in Figure 5-4, we had already used keywords to narrow the search to electric piano. Typing the word "funk" returned a list of funky electric piano loops.

To use the Search field, type in a word, and press ENTER. Any loop file containing that word in its name or keyword tags will appear in the results list.

CAUTION *The Search function resets itself whenever you select a new keyword.*

Audition Loops in the Loop Browser

Unless you like to compose via trial and error, you'll probably want to audition a few loops before adding one to your song. The loop browser lets you audition each loop, either on its own or in synchronized playback with the song.

Audition a Loop on its Own

To audition a loop on its own, double-click it in the results list. It will play back at the current song's tempo and key. Click it again to stop playback, or double-click on a different loop to play that one instead.

FIGURE 5-4	The loop browser's Search pane helps you find instruments by name. You can search through all your Apple Loops, or narrow the results by clicking on one or more keywords before initiating the search.

You can scroll through the results list with the scroll bars as a loop is playing. The selected loop need not be visible.

Audition a Loop with the Existing Song

You can get a good basic idea of how a loop sounds on its own, but once you have a few candidates in mind, it really helps to hear how various loops sound with the rest of the tracks. Fortunately, GarageBand makes your life easy by letting you hear loops in the loop browser while the song plays back—you don't need to drag the loop into the song to hear it. To hear a loop while the song plays back:

■ If necessary, move the Playhead so that it's playing over the appropriate part of the song.

■ Initiate song playback.

■ Double-click the loop in the results list.

■ If necessary, adjust the loop's loudness with the loop browser's volume slider.

TIP   *If you plan to audition a lot of loops, set the song playback to Cycle mode.*

GarageBand will wait until the song reaches a new bar before it starts playing the loop in the loop browser. This lets the loop play back in sync with the song. You can't do the reverse—start loop playback first, then initiate song playback. If you start song playback while a loop is playing in the loop browser, the loop browser will stop playing.

TIP   *If you find a few loops that you like, add them to your favorites list by clicking the box in the results list's Fav (Favorites) column. Later, you can see all the favorites together and compare them.*

Work with Loops in the Results List

The loop browser's results list (see Figure 5-5) not only displays some vital information about the Apple Loops on your system, it also lets you sort them by various parameters: Name, Tempo, Key, Beats (number of beats the loop contains), and Favorite status.

By default, the files are sorted alphabetically, A to Z (see Figure 5-6a). You can change this by clicking in any of the column headings. Click a column heading a second time to reverse the sort order (for example, Name from Z to A, as shown in Figure 5-6b).

FIGURE 5-5   The results list lets you view, audition, and sort through files. Here, we've sorted files by key.

Add Favorites

The Fav (Favorites) check box is a very powerful addition to the loop browser's bag of tricks. You can assign any loop to your personal favorites by checking the box.

Name	▼	Tempo	Key	Beats	Fav
Upbeat Electric Piano (		85	C	16	☑
Upbeat Electric Piano (		85	C	8	☐

Favorites are handy for several reasons. First, within the results list, you can sort loops by Favorites status.

TIP   *As you run through the list and find loops you like, check them as favorites. Then, after you've found a few candidates, sort the list by Favorites; you can then compare them side by side.*

Favorites in Button View

When you select a favorite, GarageBand automatically makes it available in both the Keyword and Column views in the loop browser. To see the favorites in the

(a)

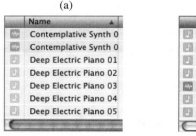

Name	▲
Contemplative Synth 0	
Contemplative Synth 0	
Deep Electric Piano 01	
Deep Electric Piano 02	
Deep Electric Piano 03	
Deep Electric Piano 04	
Deep Electric Piano 05	

(b)

Name	▼
Upbeat Electric Piano 0	
Upbeat Electric Piano 0	
Upbeat Electric Piano 0	
Upbeat Electric Piano 0	
Synth Array 11	
Spacey Electric Piano 0	
Spacey Electric Piano 0	

FIGURE 5-6   You can change the result list's sort order by clicking on a column head, such as Name (a). Click an active head a second time to reverse the order (b).

FIGURE 5-7   The Keywords view with Favorites selected

Keyword view, select the Favorites button. If you stop there, all the favorites will be displayed, regardless of other keywords associated with the loop (see Figure 5-7).

You can then refine the search by selecting a keyword. In Figure 5-8, we narrowed the search with the keyword Drums.

Favorites in the Column View

To see the favorites in Column view, select Favorites from the Keyword Type column, select the appropriate subcategory and keyword, and you will see any favorites that fit those criteria.

 *The advantage of using Favorites in the Column view is that they're restricted by keywords. However, if you want to see all favorites, regardless of keyword, ironically enough, you'll need to switch to the Button view.*

Clear Favorites

All loops you name as favorites in GarageBand will remain on your VIP list when you close a session or when you start a new one. That's great, because it lets you collect a core set of loops and use them in all your projects.

However, if you store too many files as favorites, it defeats the purpose—you'll find yourself wasting time sorting through them. You can remove individual files from the Favorites list by unchecking them in the Results menu's Fav column.

FIGURE 5-8   You can filter a favorites search by keyword.

TIP   *Use the Button view's Favorites button to see all the favorites at once.*

Filter Results by Scale Type

The Scale pop-up menu lets you filter results by—you guessed it—scale type. Choices include Any, Minor, Major, Good for Both, and None. Scale type is only important if you're dealing with harmonic material, such as chord patterns, bass lines, and melody lines. It has no impact when you're working with rhythmic material like drum and percussion loops.

Add a Loop from the Finder

When you're first getting going with GarageBand, you'll probably spend most of your time working with the files that come with the program (augmented, perhaps, by the files that come with Jam Pack). However, you can add loops to your song directly from the Finder by dragging them into the timeline. GarageBand supports files in AIFF, WAV, MP3, and (as of version 1.1) AAC formats (provided the AAC files are unprotected). If you import an MP3 or AAC, GarageBand converts it into AIFF format.

NEW IN 1.1   GarageBand version 1.1 includes an interesting upgrade to the loop browser. GarageBand can now index any audio files that you drag from the Finder directly into the browser, and is able to keep track of files that are located on multiple discs without copying them into the main GarageBand library. For more information on this powerful feature, see Chapter 13.

Create a Rhythmic Bed

NEW IN 1.1   Now that we know our way around the loop browser, we're ready to return to the task at hand—making music with some Apple Loops. Figure 5-9 shows the song as we left it in Chapter 4, with a couple of drum loops in place.

NOTE   *If you have not yet added a drum loop to the timeline, please refer to Chapter 4.*

NOTE   *To delete a track, select it in the tracks list, then choose Delete Track from the Track menu, or use the key combination COMMAND-DELETE.*

We'll stick with the Software Instrument–based Funky Pop Drum 01, but eliminate the Real Instrument Detailed Drums for now. Our song will now have two tracks: Grand Piano and Drum Kit.

 **Filter for More Relevant Results**

When you work with rhythmic material, you don't need to worry about matching keys. But with pitched material—piano, horn, guitar, and other loops—the key does matter. You can set your GarageBand preferences so that the loop browser will only search for Real Instrument loops that fall within two semitones of the song's key. Simply Choose GarageBand | Preferences | General, as shown here:

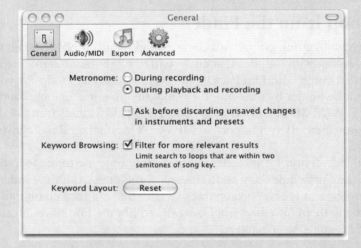

If GarageBand can make any loop match any key, why would you bother? The answer lies in the limitations of pitch shifting; the farther from its base pitch you shift an audio file (which is what Real Instrument loops are), the less natural the loop will sound. Keeping the intervals close improves the sound quality. Of course, there are drawbacks: you'll have fewer loops from which to choose. Also, a loop that's, say, seven semitones away from the root might be the *ideal* choice when you want to create a key change in your song.

Extend the Drum Loop

In Chapter 4, we extended the drum loop to cover eight bars. That's not bad as a starting point, but it's a little short for a complete song. Let's extend the basic loop to 32 bars. Remember, you'll need to drag the loop from the upper right-hand corner in order to activate the loop pointer. By the time you're done, your song should look like Figure 5-10.

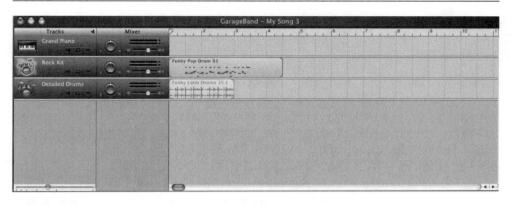

FIGURE 5-9   Drum tracks can make a good starting place when building a song.

   *When extending a region over a large number of bars, zoom out to get a better overview of the song.*

Convert a Software Instrument Loop into a Real Instrument Loop

With version 1.1, GarageBand can convert Software Instrument loops into Real Instrument loops as you drag them into the timeline. Because Real Instrument loops use less processor power than their software counterparts, this can save system resources.

There are two ways to do this. First, you can set this as a preference in GarageBand | Preferences | Advanced (see Chapter 3 for details on how to set preferences) by checking the box Convert to Real Instruments. When this is selected, every loop you drag from the loop browser will go into the timeline as a Real Instrument loop,

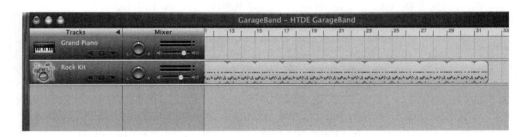

FIGURE 5-10   By extending the drum loop to 32 bars, we've given ourselves a solid musical foundation.

What Makes a Good Loop?

From a technical angle, things like sample length, frequency extension, and overall clarity figure into what makes a good loop. But sonically, certain drum loops have become standards and bear scrutiny as to what makes them tick. The Winston's "Amen Brother," James Brown's "Funky Drummer," and David Garibaldi's ecstatic drum pattern in Tower of Power's "Squibb Cakes" have been used everywhere from dance music to TV commercials.

The "Amen Brother" loop has been programmed backwards and forwards, but it is instantly recognizable: a ricocheting beat that focuses on a dry cymbal pattern and a popping snare drum. There is an elasticity and excitement, but its exact quality remains elusive. Extremely clear, it is easy to chop up and reassemble. You could say that it just feels good.

Feeling good also describes the "Funky Drummer" loop, originally recorded by Clyde Stubblefield in the mid-1960s. Slipping and sliding, it is the ultimate R&B groove and makes anyone instantly feel like "gettin' on the good foot."

Finally, the high hat jabs and frenetic sticking of David Garabaldi's "Squibb Cakes" has been reprogrammed ad infinitum, but its tremendous energy, originality, and forward motion remain intact.

For a groove to be good, it must capture the imagination, fire the ears, and shake the booty all at once.

—*Ken Micallef, Author of* The Way They Play: The Classic Rock
Drummers *(Backbeat Books)*

even if it was originally available as a Software Instrument. When it's unchecked, the file will follow its original designation. Here, we see the Software Instrument loop Classic Funk Synth being dragged into the timeline as a Real Instrument loop. Note how the icon changes to show the Real Instrument designation.

Name	Tempo	Key
Classic Funk Synth 01	100	C
Classic Funk Synth 02 (Classic Funk Synth 03)	100	C
Classic Funk Synth 03	100	C
Classic Funk Synth 04	100	C

Whichever way you have the preference set, you can change GarageBand's behavior by OPTION-dragging the loop into the timeline. That is, if the preference Convert to Real Instruments is checked, you can still place a Software Instrument loop in the timeline by OPTION-dragging it.

Play the Drum Loop

We've extended the drum loop. Now let's hear it. To initiate playback, hit the SPACEBAR or click the Play button in the transport bar. The drum loop sounds a little monotonous but we'll worry about variations later. For now, though, it provides a nice groove.

Add a Bass Track

When professional musicians use the term "rhythm section," they're often referring to the combination of bass and drums. These two instruments work together to give a song its backbone and groove.

There are several ways to take care of your rhythm section's "bottom line" in GarageBand: you can create a Software Instrument track for a sampled or synthesizer bass loop, or you can create a Real Instrument track for an audio bass loop. You can then add an Apple Loop to the appropriate track, or play a bass line of your own. Since we're focusing on Apple Loops, let's stick with the former for now, and select a bass part that goes with our drum loop.

Locate a Bass Loop in the Loop Browser

Open the loop browser and enable the Keyword view. If necessary, click the Reset button to set the view so that it shows a complete list of keywords, as shown in Figure 5-11.

Click the Bass button. A list of bass loops appears in the results list (see Figure 5-12).

If you scroll through the bass loops, you'll find a staggering number of choices. Let's narrow the list by clicking on the Rock/Blues button. This provides a nice—but manageable—selection of candidates. You can audition some loops—both on their own and along with the song—by double-clicking on them.

FIGURE 5-11   The loop browser with all keywords visible

FIGURE 5-12   The loop browser displays some bass loops. Note that keywords that don't apply to the bass are grayed out, while those that do remain dark, indicating that they're active.

Add the Bass Loop to the Song

Once you've decided on a loop, you can add it to the song. You have the option of creating a track first, or having GarageBand create a new track for the loop. We're going to do the latter. The loop Groovy Electric Bass 01 seems to go well with Funky Pop Drums 01, so let's drag it into the timeline and place it at measure 3 (see Figure 5-13). This will give us a nice two-bar drum intro. As you can see, GarageBand automatically creates an appropriate track for the bass part, called Electric Bass.

 *To make it easier to place the loop where you want it, activate Snap-to-grid and zoom in for a closer look.*

If you accidentally place the loop in the wrong position, don't fret. You can simply select it and drag it to the correct place in the timeline.

Extend the Bass Loop

The bass loop is only two measures long, so we need to extend it. The quickest way to do this is by dragging the top-right edge with the loop pointer. Unlike the drum

FIGURE 5-13   We've added the Real Instrument bass loop Groovy Electric Bass to the arrangement.

loop, however, we're going to stop at measure 11. The bass region is now eight bars long (see Figure 5-14).

Add a Second Bass Loop

You may be wondering why we didn't merely extend the bass loop to the end of the song. We could do that—and that might be preferred if we want to work out a few ideas. But since we're building a background track, it would be nice to introduce some variation. Let's return to the loop browser and select Groovy Electric Bass 02, a sparse, funky part that contrasts nicely with the rollicking Groovy Electric Bass 01.

 *Here's a timesaver: Add the bass loops to your Favorites list. This way, you won't have to search for them every time you need them.*

Drag the loop into the timeline. You can put it into blank space to create a new track, or simply place it in the existing electric bass track, as shown in Figure 5-15.

 *By placing all the bass parts in one track, you'll use fewer computer resources than you would if you created a separate track for each loop. It also makes it easier to adjust the bass part when you're mixing.*

Flesh Out the Bass Part

Now that we have some variation in place, let's complete the part. First, use the loop pointer to extend Groovy Electric Bass 02 into a four-measure part. It should now reach measure 15.

Next, copy Groovy Electric Bass 01 and place it at measure 16. There are several way to do this, and we'll describe each briefly.

 *These techniques generally work best when Snap to Grid is active. To activate Snap to Grid, choose it in the Control menu, or press COMMAND-G.*

FIGURE 5-14   Groovy Electric Bass, after we've stretched it to cover eight bars

FIGURE 5-15 The electric bass track now contains two different regions: Groovy Electric Bass 01 and Groovy Electric Bass 02.

Copy a Region with Copy and Paste Select the region. Use the Edit menu to copy it, or use the key combo COMMAND-C. Move the playhead to the position at which you want to place the region, and use Edit | Paste or COMMAND-V to place it.

 *You can paste the region while the song plays back, but GarageBand will put it at the current Playhead position. Unless you have great timing—or like the idea of randomly placing the loops—I don't recommend this.*

Copy a Region by Option Dragging Select the region in the timeline; it will appear darker than the regions around it, as shown here:

Hold the OPTION key and drag the region to the desired location. You can drag the region anywhere in the track, but its final position will be determined by the grid setting (provided that Snap to Grid is active). For an edit like this, 1/1 is a good starting point. The Playhead position has no effect on placement when you OPTION-drag.

 You can copy regions by OPTION-dragging while GarageBand plays back.

Add the Region from the Loop Browser As an alternative to copy and drag, you can also drag a fresh copy of the loop from the loop browser into the timeline. When you do, the region will default to the loop's original size.

Add More Instruments

Once you have the bass track in place, you can start adding more instruments. We'll discuss strategies for what kinds of sounds work together throughout the book. For this first song, we've chosen to augment the bass and drum parts that we've already inserted with the following Apple Loops:

- Reggae Toy Piano 01 (Keyword Electric Piano)

- Funky Electric Guitar 03 (Keyword Electric Guitar)

- RnB Horn 01 (Keyword Horns)

- RnB Horn 02 (Keyword Horns)

We add these loops as we did the others—by dragging them into the timeline. As before, the Snap to Grid feature is active, which makes it easy to place the loops so that they make musical sense.

 *You may notice that the loops are from different musical genres. That's one of GarageBand's greatest charms: it lets you mix and match styles. Don't be afraid to experiment by combining loops of different genres.*

Although these loops come from audio files that have different lengths, keys, and tempos, GarageBand automatically adjusts them so they line up on playback. You can drag them freely in the timeline, but we've chosen to position the loops so that they play back periodically (not as continuous "beds") using the techniques we've described earlier in this chapter. The end result looks like Figure 5-16. Study the image closely and you'll see that we left some empty spaces on the Electric Piano, Horn/ Wind, and Electric Guitar tracks. We've purposely left these blank so that the sounds could come in and out and trade off against one another—a good strategy when you want to add drama to your song.

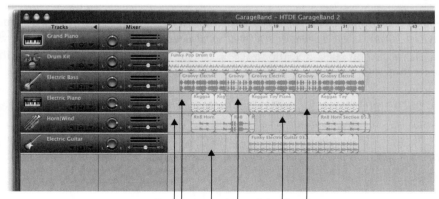

Empty space; the track is silent here.

FIGURE 5-16   The song after it's been fleshed out with a rhythm guitar track, some fast electric piano rhythms, and a funky horn part

 *As with the bass track, we put two different horn parts on the same track.*

 *Here's a great way to get to know GarageBand: Save the song, set the grid to 1/1, start playback, and try moving regions around while the music plays.*

Save That Song!

Every time you make an important change in your song, you should save it. GarageBand has several ways to save a song.

- Use File | Save (COMMAND-S) to overwrite the currently saved version.

- Use File | Save As (SHIFT-COMMAND-S) to save the song to a new location or give it a different name.

- Use File | Save as Archive to save the song *and* all the loops contained in the song into the same package file. This is the best option of you plan to take the song to a different computer, or if you want to create a backup of your song.

 GarageBand now lets you close a song without quitting the program. This makes it easier to go between different versions of a song file.

Moving On

With just a few Apple Loops, we've built a pretty cool piece of music with a nice groove. A close listen, however, shows that it needs some editing to really work as a song. The ending is abrupt; the first "verse" is shorter than the second, and the horn section sounds a little unfocused—there's potential there, but these guys need direction! If you plan to work exclusively with Apple Loops, you may want to skip ahead to Chapter 7 for a more detailed look at how to edit them, and to Chapter 13 for some less technical, more creative advice.

In the next chapter, however, we'll use Software Instruments and a MIDI controller to record a performance. If you're more interested in recording audio tracks (known in GarageBand lingo as "Real Instrument recordings"), skip ahead to Chapter 7.

Chapter 6

Record with Software Instruments

How to...

■ Check MIDI connections

■ Adjust the sound of a Software Instrument

■ Activate the metronome

■ Record a single performance

■ Re-record a small section of the track (punch-in and punch-out)

■ Enable the cycle

■ Record in cycle mode

■ Tighten up the timing after you've recorded

Musicians and nonmusicians alike can make music with GarageBand by using Apple Loops. After all, you don't need to play like Chopin to chop up some loops (though that type of composition takes its own set of skills and creative impetus). But this is only one way that GarageBand can help you create your masterpiece. One of the most powerful is by recording your own performances by triggering Software Instruments with a MIDI controller.

Obviously, if you're proficient on a musical instrument that can act as a MIDI controller, such as keyboard, wind instrument, guitar, or drums, you'll want to use this feature. And if you've had experience with a MIDI sequencer, you have a bit of a head start here. But even novice musicians can make satisfying music by playing Software Instruments. GarageBand's editing tools can help you compensate for a lack of "chops," to make the music you play yourself sound clean, tight, and correct.

How Software Instruments Work

GarageBand uses some powerful technology, but the highlight of the program from a technological standpoint may well be its inclusion of Software Instruments. With Software Instruments, you can play the program as a musical instrument, edit your performances, and create new and unique sounds.

Software Instruments can be used in two ways: first, you can use Software Instrument loops in the same way in which you use audio loops—just drag a loop from the loop browser, and place it in the song. Like their audio real instrument counterparts, these loops are "elastic"—they follow the tempo of the song. But Software Instrument loops actually give you more editing control than their Real Instrument counterparts. You can change the sound more definitively (for example, changing a piano sound into that of a guitar or saxophone). And you can change the very *character* of the performance—elements such as the pitch, timing, and volume of individual notes are all under your control.

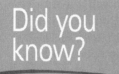

The Smart Set

6

If you plan to use GarageBand in a live context, you can prepare by creating separate GarageBand songs for each song (or group of songs) in your set. The GarageBand song would be preloaded with all the Software Instruments you'd need for a particular piece of music, but the tracks themselves would contain no data, as shown here.

You can use the mouse or the computer's arrow keys to move from track to track. Any edits you make to the Software Instrument tracks, including effects settings, will be stored as part of the song. Just be sure to leave enough time for the GarageBand song file to load, and set latency to Minimum Delay When Playing Instruments Live in GarageBand | Preferences | Audi | MIDI.

You can also record your own performances with Software Instruments. These recordings can be edited and stretched, just the like prerecorded Apple Loops. You can combine both kinds of material in your song. You can also use a Software Instrument to jam along with the tracks you've built with Apple Loops This is great in a live performance situation, where you want to play fresh material over prerecorded background tracks.

Finally, you can simply play GarageBand's Software Instruments in a live performance context. For your live performance GarageBand song, you could create a "bank" of Software Instrument tracks, each preloaded with a different Software Instrument. During your performance, switch among the tracks to hear different sounds (see preceding "Did You Know").

Play a Software Instrument

Whether you're going to just jam along with some backing tracks or record some tracks of your own, you'll need to get some sound happening with the Software Instruments. The first step is to make sure that GarageBand is receiving MIDI from your controller.

Set Up the MIDI Controller

Although you can play Software Instruments by triggering GarageBand's built-in keyboard with your mouse, for a real performance experience, you'll want a more elegant controller.

NOTE *You can access the built-in keyboard from the Window menu, or by using the key combination COMMAND-K.*

MIDI controllers come in many shapes and sizes, from piano-like keyboards with 88 weighted keys, to guitar, wind, and drum controllers that transmit MIDI messages. The keyboard is the most common, and devices like the USB equipped M-Audio Ozone (see Figure 6-1) are more than up to the task.

The advantage of a USB controller like the Ozone (and others) is that it can connect directly to the computer: no outboard interface is needed. The Ozone also sports a built-in audio interface, so you can use it for high-quality sound recording and playback as well as MIDI control.

Set Up Your MIDI Interface and Controller

Before you can get your MIDI controller to work with GarageBand, you have to get it to transmit MIDI to the program. MIDI signal reaches GarageBand from your controller via a separate device called—sensibly enough—a MIDI interface.

FIGURE 6-1   M-Audio Ozone USB MIDI controller and audio interface

Unlike with audio, Apple computers do not have built-in MIDI inputs. So while you can use GarageBand's audio features without a third-party interface if you wish, you cannot use a MIDI controller without a MIDI interface.

In a traditional MIDI setup, you would connect the MIDI output from your controller to a MIDI input on the interface. A MIDI output on the interface connects to a MIDI input on the controller, and the interface connects to the computer via the USB port (as shown in Figure 6-2).

MIDI connections are made with MIDI cables, which have a five-pin connection scheme, as shown in Figure 6-3. A MIDI cable always has male connectors on both ends; the interface has female connections for both inputs and outputs. MIDI cables are available at any musical instrument dealer. As with audio cables, quality is important: get the best cable you can afford.

NOTE   *Although MIDI uses a five-pin connector, only the middle three pins are active.*

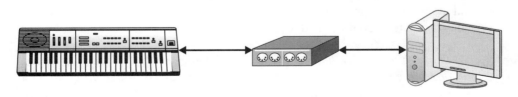

FIGURE 6-2   MIDI connection diagram

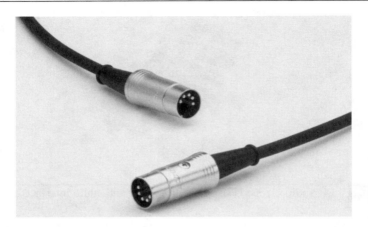

FIGURE 6-3 A MIDI cable uses a five-pin connector (image courtesy of Pro Co Sound)

However, a device like the Ozone is both controller *and* interface, so you need make only one connection between the Ozone and the computer via USB (which means that you won't need a separate MIDI cable to connect it to your computer).

Whether you're using a separate controller/interface setup or an all-in-one like the Ozone, you'll need to install the appropriate drivers so that your computer can recognize the external hardware.

 *Because of the variety of options available for MIDI controllers and interfaces, we won't get into a step-by-step interface setup. However, we will address some potential issues in the Troubleshooting guide in Chapter 14.*

Open Audio/MIDI Setup

Audio/MIDI Setup (see Figure 6-4) gives you a graphical view of all the MIDI devices connected to your system. Here, you can view and configure your interfaces and controllers so that every application in OS X can recognize them. Audio/MIDI Setup is found in the OS X Applications | Utilities folder; although it's not a program I use every day, I like to keep it in the dock.

Those of us who've had experience working with MIDI in previous Apple operating systems know that in the past, you needed a bridge program, such as Opcode's Open Music System (OMS) or Mark of the Unicorn's Free MIDI (very few pro applications used Apple MIDI Manager). Thankfully, those days are over, as are the bugs and incompatibilities that went with them!

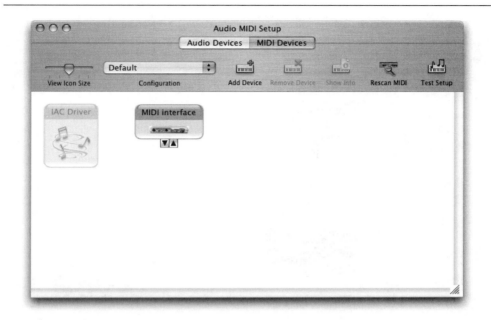

FIGURE 6-4   The Audio/MIDI Setup utility, with the MIDI Devices pane showing

One of the nice things about the utility is that it lets you set up different configurations for different applications. For now, let's stick to one default setup. The utility shows all MIDI interfaces installed on your system. To add a controller, click the Add Device button, then manually drag from the controller's outputs to the interface's inputs, as shown in Figure 6-5.

Once the controller is connected, you can use the Test Setup button to make sure that it's being seen by the computer. Play the controller; the interface's MIDI input arrow should light up.

 *It may sound obvious, but make sure that the controller and interface are powered on and that the connection between the controller's output and the interface's input are working.*

Play a Software Instrument

Now that the controller is working, you're ready to play a Software Instrument. You can start on any available Software Instrument in the song. (If you haven't already done so, create a Software Instrument track, as described in Chapter 4.) Simply select it in the track header and play the controller. You should be hearing sound.

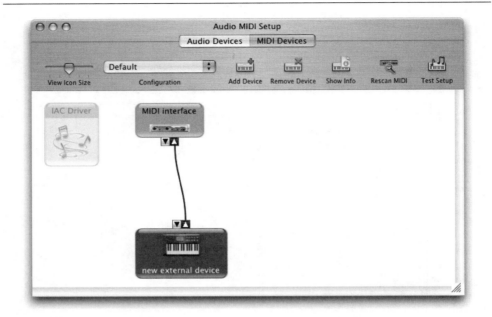

FIGURE 6-5 Adding a controller

NOTE *When GarageBand is receiving MIDI, you'll see a small light flash in the time display, just to the left of the tempo indicator.*

CAUTION *Make sure that the Software Instrument track is not muted, and that its audio is at a listenable level.*

Adjust the Sound Level and Position

One of the most critical things in a performance is being able to hear yourself clearly in relation to the other instruments. You can adjust your track's level relative to the others by using the volume slider in the track header. Remember, you can always put the volume back to a level that better fits the overall mix after you're done playing or recording the track. As you play, you should see the level meters fire. These verify that signal is coming through the track.

Voices from the Community

Guitarists' Gateway to GarageBand

Most of the music industry has gone high-tech, but sometimes it seems that guitarists are still stuck in the 1950s. Traditionally, the electric guitar has had only passive magnetic pickups as a sound source, and that fact has not changed in the last 50 years. The question I like to ask "traditionalist" guitarists is this: Do you still watch a black-and-white TV?

Fortunately, not all is retro in the guitar world. The iGuitar by Brian Moore Guitars—and other technology-equipped guitars such as those made by Godin and others—features a 13-pin output in addition to the traditional magnetic pickups. (Special "divided pickups" with 13-pin outputs, such as the Roland GK-2AH, are also available as retro-fits.)

Unlike magnetic pickups, which send audio signal for all six strings at once, a 13-pin output senses each string individually. It then translates each string's vibration into an independent data signal that a computer (or other compatible sound device) can use to control electronic instruments. The 13-pin standard, which was created by Roland (and adopted by Yamaha and Axon), gives you the power to play GarageBand's Software Instruments—such as piano, strings, bass, and all of the interesting synth sounds—with your guitar.

Although this technology has been around for a while, recent improvements have made it better, faster, and more powerful. The new Roland GI-20 GK-MIDI interface converts the 13-pin signal to USB, and sends a fast MIDI signal to your Mac with almost no latency (yes, its fast!). It is nothing short of remarkable! The electric guitar has been in "black and white" for over 50 years, and now it can be heard in full color!

Previously, the synth-minded guitarists had to struggle to write and record "electronic instrument" parts on a keyboard. Now with the iGuitar, a GI-20, and GarageBand, you can write and record more intuitively on your natural instrument, and incorporate the expressive techniques that make the guitar so special in your work. And now that the guitar can communicate with the computer via USB, it is possible to play directly to notation and TAB programs like Sibelius and Finale.

Like traditional electric guitars, the iGuitar still has regular (magnetic) pickups for all the traditional guitar sounds, plus a piezo pickup that offers a warm, harmonic-rich acoustic sound via a stereo output—as well as being the pickup for the 13-pin output. It is Roland GK–compatible with some tracking improvements.

In summary, the iGuitar and instruments like it let the guitarist get the most out of GarageBand, with great traditional electric guitar sounds and effects, life-like acoustic sound from the piezo pickup, and control of all the Software Instruments inside GarageBand. With these new instruments and programs, there are infinite creative possibilities for guitarists!

—*Patrick Cummings, president, Brian Moore Guitars and iGuitar designer*

NOTE   *If the level meters are firing and you're still not hearing anything, double-check that your monitoring system is on, that GarageBand's master volume is up, and that the computer's audio interface's volume is up. Also, check the Audio pane of the System Preferences to make sure that the correct audio output is selected.*

TIP   *If you've got your track's volume up all the way and it's still not loud enough, lower the volume of the other tracks, then boost the master volume control, which is located at the bottom right of the screen.*

Adjust Pan

Adjusting an instrument's volume is only one way you can make it easier to hear. Later, we'll discuss some of the ways to fine-tune a sound, but now, let's look at a simple way to separate the instrument you're playing from the rest of the audio in your song. The pan control, which lets you move the track between your left and right speakers, is very effective when you need to focus on a track. Try panning the

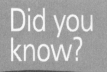

Find Your Own Comfort Zone

When you're playing or recording your own performance, the most important thing is that you're comfortable with the sound. There's no definitive setting for your mix when you're tracking—it's okay to have the balance completely out of whack at this point, because all you're concerned with is getting the best performance. You'll have plenty of time to adjust the mix later.

instrument you're playing to one side, and panning the backing tracks to the other. You should be able to focus on your own sound, without having to put the volume at an uncomfortable level.

Alternatively, you can use the Solo button to isolate the track—and therefore the instrument—in question. Once you have perfected your sound, deactivate Solo to hear the instrument in context with the rest of the tracks. You can toggle Solo on and of with the S key on your computer keyboard.

Play in Time

Like other sequencers, GarageBand lets you edit and arrange your work on a grid, which is based on bars and beats. But in order to take advantage of these features, you need to play in a way that is consistent with musical time. In other words, you need to adhere to the song's tempo as closely as possible.

Unless you've got a nuclear clock hard-wired to your brain, you'll need some sort of timing reference to play along with. Fortunately, GarageBand's built-in metronome is there to save the day. If you don't like playing with a metronome, you can play along with an Apple Loop—preferably a steady drum or percussion loop—instead.

Use the Metronome

To activate/deactivate the metronome, select it in the Control menu, or use the key combination COMMAND-U.

As we mentioned in Chapter 2, you can set the metronome's behavior in the General preferences window. The metronome can be set to play only during recording (in which case it's disabled during normal playback, even when the metronome option is checked in the Control menu). If you select the During Playback and Recording option, the metronome is always active, unless you disable it manually.

Let's assume you have the metronome set to be active for both playback and recording. Initiate playback (by hitting the SPACEBAR or clicking the Play button in the transport bar). You will hear the metronome play a steady pulse, one "click" per beat. As you listen to playback, you'll notice that one out of every four beats is a little higher in pitch than the others: this indicates the first beat of the measure, or *downbeat*.

 *This assumes that you're working in a 4/4 time signature. If you're working in 3/4, for example, the high-pitched downbeat would be one every three beats; in 6/8, it would be one in every six. GarageBand automatically adjusts the metronome to match the time signature.*

Play along and follow the count; try to stick as close to the tempo as possible. Once you're comfortable, you're ready to record.

 ## It's a Question of Time

Before you begin recording, you should ask yourself the following questions.

Am I Comfortable Playing at this Tempo?

At this point, we're trying to find a tempo that will let us play comfortably. Even if you want your song to end up at a fast tempo, you don't need to record it that way. Remember, GarageBand lets you change the tempo later. If the metronome is too fast, adjust the song's tempo until you can keep up.

CAUTION *Once you've recorded audio (see Chapter 7), you can't change tempo as easily. Try and lock your project into its final tempo before recording audio.*

Am I Able to Keep the Count?

Playing with a metronome can be extremely difficult when you're not used to it. Even accomplished musicians—especially those who play classical music and jazz—can find a metronome too restrictive. If you're having problems, try counting out loud or tapping your foot as you play.

Is the Metronome Making Me Uptight?

If you've practiced with the metronome a few times and you still don't feel comfortable, you may be better off using an Apple Loop as a timing reference. We'll discuss that momentarily.

Play Along with an Apple Loop

The metronome isn't always the best accompaniment. As I mentioned above, some musicians find playing to a metronome about as inspiring as watching paint dry, while others find it a little intimidating. But even if you have no problem playing to a "click," (musician lingo for metronome), there are times when you might want something a little more inspiring as you play your tracks. A simple drum loop, for example, might have a more musical feel than the metronome.

Fortunately, it's easy to create a rhythmic reference track: Simply locate a loop that suits your style in the loop browser, drag it into the song, and stretch it with the loop pointer. Real Instrument and Software Instrument loops work equally well.

 *See Chapter 5 for a more detailed look at Apple Loops and the loop browser.*

TIP   *To use a loop as a backing track, you don't need to create a full-fledged arrangement. In fact, you can discard and replace the loop after you've recorded your Software Instrument track(s).*

Remember, GarageBand can automatically adjust the tempo of Apple Loops to fit that of the song. So, just as with the metronome, you can try the loop at different tempos to find your own comfort zone.

TIP   *You don't need to choose between the metronome and an Apple Loop for accompaniment. You can have both active at the same time.*

Use the Count-In

Ever listen to a band play live, and the drummer clicks his or her sticks and says "a-one, a-two, a-three, a-four" before the song starts? This is known as the "count-in." A count-in not only counts down to that first beat; it gives the band an idea of the song's tempo as well, so that everyone can come in together and play in time. (There's nothing worse than a count-in that's at the wrong tempo.)

GarageBand's count-in is similar, though, unlike some drummers I've played with, it can always be relied upon to be accurate. The count-in is essential if you want to be ready to play a song right from the beginning, because it gives you a one-measure countdown to the start of the song.

6

You activate the Count In feature by selecting it in the Control menu. (As of version 1.1, there's no key combination to activate Count In.) Initiate recording; you will hear the metronome click at the song's tempo. A static red line, representing the Playhead, appears at the beginning of the first measure in the timeline (see Figure 6-6). Count-in can also be used for punch-in recording, which we'll cover later in this chapter.

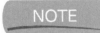 *Count In only works when the metronome is enabled, and only when GarageBand in is record mode. There is no count-in on playback.*

Record a Software Instrument Track

Hopefully by now, MIDI is working, the Software Instruments are in place and sound the way you want them to, the metronome—or a drum loop—is set up for accompaniment, the song is at comfortable tempo, and the count-in is enabled. Great: You're ready to record a track.

FIGURE 6-6   Count In is enabled. The Playhead is waiting at the start of the song as the metronome gives a one-measure countdown.

GarageBand makes it easy to get a track ready to record—all you have to do is select the track in the track header and play the controller. If you hear the instrument, you're ready to go. To record:

- Press R on the your computer's keyboard.

- Click the Record button in the transport bar.

These steps are used in all of GarageBand's recording modes. When you're finished recording, press the SPACEBAR or click on the Play button in the transport bar to stop playback.

NOTE *You can stop recording—while letting the song continue playback—by pressing the Record button again, or by pressing the R key on the keyboard.*

After you're done, you'll see a new region in the timeline, as shown in Figure 6-7. This region can be stretched and looped, just like an Apple Loop.

6

FIGURE 6-7   A new Software Instrument region appears in the timeline.

GarageBand 1.1's new Duplicate Track feature makes it easy to compile different takes of the same part. Let's say you record a piano part that you like, but think you can play it better. If you were to record over the original part, it would be lost. However, you can record a new version of the part on a new track, then compare the two takes and choose the one you like best.

- Select the track that has the take you want to replace.

- Mute the track by hitting the Mute button (or pressing M on you computer's keyboard).

- Go to Track | Duplicate Track (or use the key combination COMMAND-D).

GarageBand will create a track with the same instrument settings as the original, but will not copy any regions in the timeline. The new track will be automatically selected and ready for you to play. Once you've finished the next take, you can toggle the mute status of the two versions. If neither strikes your fancy, use the Duplicate Track command to take another shot, or simply edit the two tracks so that they create a single performance. We cover editing in depth in Chapters 8 and 10.

Recording Options

Although you can always record a track from the song's beginning, this isn't always the best place to start. GarageBand has several advanced options that let you optimize recording for the situation at hand.

Record in the Middle of a Track

Let's say you've recorded a great intro to your song, but the first verse is about as inspiring as an expired parking meter. You don't have to re-record the whole track. Instead, you can set GarageBand to begin recording only at the first verse. There are a couple of ways to do this.

 You can manually enable Record while the track is playing back. This only works if you have superhuman timing—or if there's a large gap between the existing part and the one you're about to play.

The easiest and most basic method is to punch-in. To punch-in:

■   Enable count-in.

■   Move the Playhead to the position at which you want to record.

■   Initiate recording.

You'll get a one-bar count-in from the metronome. You can see the Playhead flash at the insert position, as shown in Figure 6-8. Be ready to play! As soon as the count-in ends, GarageBand is recording.

 Be sure to stop recording, or "punch-out" before you go over material you want to keep.

Recording with the Cycle

GarageBand's Cycle is a powerful feature. It lets you choose a section of music to repeat in a loop. This has many uses, but one of the most powerful is in recording

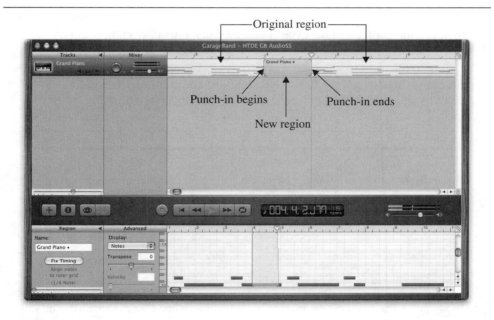

FIGURE 6-8   You can record in the middle of a track by enabling the count-in and placing the Playhead at the desired position in the timeline.

Software Instruments. With Cycle enabled, you can record a part in layers, so that each time through the cycle region, you add material without erasing what was previously there. This is especially effective when you're trying to build drum parts, but is also useful if your instrumental abilities are not quite up to your compositional vision.

Activate the Cycle

Enable Cycle by clicking on the Cycle button in the transport bar, or by pressing the C key on your Mac's keyboard. The cycle region will appear at the top of the timeline (see Figure 6-9). A yellow bar indicates the measures that are within the cycle.

Set the Cycle to the Appropriate Position

There are several ways to adjust the position and duration of the cycle. To change its position, click in the middle of the cycle (the arrow cursor will remain, and the cycle will be highlighted) and drag it to a new location. This will move the cycle, but not change its length.

> **TIP**   *Moving the cycle is very handy when you're writing a song. You can, for example, create an eight-bar cycle, use it to record the intro, then move it for the first verse, move it again for the chorus, and so on.*

To adjust the duration of the cycle, place the cursor at either end. The resize pointer will appear (as shown here). From the end of the cycle, drag to the right to lengthen it and to the left to shorten it. From the beginning of the cycle, drag to the left to lengthen it, and to the right to shorten it. Figure 6-10 shows the cycle before and after a length adjustment.

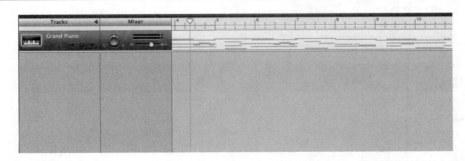

FIGURE 6-9   The cycle region appears in the timeline when Cycle is enabled. The yellow bar indicates the boundaries of the cycle.

(a)   (b)

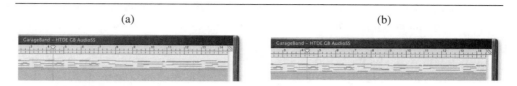

FIGURE 6-10   We've taken a four-bar cycle, beginning on measure 5 (a) and doubled its length by dragging its end boundary further to the right (b).

NOTE   *You can move and adjust the duration of the cycle while GarageBand is playing, but not while it's recording.*

Record the Region

OK. Now that the cycle is set to the desired position and duration, we're ready to record. As I mentioned earlier, the cycle is especially effective for drum tracks. Let's create a new Software Instrument track for drums. The song should look something like Figure 6-11. I've set the cycle region for two measures.

Activate the metronome—this is especially important when you're recording drum tracks. You can test the tempo by playing along.

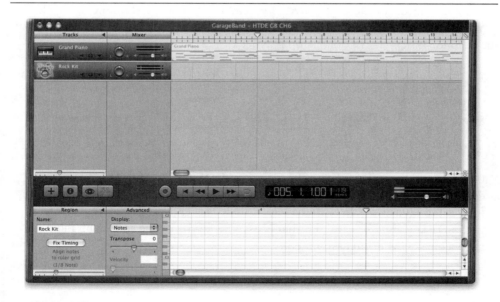

FIGURE 6-11   Our song, with Cycle enabled and a Software Instrument drum track selected. We're ready to record some drum parts.

TIP   *When you're recording in the Cycle, the count-in is optional. If you miss the first measure, you can always catch it the next time around!*

When you're ready, press R on the keyboard to activate recording. Play a part on the bass drum and snare. For this example, I'm going to do a simple beat: I'll hit the bass drum (a.k.a. the "kick drum" or the "kick") on the 1 and 3 of each measure; the snare on beats 2 and 4. The track should sound like a nice, steady boom chick, boom chick, boom chick, boom chick.

TIP   *You can stop playing and leave GarageBand in Record; you'll hear the part you just created play back without any of it being erased.*

Now that the kick is in place, let's add some hi-hat. For my track, I'm going to play eighth notes.

NOTE   *Remember: there are two eighth notes for every beat (see Chapter 2 for more about musical notes and their duration).*

The hi-hat track will sound like ta-ta, ta-ta, ta-ta, ta-ta, and should fill in some of the spaces between the kick and the snare hits. Now the drum track is sounding good, but it needs a little more flavor. Let's add a cymbal (C#2 on the controller keyboard) to the beginning of the first measure, and an extra snare hit to the end of the second. When you're done, stop playback.

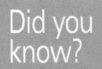

Following the Same Drummer

GarageBand basically follows the General MIDI (GM) convention in assigning drum sounds to specific keys of the keyboard, although there are some variations from kit to kit as well. In GM, the bass drum is assigned to the C1 key, the snare to the D1 key, and the closed hi-hat is assigned to F#1. The following table shows basic GM drum assignments.

Note	Instrument	Note	Instrument	Note	Instrument	Note	Instrument	Note	Instrument
C1	Kick	C2	Hi Mid Tom	C3	Hi Bongo	C4	Long Whistle	C6	Open
C#1	Stick	C#2	Crash Cymbal	C#3	Low Bongo	C#5	Short Guiro	C#6	Open
D1	Snare	D2	High Tom	D3	Mute Hi Conga	D5	Long Guiro	D6	Open
D#1	Clap/Snare 2	D#2	Ride Cymbal	D#3	Open Hi Conga	D#5	Claves	D#6	Open
E1	Electronic Snare/Snare	E2	Chinese Cymbal	E3	Low Conga	E5	High Wood Block	E6	Open
F1	Low Tom	F2	Ride Bell	F3	High Timbale	F5	Low Wood Block	F6	Open
F#1	Closed Hat	F#2	Tambourine	F#3	Low Timbale	F#5	Mute Guica	F#6	Open
G1	Hi Floor Tom	G2	Splash Cymbal	G3	High Agogo	G5	Open Guica	G6	Open
G#1	Pedal Hat	G#2	Cowbell	G#3	Low Agogo	G#5	Mute Triangle	G#6	Open
A1	Low Tom	A2	Crash Cymbal 2	A3	Casaba	A5	Open Triangle	A6	Open
A#1	Open Hat	A#2	Vibraslap	A#3	Maracas			A#6	Open
B1	Low Mid Tom	B2	Ride Cymbal 2	B3	Short Whistle			B6	Open

6

GarageBand 1.1 exhibits some odd behavior when you take the track out of Cycle Record. If you reenable Cycle over the same track, you will hear it play back as you record new material (just as you did on the first cycle through). But GarageBand will actually erase the original material if you cycle through a couple of times. You will be left with only the new material. That means that if you want to record the drum track illustrated, you must keep GarageBand in record until you have finished playing the complete part. Thankfully, there is a workaround. You can manually punch-in and -out of a track while Cycle is active, and when you do, the material you add will be added to (or merged with, in MIDI terminology) what's already there. Just be sure to get out of Record before the cycle goes back to the beginning!

Tighten Up Your Performance

Unless you have perfect timing, you may find that your drum track sounds a little bit off with the click. GarageBand's Fix Timing feature performs a technique known as *quantizing* to move individual notes so that they line up with a specific grid position. You can determine the grid position that best suits your song. If, for example, your grid position is set to 1/8 Note, every note will be assigned to the closest eighth-note position; if your grid position is 1/4 Note, GarageBand will move every note to the nearest quarter note, etc.

Fix Timing

In order to fix a region's timing, you need to open the region in the Software Instrument editor. Select the region and click the Edit button below the timeline (or use the key combination COMMAND-E). Figure 6-12 shows the track editor open for the drum track.

The notes in the track editor are displayed as bars in a grid. In Chapter 8, we'll go into more detail about Fix Timing and other editing techniques. But for now, let's grab a region and tighten it up before we go on to record more music. (Fix Timing is one edit you may want to make as you're recording so that your song develops with solid groove.)

If you open the track editor and see no MIDI data, don't despair: the notes in your region are probably outside of the display's current view range. Use the scroll bars (see Figure 6-13) to set the window to the proper perspective.

Set the Track Editor Grid Value

Like the timeline, the editor uses a grid based on bars and beats. You can set the editor to its own grid value, independent of that of the timeline.

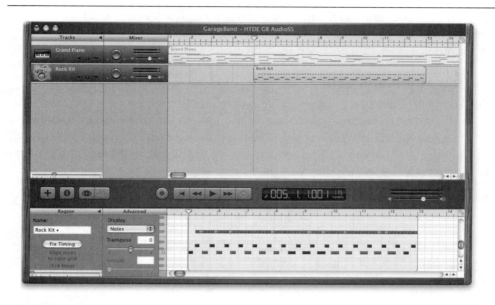

FIGURE 6-12   The Software Instrument track editor

NOTE   *This is an important feature because the kind of editing you do on the timeline often requires a large grid value such as 1/1 Note (which means one measure), whereas the finer editing you do in the editor can benefit from a smaller grid value, such as an eighth- or sixteenth-note.*

(a)   (b)

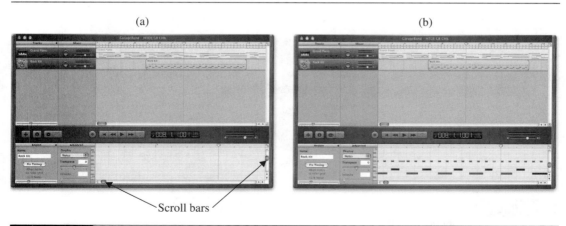

Scroll bars

FIGURE 6-13   If the region you've selected in the editor appears empty (a), use the scroll bars to find the data (b).

To set the grid value in the track editor, click the Track Editor Grid button, which reveals the pop-up menu shown in Figure 6-14. Since the smallest note value we played was an eighth note, we'll set the grid value to 1/8.

Use the Automatic Grid

The Automatic check box in the Grid pop-up menu (shown here) lets you use the zoom slider (on the bottom left of the edit window) to determine the grid setting. As you move the slider, you'll see the current grid value displayed just under the Fix Timing button. If you want to zoom in close and still edit to a larger grid setting (or vice versa), reselect the desired grid value in the pop-up menu.

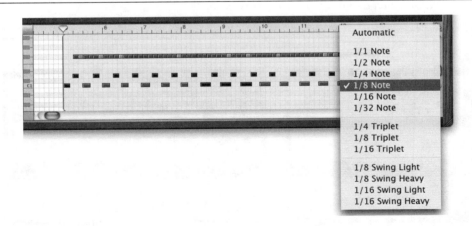

FIGURE 6-14   The Track Editor Grid button lets you set the grid value for the editor that's independent of that of the timeline.

Grid Irony

Most of GarageBand's editing features are governed by the status of the Snap to Grid setting in the control menu (or via the key combination COMMAND-G). When Snap to Grid is on, anything you drag will be moved by the current grid setting; when it's off, you can move things freely. However, Fix Timing works whether or not Snap to Grid is active.

Fix Timing

Once you've selected a region and set the editor's grid value, you can hit the Fix Timing button to tighten up the track. Look closely, and you'll see the notes move on the grid, as shown in Figure 6-15.

CAUTION *Use care when setting the grid value; the wrong setting can yield some unexpected results. Always listen to the track after you fix timing. If the results aren't what you were looking for, undo and try again with a different grid value.*

Play the Track with a New Sound

One of the most important ways in which a Software Instrument differs from a Real Instrument is the degree to which you can change the sound after the track has been recorded. Take our drum track, for example. Although it's producing some very specific drum sounds, these are triggered by MIDI notes, and the same notes can be assigned to another instrument. As an example, try assigning the drum track to a melodic instrument like piano. The result isn't exactly pleasing to the ear—unless

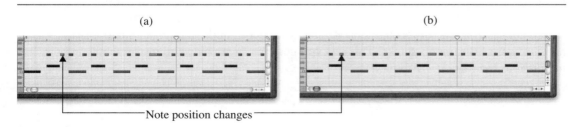

(a)   (b)

└── Note position changes ──┘

FIGURE 6-15   A drum part before (a) and after (b) we've used GarageBand's Fix Timing button.

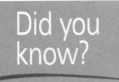

Voice Control

Software Instruments require a lot of processing power. This is especially true of those that are created with GarageBand's modeling generators, such as the synths, organs, electric pianos, and others. If GarageBand is struggling to play back your Software Instrument tracks (common problems include distorted playback, crackling, or stuttering), you may be able to improve performance by reducing the number of voices per instrument in the Preferences | Advanced pane. By default, GarageBand automatically calculates the number of voices to make available based on its analysis of your computer's processing power, but if you have a large number of tracks—or processor-hungry effects—you may want to override GarageBand's judgment and reduce the number of voices in the Preferences menu.

you like to compose marching music for robots—but it does demonstrate how the concept works. We can alter the track a second time by changing the acoustic kit to something more electronic, such as Twang kit.

When you're working with more melodic material, this kind of editing can be even more powerful. You can start out with a grand piano sound, and then try the track with an organ, horn section, set of vibes, guitar—whatever you have available. You can also copy a performance from one track to another, and layer the two to create a unique sound—for example, the popular combination of piano and strings. This kind of after-the-fact sound manipulation is at the heart of working in a sequencer environment.

Moving On

You can create some very complex songs and arrangements with GarageBand's Software Instruments—with or without the addition of Apple Loops. These powerful features can take you on a long musical journey. However, GarageBand isn't a completely closed ecosystem. One of its charms is its ability to record audio alongside the loops and Software Instruments tracks. This lets you get your own voice and instrumental genius into the mix. It's also next.

Chapter 7

Record Audio Tracks

How to…

- Prepare for Real Instrument (audio) recording
- Create a blank track
- Route audio to GarageBand
- Check levels
- Monitor the sound
- Adjust the sound of the input
- Record a first track
- Overdub
- Adjust the sound of an audio track
- Punch in and out on an audio track
- Loop an audio track

Not so long ago, when someone said they were going to make a recording, everyone assumed they were talking about recording audio performed by real musicians. Concepts like sampling and sequencing were still considered very specialized and unnatural. In those days, the most common recording medium was analog tape, which had taken over from recording media like wire and wax to help transform the music industry.

The use of tape led to the development of the multitrack recorder, which eventually led to the development of the digital tape recorder. These, as we've already said, are linear devices: everything you record goes onto tape at a specific point in time, ever to stay there unless someone with a razor blade and splicing tape comes to cut and splice it. Hard disk–based recording—and the random-access editing that it affords—revolutionized the music and audio production business because it made it easy to change the audio after the fact. Once you've used a hard-disk recorder, it's hard to imagine ever again having to record everything in some linear order.

Like other hard disk recorders, GarageBand lets you record audio in any order you like. If you think the guitar lick you played in the opening bars of the song really belong in the middle of the second chorus, you can simply grab it and move it there. Don't like it? Move it back. That's powerful stuff for any creative person!

But before you can exercise your freedom of artistic choice, you need to get audio into your computer.

Get Audio to GarageBand

Despite the fact that it lives inside your computer, GarageBand is not that different from a traditional tape recorder. (We realize we date ourselves here; many of you have probably never used a tape recorder.) Before it can record anything, it needs to hear some sound at its inputs. Figure 7-1 shows a basic block diagram of how this works.

> NOTE *One of the things that makes audio recording a challenge—and an art form— is the number of variables that can go in between the source and the recorder. We'll get into some of them in Chapter 10.*

7

When you play an analog source—such as our bass guitar—its audio signal needs to be converted to a digital format that your computer can handle. This is known as analog-to-digital conversion, or A/D. The analog audio inputs of your Mac have built-in A/D converters, as do most third-party interfaces. Some inputs, be they on the Mac or in a third-party interface, are digital. These cannot convert an analog signal; you must first digitize the signal by running it through an A/D converter before it can be plugged into a digital input.

> NOTE *If you are feeding a digital signal, such as the digital output of a digital mixer or keyboard, to a digital input, no analog-to-digital conversion is necessary.*

Set the Audio Input

GarageBand can accept audio signal from any Core Audio device that's installed in your system. These include your Mac's built-in audio, as well as third-party devices, which can connect to the computer via USB, FireWire, or a PCI slot. To set the audio input:

1. Open Preferences from the GarageBand menu, or press COMMAND-comma.

2. Select the Audio/MIDI tab.

3. Use the pop-up menu to choose the input (see Figure 7-2).

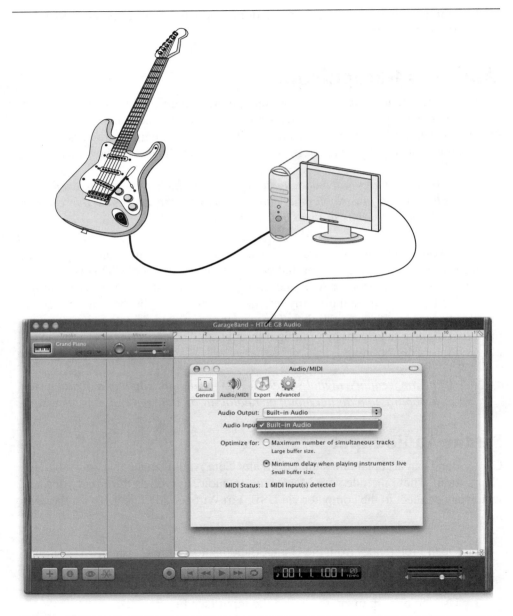

FIGURE 7-1   A typical recording signal path. The source—in this case, a bass guitar—
feeds the computer's audio input, which in turn feeds GarageBand.

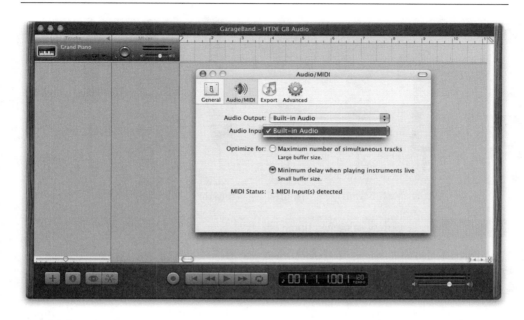

FIGURE 7-2   You can choose an input in the audio preferences.

NOTE   *The number of available inputs depends on the specific devices connected to your system. For a detailed look at your audio devices and their properties, open the Audio/MIDI Setup utility (Applications/Utility/Audio MIDI Setup).*

If you have more than one audio device, you can switch inputs to suit your needs at any time in a song. For example, you can start out using your Mac's built-in inputs, then switch to a third-party device for the next track.

It's All About Connections

It's an old adage in the music biz—it's not what you know, it's *who* you know. Connections are everything. Well in audio, connections are also important; you've got to have the right ones for the right job. Audio connections come in many shapes and sizes, and can carry analog or digital signals. Analog connections can be unbalanced or balanced. Figure 7-3 shows a rendering of some of the most common types of connections.

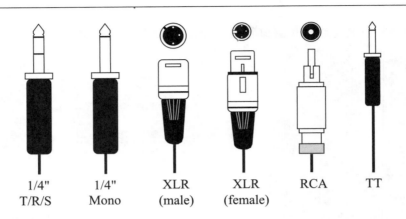

| 1/4" | 1/4" | XLR | XLR | RCA | TT |
| T/R/S | Mono | (male) | (female) | | |

FIGURE 7-3 A variety of connections

Unbalanced Connections

Unbalanced cables use only two wires: the signal and the ground. These types of cables are often used for home studio applications. Your Mac's analog audio inputs are unbalanced. The most common unbalanced connections are 1/4 inch (which is the standard connection for instruments like electric guitar and bass), RCA phono plugs (the type used to connect home electronics equipment), and the 1/8-inch minijack, which is most likely what you'll find on your Mac and your Walkman. Some unbalanced connections are stereo—the Mac's input, for example. With these, one jack is used to connect two channels of audio.

NOTE *RCA-type connections are often grouped in pairs to handle stereo signals, but the individual connections are mono.*

Balanced Connections

A balanced connector uses three wires: two carry the sound; one carries the ground. Audio professionals favor balanced connections because they reject noise and offer better signal quality over a long cable run. Many of the latest generation of computer-audio interfaces are equipped with balanced connections, whether in the form of 1/4-inch TRS (or tip/ring/sleeve) jacks (for line-level signals) or XLR jacks (which are most commonly used to connect microphones, but are also frequently used to connect professional audio components). In fact, even if you're working in a strictly consumer environment, your microphone may indeed have an XLR-balanced connector.

In order to plug a microphone with a balanced connection into an unbalanced input, you'll need a special device called a mic transformer (see Figure 7-4), which creates an unbalanced signal that can be received by the input.

Digital Connections

Digital audio connections were once the domain of professional studios, but they are becoming more and more common on home audio gear. Apple G5s have built-in digital audio (using a digital audio transfer format called S/PDIF, which stands for Sony/Phillips Digital Interface), and most third-party interfaces also include digital audio inputs and outputs. You might use a digital input to connect an outboard mixer or preamplifier to your system. Digital connections come in several varieties, but the most common are RCA-type connectors (used commonly for S/PDIF connections)—which look like their analog counterparts—and optical TOS link connectors.

7

You cannot connect an analog source to a digital input (nor can you connect a digital output to an analog input). Doing so won't damage your gear, but you won't get any sound.

Level Matching

When you cable together two pieces of audio gear, the connectors aren't the only things you need to worry about. The strength, or "level," of the audio signal also needs to match. In analog audio, there are four signals levels: +4dB line, −10dB line, −20dB instrument, and microphone.

FIGURE 7-4   A mic transformer (courtesy of Pro Co Sound)

A *line-level* signal is used to connect devices like mixers, outboard recorders, and preamps. It's generally louder, or "hotter," than other signals. An *instrument-level* signal is used to connect guitars and basses. It's not as loud as a line-level signal, and usually needs to go through a circuit called a preamp before it can be plugged into a line-level signal. A *mic-level* signal is quietest of all. Microphones put out a mic-level signal that almost always needs to go through a preamp before it can be plugged into a line-level input.

 *Some line-level inputs use XLR connections—just like mic-level inputs. But if you plug a mic into a line input, you won't hear much, if any, signal. Consult the documentation for your audio gear to make sure that you're connecting to the correct-level inputs.*

Signal matching is important because too hot a signal can cause the input to overload, which in turn makes the track sound distorted; too quiet a signal, and the track may be barely audible, or worse, the good signal—your music—may be low compared to other noise.

 *The relative loudness of your audio compared to noise is known as the signal-to-noise ratio. The higher the signal to noise, the better.*

A Last Word

If you go beyond the very basics of audio, you're likely to encounter many different types of connections. In my small home studio, I have balanced 1/4-inch, unbalanced 1/4-inch, XLR line, XLR mic, RCA analog, RCA digital (S/PDIF), TOS link optical, and 1/8-inch minijacks, and a *box* full of adapters and converters. In order to make all my gear work together, I had to invest some time to learn about each one's input and output levels and connections. It's dry stuff, no doubt, but it is essential information if you want to get optimal sound.

Plug an Instrument into Your Computer

We've talked a lot about different interfaces, and we'll examine some of these options in Chapter 12 and show some wiring options in Appendix C, which is online. For now, let's assume you're plugging directly into your Mac's built-in analog input. This is the default setting in GarageBand's Audio/MIDI preferences.

 *To plug an instrument such as a guitar or a bass directly into the Mac's input, you'll need a 1/4- to 1/8-inch converter plug, such as the one shown in Figure 7-5.*

Create a Blank Audio Track

Before you can record audio, you need to create a track for it. In GarageBand, audio goes onto Real Instrument tracks only—you cannot record audio onto a Software Instrument track. To create a new Real Instrument track:

1. Open the New Track inspector by hitting the + button in the GarageBand window, choosing Track I New Track in the Track menu, or by pressing OPTION-COMMAND-N.

2. Choose the Real Instrument Tab.

3. Select the instrument type.

4. Set input and monitor options.

Figure 7-6 shows the New Instrument inspector. As you can see, there are lots of options. The best one to choose depends on the source material: is it mono or stereo? Will you need to hear it as it plays through GarageBand, or can you monitor it some other way?

If you plug your guitar or bass directly into your Mac—without using a mixer or preamp, your only choice will be to monitor it through GarageBand.

FIGURE 7-5 A 1/4- to 1/8-inch converter plug lets you plug a guitar or bass directly into your Mac.

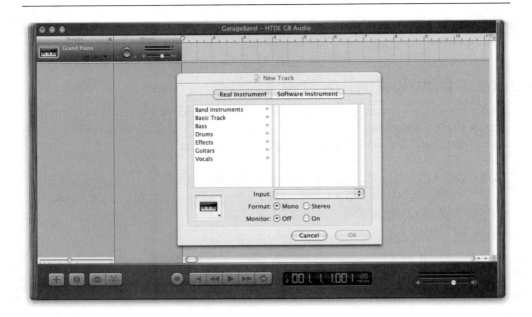

FIGURE 7-6   The New Instrument Inspector

Set Up the Audio Track

The settings in the New Instrument Inspector fall into two categories: those that affect the track's playback, and those that affect how the track's audio is recorded into GarageBand.

Set Instrument

The Instrument settings only affect playback. These are used to color the track by adding EQ (equalization) and effects. You can record a track with one instrument setting, and play it back with another. The actual audio going to disk is unaffected.

For now, let's start with a blank slate. Choose Basic Track | No Effects (see Figure 7-7).

NOTE   *You need to choose an audio instrument setting before you can set up input parameters.*

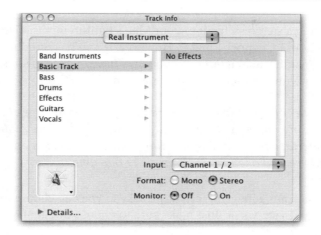

| FIGURE 7-7 | Choose No Effects to hear your audio without coloration. |

Choose Mono or Stereo Recording

GarageBand can record one track at a time, in either mono (one-channel) or stereo (two-channel) streams. Mono sources include electric guitar, bass, and most microphones; stereo sources can include preamps, electronic keyboards, outboard mixers, home stereo equipment, and others.

It goes without saying that you should choose an input type that matches your source. If you're recording an electric guitar or bass directly into your Mac, choose a mono track; if you're routing that same guitar's signal to the Mac from a stereo guitar preamp, you can go stereo. Since we're recording an electric bass, we're going to go mono.

 *Try to avoid creating stereo tracks for mono sources. When you do, you're wasting disk space (stereo tracks take up double the space on your hard disk). When you record a mono source to a stereo track, the track may also sound out of balance, with audio only on one side of the stereo field.*

Select Input

If you're recording a stereo signal into your Mac's built-in inputs, GarageBand will automatically choose Channel 1 and 2. However, if you're-recording in mono—or working with a multichannel interface—you may have to change some settings here. You set the input with the Input pop-up, shown in Figure 7-8.

The number of inputs you choose among depends on the type of audio interface you're using and how it's configured to work with Core Audio. But even if your interface is capable of handling many channels at once, GarageBand can only record one or two channels at one time.

In GarageBand, any input can feed any track, so you can choose input channel 2 to feed track 1, and vice versa. Just make sure to choose the input that your source is plugged into.

Set Monitor

GarageBand's Monitor option (see Figure 7-9) determines whether the audio you route to the input will be routed to GarageBand's outputs as it's being recorded.

FIGURE 7-8   The Input pop-up

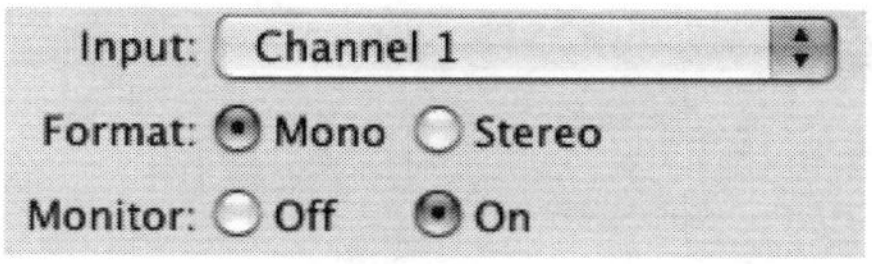

Input: Channel 1

Format: ● Mono ○ Stereo

Monitor: ○ Off ● On

FIGURE 7-9 The New Track Monitor option

Set the Monitor to On if:

■ You are plugging directly into the computer and have no other way of hearing the audio.

■ You wish to hear the audio through GarageBand's effects as you record.

Set the Monitor to Off if:

■ You are plugged into another monitoring system, such as an outboard mixing board.

■ You are hearing a latency (see the next sidebar "Falling Behind") delay in the signal as you monitor.

Click OK

Your new track now appears in the Tracks list, already selected and ready for you to record. Although we could start recording right away, there are a couple more things you might want to consider before turning on the "red light."

Name the Track

When you create a new track, GarageBand automatically names it after the current effects setting: in this case, "No Effects" (see Figure 7-10)—not very descriptive. When you record to the track, the resulting region will bear the name of the track. I don't know about you, but it saps my morale to see one of my audio tracks named "No Effects."

You can, however, name a track before you record. Open the track editor (see Figure 7-11); under the track column, you'll see the Name field. Type in a descriptive name. You'll see the results reflected in the Track List (see Figure 7-12).

7

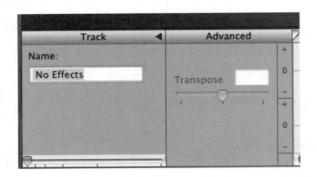

FIGURE 7-10   No Effects? C'mon, we can come up with a better name than that!

Falling Behind: Latency

Latency—an audible delay as a signal passes through the audio system's input on its way to the output—was once the bane of all "native" computer audio systems.

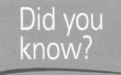 *Native audio systems use the computer's CPU for audio processing.*

With a high latency, there would be a long delay between the note you played and the note you heard back. As a result, it was almost impossible to record into a computer-based audio system without having some sort of outboard mixer or monitor.

These days, latency can be so low as to be inaudible. However, to get low latency, you need to set your audio system to a low buffer size. The lower the buffer size, the harder your Mac's CPU must work to process audio. If you have a lot of tracks open—especially if you have effects on those tracks—this can adversely affect audio playback. Fortunately, even at GarageBand's "large buffer size" setting, latency isn't so bad that you can't play along in real time. However, in most cases, you'll want to record with the lower latency setting, and then switch to the larger buffer (if necessary) as you start preparing to mix by adding effects, which may tax your computer's processor.

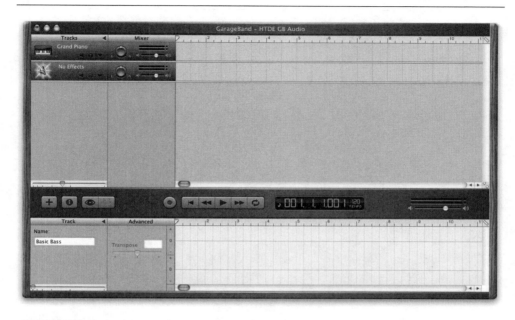

FIGURE 7-11   We've changed the track's name from No Effects to Basic Bass in the Track Editor window. All regions we record on that track will now bear the name Basic Bass (unless we rename the track again).

 With version 1.1, GarageBand lets you name a track in the track header. Click the name and hold the pointer. The name field will appear (shown here). Type in a new name (or edit the existing), and click RETURN.

Adjust Input Levels

Now that the track is set up, you should perform one last but vital step before recording: check the audio level. Every track in GarageBand has an audio meter (see Figure 7-13), which shows the level of the audio that's being routed through the track. When you're ready to record, the selected track's meters will show the level of the incoming audio. When you finish recording, the track's meters will show the level of the audio as it plays back.

FIGURE 7-12 After we changed the name in the track editor, the new name appears in the track header.

TIP

Try and keep the signal at or near the yellow (right) side of the meter, without hitting the red. Red indicates an overload, which can cause distortion.

Read the Meters

The meters give you an important visual reference to your audio tracks. In GarageBand, the meters fire from left to right. Play your instrument. If only the left few segments fire, your signal is too low. A track with a low signal can be hard to work with at mix time, and can sound noisy when boosted to match the other tracks. That's because when you boost the good part of the  signal—your music—you're also boosting the bad part—for example, the ambient noise from the computer fan, guitar pickup hum, or the sound of the neighbor's dog barking.

Raise the input level on your instrument. But be careful not to go too far, or you'll end up in the red zone, on the right hand side of the meter. This shows that the signal is too hot, and is likely to cause distortion.

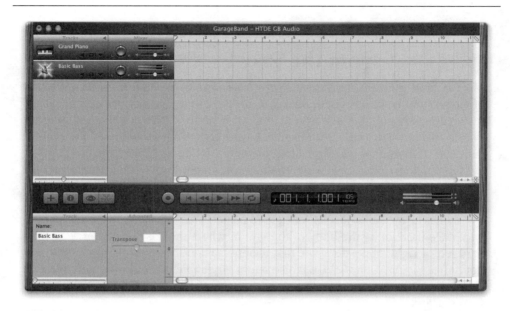

FIGURE 7-13   When you're ready to record, the audio meters indicate the level of signal coming into the track.

Reduce the level of the input slightly, so that the signal spends most of its time in the yellow zone. This will give you a nice healthy track, without noise or distortion.

Figure 7-14 shows three audio waveforms: one recorded too low, one too hot, one just right.

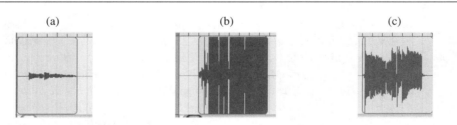

(a)   (b)   (c)

FIGURE 7-14   These waveforms represent three different files. The first (a) was recorded too low; it will be hard to work with. The second (b) is too hot. See how the top of the wave is cut off? That file is "clipped" and will sound distorted. The third (c) is just right. The waveform is high but never clips.

Be Like Mic! Recording Tips from the Pros!

I like to think of the microphone as a set of ears. If you stand in front of an instrument or singer, and it sounds good, then it is good. Let the microphone capture it. If it's an acoustic guitar, walk around, bend down, do whatever you need in order to find that "sweet spot." With drums, let the room (hopefully, it's a good one) help you. Experiment with spreading the mics out, moving them up, down, back.

Let's take a quick look at stereo and mono recording. With a single vocalist, one mic works fine—that's mono. Going back to that acoustic guitar, try two microphones: Place one in front of the sound hole, near the fretboard, about 6–8 inches away. Pan it just left or right of center. Then take a second microphone and place it down by the body of the guitar, where the bass resonates. Pan that hard left or right, opposite of the first channel. This is stereo miking—providing not only a bigger soundfield, but also a more dynamic track to mix with. Note that this works with most instruments. Just be sure to create a stereo track in GarageBand.

Some microphones are multipattern, meaning they can actually record the acoustic space differently. A cardioid pattern records directly in front of the source, with little response to the side. This is great for vocalists, and the legendary Shure SM-58 microphone features a cardioid pattern. But some microphones can be switched to record in omni mode, basically capturing the sound in a 360-degree circle around the mic. Omni recording is great for a concert hall, overhead drums, and can make a great acoustic bass recording. Figure-8 pattern records almost like two cardioids, one on each side of the mic. Place two singers on either side of the microphone, facing each other, and you'll capture each one equally. It's important to experiment with microphones and find what fits your music best. Then you'll know it's right.

—Rich Tozzoli is a producer/engineer/composer who specializes in multichannel audio production. He has mixed over 25 surround sound titles, including work with the likes of Carly Simon, Blue Oyster Cult, The Marsalis Family, and David Bowie. Also Senior Editor of Surround Professional *magazine, Rich's new book,* Surround Sound Mixing With Pro Tools, *is due out this fall.*

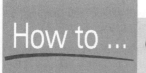

Give Yourself a Boost

If you do happen to record an audio track at too low a level, all is not lost. An audio track can be boosted after the fact. See Chapter 13 for tips on how to fix an anemic audio track.

CAUTION *GarageBand doesn't have an input level control of its own. A track's volume slider sets the track's playback volume, but has no effect on the audio as you record it onto the track. You must use the input level controls on your audio interface (for example, in your Mac's Sound control panel)—or on the source itself—to adjust your input audio level.*

7

Record a Track

Okay: we've got a newborn track, which is being fed with a nice healthy audio level. The track even has a descriptive name. We're just about ready to start tracking.

Create a Tempo Reference

As we did in Chapter 6, we're going to work with a tempo reference. This is important if we want to add Apple Loops to our project. Playing to a predetermined tempo will also make it easier to edit our work on the grid.

To record to a tempo, you'll need a reference. You have two options: you can play along with the metronome, or with an Apple Loop.

Play Along with the Metronome

The metronome provides a steady click track that marks time without adding any "feel" or groove to the track. The metronome gives you freedom—you won't be influenced by any particular pre-recorded groove or key—but it can also be a little less than inspiring. To enable the metronome:

- Press COMMAND-U.

- Select Metronome in the Control menu.

Click Play and play along. You'll hear the metronome through your monitors. How does the music feel? Are you comfortable at that tempo? Does the song drag or move too fast? You can use the tempo slider to adjust the tempo as you play, and the metronome will follow along.

 *At this point, it's important to be sure that the tempo suits the song. Once you record audio, you'll be locked into that tempo. Unlike Apple Loops, the Real Instrument recordings you make are not "elastic"—unless you convert it to an Apple Loop with the Loop Utility, which we'll discuss in Chapter 13.*

Play Along with an Apple Loop

If you find the metronome too sterile, you can play along with an Apple Loop instead. One good, basic drum loop can form the backbone for many a song. Later, after you've recorded a few tracks, you can expand on the basic loop with something more elaborate, or replace it altogether.

 *If you don't like the metronome sound and don't want to play along to an Apple Loop, create your own basic beat with a Software Instrument track, and loop it.*

Record Your First Track

Once you're comfortable with the tempo, you're ready to record. If you're recording from the beginning of the song, you'll probably want to activate Count In (as we did in Chapter 6). Select it in the Control menu.

To record:

- Press the R key, or click the Record button on the transport.

- Play your instrument.

When you're ready to stop playing, stop GarageBand by pressing the SPACEBAR or clicking the Play key in the transport. A new Real Instrument region will appear in the timeline. The region is purple, indicating that it's not an Apple Loop. I also like to keep the track editor open while I record; it gives me a detailed view of the audio waveform as it's going to disk.

 *Don't leave the machine in record mode for too long after you've stopped playing. GarageBand will record the silence, and waste disk space in the process.*

Congratulations: you've recorded an audio track. You timeline should now look something like Figure 7-15.

FIGURE 7-15   The timeline with an audio track in place

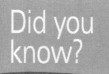

If you don't like the results of your audio track, you undo your recording by choosing Edit \ Undo or pressing COMMAND-Z. The track will be erased from your hard disk the next time you quit GarageBand.

Did you know?

Where'd It Go?

When you record an audio track, GarageBand creates an AIFF file, which it stores in the song's package file. To view the individual AIFF files, locate the song file in the Finder (GarageBand files have a ".band" extension). CONTROL-click the file and choose Show Package Contents from the pop-up menu. Open the Media folder, and you'll see your audio. We'll look at ways to work with your audio files in Chapter 13.

Add a Second Track

Now that you have one audio track down, you can add more. GarageBand is, after all, a multitrack program. Before you record, you'll need to make a new track, set up its inputs, and give it a name, as we did for the Bass track. This time, we're going to add some guitar. After we plug a guitar into the input and adjust levels, we're ready to go.

 *You can use Undo to restore the previous recording, but doing so will erase the new recording.*

Like the first track, we're going to record this one from the beginning. If it's not already there, position the Playhead at the start of the song by clicking the Go to Beginning button on the transport or by pressing the HOME key on the keyboard.

Put the machine into record mode, wait for the count in, and start playing. Figure 7-16 shows the song with two audio tracks.

FIGURE 7-16   We've added a guitar part to our song.

Add an Effect as You Record an Audio Track

As we mentioned above, GarageBand lets you monitor your audio inputs through effects, even though the audio that's recorded to disk is "dry" (without effects). Why would you want to monitor through effects? The sound you're playing with can affect your performance. For example, if you want to lay down a hard rock guitar solo, it won't do to play through a squeaky clean sound. You'll need to add some distortion. You can also use effects like delay to create parts that would be otherwise impossible (U2's guitarist The Edge has made a career of doing just that). Singers like to hear their voices in the shower, and reverb gives a similar effect, making your voice sound larger than life—and hopefully inspiring you to hit the high notes.

Set Up the Effect

GarageBand is flexible in that it lets you adjust a track's audio effect at any time. Later, we're going to learn how to apply effects to previously recorded material, but now, let's get some sonic inspiration by adding an effect to a track that we're about to record. Create a new track. This time, when the New Track inspector pops up, we're going to choose an effect. Since we've still got a guitar plugged in, let's select the Guitars category and then an Amp Simulation effect with a distorted tone, as shown in Figure 7-17. You should hear the guitar with a nice rock 'n' roll crunch.

TIP   *Be sure that you have the correct input selected and that Monitor is on.*

Once you've found an effect to your liking, click OK (later, we'll learn how to create and save our own effects settings). Note that the track now bears the name of the effect—in this case, Modern Rock.

Play along with the track to see how the effect blends with the other sounds. When you're satisfied, record as you did the tracks above. If you don't like the effect, remember that you can always change it later. For now, it's time to rock out!

Punch-In: Record in the Middle of a Track

So far we've recorded audio from the beginning of the song. But as we explained in Chapter 6, there are many occasions where the beginning is not the best place to start. GarageBand can record anywhere in the timeline, and can automate the recording process, with or without the cycle engaged.

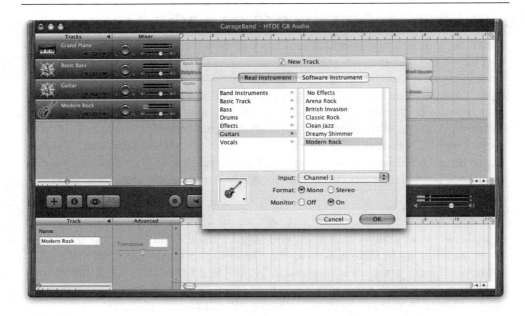

FIGURE 7-17   We've chosen a guitar effect. Note that Monitor must be on in order for you to hear the effect.

NOTE
For a detailed look at using the cycle region, refer to Chapter 6.

Manual Punch-In and Punch-Out

There are several ways to begin recording from the middle of a track. The simplest is to start playback, then put GarageBand into record mode as the music is playing. The trick is to get the machine into record mode before the part starts, and get it out before you erase anything you wanted to keep.

The advantage is that you can decide on the fly when you want the recording to begin and end. The disadvantage is that it's tough to do when you're working alone, unless you're adept at pressing the R key with your toe or nose.

TIP
Manual punch-in is most effective when the person operating the controls is not the one playing.

To punch-in manually:

1. Start playback.

2. Enable recording by pressing the R key or the Record button.

3. Play the part.

4. Stop playback, or disable recording by pressing the R key or Record button.

Automatic Punch-In; Manual Punch-Out

GarageBand can start recording from the Playhead position, no matter where that is in the song. You can use this feature, along with count-in, to set up an automated punch-in. This way, you can have your hands on the instrument and let GarageBand worry about hitting the spots.

To punch-in automatically:

1. Position the Playhead at the desired record location. (Remember: the grid setting affects the Playhead position, so adjust the grid according to your needs.)

2. Enable count-in.

3. Enable recording by pressing the R key or the Record button. GarageBand will give you a one-measure count-in (you'll hear the song, not just the metronome) and will go into record mode when the Playhead reaches the right spot.

4. Play the part.

5. Stop playback, or disable recording by pressing the R key or Record button.

When you're done, your track will look something like Figure 7-18.

Automatic Punch-In and -Out with the Cycle

The cycle is a powerful feature for both audio and Software Instrument recording. We discussed it as it relates to software instruments in Chapter 6; it works a little differently on Real Instrument tracks. As you'll recall, when you record a Software Instrument in the cycle, GarageBand remains in record mode, and each pass lets you add MIDI information to the layer, until you click Stop.

When you're working with Real Instrument recordings, the cycle *does not* merge what you play as it goes around. Instead, GarageBand goes into record mode when it reaches the beginning of the cycle, and drops out of record when it reaches the end.

FIGURE 7-18 We've punched-in on the guitar track Modern Rock. Note that the region begins on measure 5.

This lets you automate the punch-in and -out process. This is especially useful when you want to fix a mistake without recording over the audio before or after the offending part.

To punch-in and -out automatically:

1. Set the cycle region so that it starts where you want the recording to begin, and ends where you want the recording to stop. (Remember: the grid setting affects the cycle position, so adjust the grid according to your needs.)

2. Enable count-in.

3. Enable recording by pressing the R key or the Record button. GarageBand will give you a one-measure count-in (you'll hear the song, not just the metronome) and will go into record mode when the Playhead reaches the right spot.

4. Play the part.

5. When GarageBand reaches the end of the cycle region, it will drop out of record mode, though it will continue to play back until you click Stop.

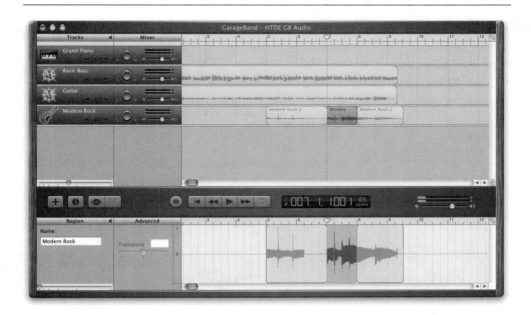

FIGURE 7-19   The guitar track after a cycle recording. Note how the new region begins on measure 7 and ends on measure 8.

Figure 7-19 shows the guitar track after we've recorded in cycle mode. We set the cycle to start on measure 7 and end on measure 8; as you can see, the new region is exactly one measure long.

You can fine-tune the cycle region by adjusting the timeline grid. If you want to start a little before a measure, for example, set the grid to 1/8 or 1/16, and drag the cycle so that it begins before the measure starts, as shown next.

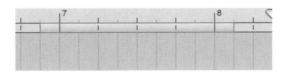

Once you've made a few Real Audio recordings, you'll see that they work much like Real Instrument Loops—you can edit them very freely. The big difference, as we've said, is that you can't change their tempo without the help of the Loop Utility.

Moving On

Congratulations. You've reached a real milestone in learning GarageBand: you've now worked with loops, software instruments, and your own audio. From here, you can get into some advanced editing, arranging, and mixing.

Part III

Create a Finished Master

Chapter 8

How to Edit

How to...

- Split and join regions in the timeline
- Move a region
- Work with Software Instrument tracks
- Fix timing
- Move individual notes in pitch and time
- Move groups of notes
- Adjust loudness (velocity) of individual notes
- Adjust modulation
- Adjust pitch bend
- Adjust sustain
- Edit Real Instrument Regions
- Move parts of an audio region to create a new performance

So far, we've built basic songs in several ways: with Apple Loops, by recording Software Instruments, and by recording our own Real Instrument tracks. We've worked with regions in the timeline to transform a basic arrangement into something more elaborate. In fact, you can do quite a bit without ever opening the GarageBand edit windows.

But as any seasoned veteran of computer-based audio will tell you, the ability to go deep into a track can turn a good-but-flawed performance into an excellent piece of music.

The actions listed at the top of this page are on the "inside" level; unlike the edits we've discussed thus far—which deal with complete regions and parts of regions— these edits happen within the confines of the region itself. Think of it this way: Editing in the timeline is similar to moving cars around a parking lot. Working in the editors is more like getting under the hood and fixing the car's drivetrain. Of course, you can combine this type of inside editing with the more global approach of moving regions around in the timeline. You can get the cars running smoothly *and* park them in the right locations.

But before we jump down to the edit window, let's take a look at two powerful timeline editing commands: Split and Join.

Split and Join Regions in the Timeline

Many of the edits you do in GarageBand can happen in either the timeline or the track editors. In fact, one of cool things about the program is the way you can switch between these edit modes freely; if you want to work on several tracks at once, or work on a large section of time in your song, use the timeline; for a more focused look at one track or section of music, use the edit window. Any edits you make in one are instantly updated in the other.

We've already discussed how to move, cut, copy, paste, loop, and resize regions in the timeline. Split and Join are two other powerful timeline commands that let you edit your music in the timeline. Each is available in the Edit menu or via shortcut keys.

Split

Split (COMMAND-T) divides a selected region into two new regions at the playhead position, as shown here:

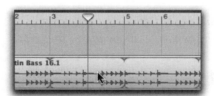

Only selected regions are affected by the Split command; even if the playhead is over an unselected region, it won't be split. However, you can split regions on two or more tracks at the same time (provided you have selected them), and you can split both Software and Real Instrument regions at the same time. Once you split a region, (shown next) you can work with the resulting "offspring" regions as you would any other—in other words, you can resize, loop, copy, delete, move them around in the timeline, and even assign them to a new track.

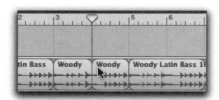

 *Split is also a quick tool for resizing a region: Split the region to create the new boundary, and then delete the unwanted portion from the timeline.*

Join

The Join Selected command (COMMAND-J) lets you combine two regions into a new region. Join only works in the following situations:

- Real Instrument recordings that are both contiguous and on the same track
- Software Instrument regions that are on the same track
- Instruments of the same type (Real and Real, Software and Software)

You cannot join Software and Real Instrument regions to one another, nor can you join two Apple Loop regions, even if they originated from the same loop file. When you try to join invalid material, the command will be grayed out in the Edit menu.

 *If you try to join noncontiguous audio regions, GarageBand warns you that doing so will generate a new audio file.*

To use Join, select the regions you wish to join (shown here), and issue the command.

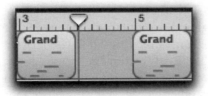

The result should look something like this:

Depending on the Zoom level and the grid resolution, you can use the timeline for some detailed edits. In fact, split and join can be used together to create some interesting variations on Real Instrument Recordings and Software Instrument loops. However, to really get inside your music, you'll probably want to open the editors.

NOTE   *Edits you perform in the timeline affect the entire region; edits you perform in the editors affect units as small as one note.*

About the Editors

In Chapter 1, we had a quick look at GarageBand's editor window, which is located below the timeline (see Figure 8-1). As you can see, the information the editor displays will differ depending on whether the track is a Software Instrument or Real Instrument. You open the editors by clicking the Track Editor button by selecting it in the Track menu, or by double-clicking on a region in the timeline.

Before we get too deeply into editing techniques, let's refresh our grasp of the editor windows' geography.

The Software Instrument Display

The Software Instrument editor (see Figure 8-2) is designed to give you an immediate look at how individual musical events are positioned in time. This grid-like display

(a)   (b)

FIGURE 8-1   The Editor window shows a Software Instrument region (a) and a Real Instrument region (b).

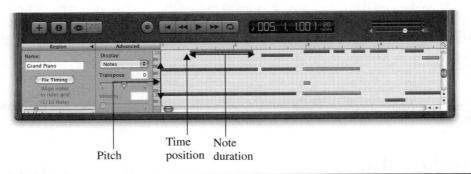

Pitch   Time   Note
position duration

FIGURE 8-2   The Software Instrument editor is set to show notes.

is fairly standard in the world of music software, and if you've ever used a software sequencer, you'll immediately know the territory. The vertical, or y, axis shows pitch; the horizontal, or x, axis shows time. Each bar in the screen represents a single note. The longer the bar, the longer the note. You can change the Software Instrument editor's display to show velocity, modulation, pitch bend, and sustain. We'll look at these other parameters in a moment, but first, let's take a quick peek at the Real Instrument editor.

The Real Instrument Display

The Real Instrument editor (see Figure 8-3) is similar to the Software Instrument editor, but it shows amplitude (or loudness) and time, instead of pitch and time. There are fewer parameters to edit with Real Instrument tracks, but you can do some serious editing here also.

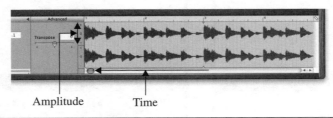

Amplitude   Time

FIGURE 8-3   The Real Instrument editor

Work with Software Instrument Tracks

Although there's plenty you can do to edit Real Instrument tracks, Software Instrument tracks offer the greatest opportunity for getting "under the hood." That's because the performances you record into a Software Instrument track consists of different kinds of data, which in turn is used to trigger a sound. After you've recorded a track, or loaded up a Software Instrument loop, you can still:

- Fix the timing of the whole region, or of individual notes within the region.

- Change the pitch of individual notes or groups of notes.

- Adjust the velocity (which usually affects the loudness) of individual notes or groups of notes.

- Edit MIDI controller effects such as modulation and pitch bend, and move or remove incorrect notes.

- Adjust the sound and character of the Software Instrument.

The Software Instrument editor has a separate view for four different types of data. The Notes display shows the notes themselves. Here, you can adjust the note's timing, pitch, and loudness. You can also move and copy individual notes. There are also separate displays to show pitch bend, modulation, and sustain pedal data. In these windows, you don't see notes, but instead see an envelope curve (similar to the volume curve in the timeline).

The Notes Display

By default, when you first open a region in the Software Instrument editor, you'll see the Notes display (see Figure 8-4). The notes are represented by bars on a grid.

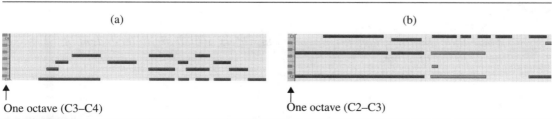

(a)   (b)

↑
One octave (C3–C4)   ↑
                                      One octave (C2–C3)

FIGURE 8-4   The notes editor shows a little more than one octave. Here, we see the range C3–C4 (a). You can see more information by using the scroll bars to adjust the display (b). We now see the octave C2–C3.

This is probably where you'll spend most of your editing time. The display shows a pitch range of about one octave.

 *An octave spans eight notes in a diatonic scale—the one you may know by singing the familiar do, re, mi, fa, so, la, ti, do—but there are actually twelve notes in a chromatic scale. Each note is one half-step apart.*

You can select what the editor shows with the Display pop-up window. When you switch tracks, GarageBand will stay in the same edit mode from track to track. So if you're editing notes on one track and switch to another, the display will still show notes. If you're editing pitch bend on the first track, the next track you select will also show pitch bend.

Find the Notes

When you first open a region editor, it may not show any notes. Don't worry—nothing is missing. It may just mean that the note editor is showing an octave that doesn't contain any notes, or is displaying a section of the song in which the region is "resting." To see notes that are outside of the current pitch range, use the scroll bar to the right of the window to change the pitch range (see Figure 8-4).

 GarageBand does not let you zoom in or out on the editor's pitch range (a feature that is available on many sequencers).

To see the notes in a different part of the song, either use the scroll bar at the bottom of the window or move the Playhead to a position in which the region contains some notes.

 The editor windows have their own zoom sliders, which are independent of those in the timeline.

Did you know?

The Key to the Keys

Like a lot of sequencers, GarageBand uses a type editing display called a *piano roll*. The name comes from the days of the mechanical player piano. Back then, a roll of paper would be stamped with little holes, which would match up with a special drum in the piano. As the paper passed over the drum, the drum would turn and drive the keys. In that way, the player piano is an old-time (or is it olde tyme?) version of the modern sequencer.

The piano roll display uses an illustration of a keyboard to show note position. That's great if you're a keyboardist, but not everyone knows how to read the keys. As you can see, each consecutive key represents a half-step (or a full degree of the chromatic scale).

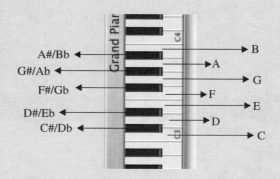

As you can see above, each of the black keys actually has two names. For example, the key between C and D could be called C-sharp (C#) or D-flat (Db). Sharp means "higher"; thus, C# is one half-step higher than C. Flat means "lower." Db is one half-step lower than D (it is also one half-step higher than C). The correct name to use depends on the context and the key of the music, and is outside the realm of this book, but it is important to know what you're looking at.

The distance between the C's is one octave. The note names will then repeat at the next octave up or down. Since the notes repeat on a piano keyboard (and on a piano roll), it can be a little bewildering to open up an editor and simply see some notes as they are displayed in the grid. The following image is taken from a two-handed piano part. At first glance, it's difficult to tell which "hand" we're looking at. Fortunately, the piano roll gives us the answer because it not only tells us which notes we're seeing, but which octave they are in: the left hand is in the lower octave.

NOTE   *The octave numbers run from –2 to 8, with lower numbers indicating lower octaves. Middle C on a piano is also known as C_3.*

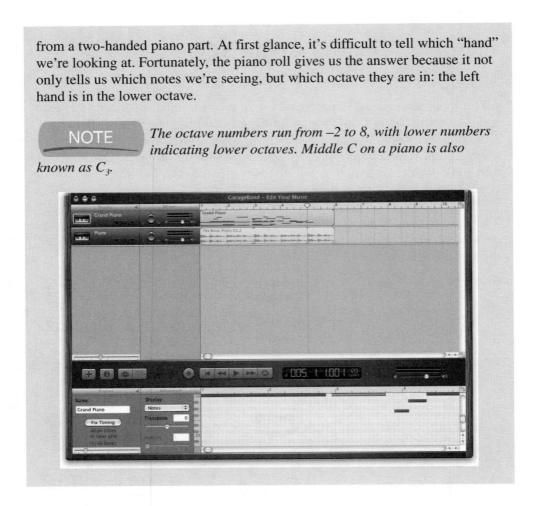

Work with the Entire Region

One of the nice things about GarageBand is that it lets you work with entire regions, or with the elements within a region. With Software Instruments, you can use the edit window to do the following to an entire region:

- Fix timing
- Transpose, or change pitch
- Rename

To work with an entire region, you must first select it in the timeline by clicking on it with the mouse.

NOTE   *Although you can select more than one region in the timeline by SHIFT-clicking, you can only edit one region at a time in the editor.*

Once you select a region, the editor comes to life. In keeping with GarageBand's color scheme, a Software Instrument will bring up a green display, a Real Instrument loop a blue display, and a Real Instrument a purple display.

CAUTION   *If the display is grayed out, it means that no data has yet been selected for editing.*

Work with Notes Within a Region

Although you can perform a lot of edits on a complete region basis, you may also want to get inside and work on individual data within a region. To do this, navigate to the part of the region you wish to edit and, from within the editor, select the notes you want. You can select individual notes or groups of notes a couple of different ways.

CAUTION   *When you edit the notes in a looped region, the edit will affect* all *instances of the loop. For example, let's say the first note of the loop is an F and you move it to G. In subsequent instances of the loop, the first note will be G as well. If you want to limit the edit to one part of the loop, separate the loop by placing the Playhead at the appropriate position and using the Split command.*

Select Notes with the Pointer

To select an individual note with the pointer, simply click on it with the cursor. You can SHIFT-click to select more than one note at a time, as shown in Figure 8-5.

TIP   *SHIFT-clicking is a good way to select noncontiguous notes.*

Select Notes by Dragging

You can also drag the cursor to select a group of notes. This is a great way to select a cluster of nearby notes, as shown in Figure 8-6.

8

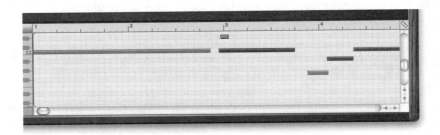

FIGURE 8-5   You can select more than one note at a time by SHIFT-clicking on them in the editor. The dark notes are selected.

Fix Timing

GarageBand's Fix Timing command performs a function generally known as "quantizing." Quantizing is a function that moves a note to a specific grid position. If, for example, you set the grid resolution to 1/4, Fix Timing will position every note to the nearest quarter note.

NOTE   *GarageBand lets you set the editor's grid resolution independent of that of the timeline. To do this, use the Timeline Grid pop-up (see Figure 8-7).*

The correct grid setting is critical to getting the best results when you fix timing. Set the grid to too high a value, and you'll lose the nuances of the performance. Set it too low, and you won't hear much difference. In order to choose the right grid position, you need to know a little bit about the music in the region. The grid position should match the smallest note in the region. For example, if you are playing a part that consists of eighth, quarter, and half-notes, you should set the grid to 1/8. If, however, you have a flourish in that passage that includes a couple of sixteenth notes, you'll

FIGURE 8-6   Drag the cursor to select a cluster of notes.

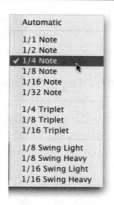

FIGURE 8-7   The Editor's Grid pop-up menu lets you set a grid resolution independent of the timeline.

need to set the grid to 1/16. Otherwise, the sixteenth notes will be "fixed" into 8th notes. Figure 8-8 shows an example.

Whenever you use Fix Timing, it's a good idea to listen to the results before moving on. If your performance loses its feel, you should undo and try another quantize value.

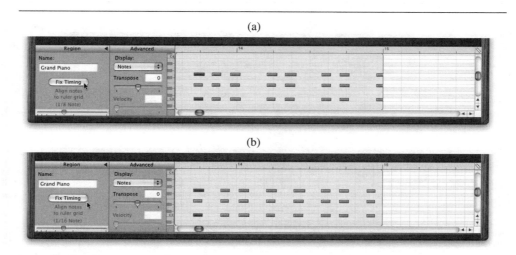

FIGURE 8-8   In this region, we used Fix Timing with the grid set to two different values: 1/8 (a) and 1/16 (b). Note how example b preserves the 16th notes, which are moved in example a.

Fix the Timing of a Region

To fix the timing of an entire region, select the region in the timeline, set the grid value, and click the Fix Timing button.

Fix Timing of One Note or Groups of Notes

Starting with version 1.1, you can use Fix Timing on one note or on groups of notes within a region. Assuming you have the grid set to the appropriate value, select the notes using one of the methods we discussed, and click the Fix Timing button. Figure 8-9 shows a group of notes before and after we've fixed timing.

 *The use of Fix Timing on individual notes or groups of notes is especially useful when you have a passage that has a varied rhythmic character. For example, if you have a quarter-note chord followed by an eighth-note lead line, quantize the two parts separately.*

Use Swing Timing

Duke Ellington said, "It don't mean a thing if it ain't got that swing." As you know, Fix Timing works on a grid. But a straight, rigid grid is not always appropriate for every type of music. For example, most jazz is said to "swing." Instead of the eighth notes being evenly spaced, so that each one is half a beat, in swing timing the first

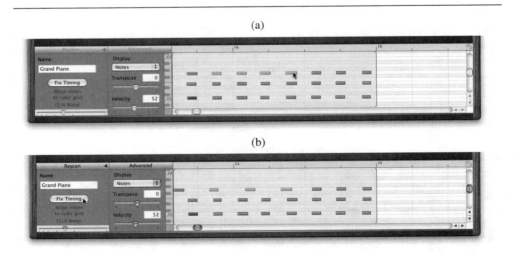

FIGURE 8-9   Here we've selected a group of notes (a) and used fix timing to a 1/4 grid (b).

eighth note is longer—more like a dotted eighth (one eighth plus one sixteenth)—and the second eighth note is shorter, closer in timing to a sixteenth note. Swing timing is appropriate for some jazz, for music that has a "triplet" feel. Figure 8-10 shows an example of a piece of music with an eighth-note swing feel.

 *You can Fix Timing manually by dragging one or more notes to the nearest grid position.*

Change the Duration of a Note

You can change the duration of a Software Instrument note by dragging on the end of it with the mouse (see Figure 8-11). As with other edits, you can do this on one or more selected note.

Change Pitch

GarageBand gives you a number of ways to change the pitch of your Software Instrument performances. You can change the pitch of an entire region, of a single note, or of a group of notes within a region.

8

(a)

(b)

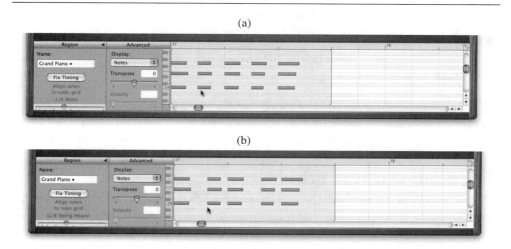

| FIGURE 8-10 | The swing grid lets you Fix Timing when the music doesn't follow a rigid pattern. Here, we've taken a straight eighth note pattern (a) and given it a shuffle feel by applying heavy 1/8 swing (b). |

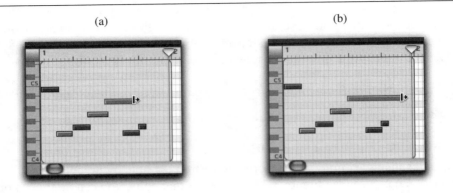

(a)   (b)

FIGURE 8-11   You can select an individual note (a) and change its duration with the mouse (b).

Transpose a Region

The Transpose command lets you change the pitch of all the notes in a region. Transpose works in single increments of the chromatic scale. You can transpose up to 36 steps, or three octaves, up or down.

Twelve degrees of the chromatic scale equals one octave.

To use Transpose, select a region in the timeline, and set the transpose value in the Transpose pop-up menu.

You can split a region and transpose each resulting section to a different value. This is especially handy when you're working with Apple Loops; you can use Transpose to create more variety as the track unfolds over time.

Drag a Note to a New Pitch

While GarageBand's Transpose feature is effective when working with an entire region, there are many instances when you might want to move an individual note or a group of notes. The most obvious application for the one-note fix is to correct a mistake. But you can also use it for purely creative purposes; for example, you can add some variation to a Software Instrument loop by dragging one or two notes to a new position. To change a note by dragging:

■ Select the note in the Editor window.

■ Drag it up (to raise pitch) or down (to lower pitch).

(a)   (b)

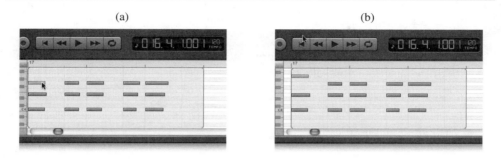

FIGURE 8-12   You can select an individual note with the mouse (a) and drag it to a new pitch (b).

As mentioned earlier, you can select one note or groups of notes. Figure 8-12 shows how to drag a single note to a new pitch.

You can drag notes beyond the limits of the pitches displayed in the editor. For example, if the editor is currently showing the octave C2-C3, you can still drag a note down to C1, or up to C5, or up to D6, etc.

Adjust the Loudness of Individual Notes

In the next chapter, we're going to talk about mixing, and one of the most basic jobs you do at mix time is to set the level of each track in your song. But a track's volume envelope isn't always the best way to control loudness. When you're working with Software Instruments, you can adjust individual notes' loudness with the velocity parameter.

Velocity is a MIDI parameter that measures the force with which you play a note. Like other MIDI data, it follows a 127-step scale, with lower numbers being lower in velocity. Figure 8-13 shows the velocity field in the Software Instrument editor.

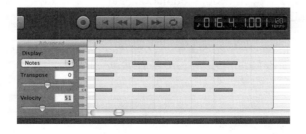

FIGURE 8-13   You can use the slider or type into the velocity field to change the velocity of an individual note or a group of notes.

NOTE

Traditionally, velocity is used to control the loudness of a note, but some devices let you use velocity to control tone or other parameters.

To adjust velocity, select one or more notes: the velocity display will show the velocity of the last note you select.

■ Use the velocity slider to raise or lower velocity.

■ Type in a velocity value.

NOTE

If you edit the velocity of more than one note at one time, all the notes will be adjusted by the same value, but will retain their relative differences. For example, if you have two notes, one with a velocity of 50 and the other with a velocity of 90, adjusting the velocity by 30 will add that number to each note, resulting in a note with velocity of 80 and one with a velocity of 120. The exception to this is when one of the notes is close to the higher or lower limit of the scale (1 or 127, respectively). For example: Adding 10 to the velocity of a note that's already at 125 will cause it to be at 127.

Copy Individual Notes

Many of the leading sequencers on the market let you "step" record, a technique where you insert notes in a MIDI track without actually playing them in real time. GarageBand doesn't have a step-record feature, but you can do something similar by copying individual notes and moving them around in the editor. Figure 8-14 shows how it's done.

You can OPTION-drag groups of notes as well, as shown in Figure 8-15.

Edit Controller Data

With Software Instruments, the actual notes are only one part of the picture. You can also use MIDI controllers to add some flavor to your sound. GarageBand supports three MIDI controllers: pitch bend, modulation, and sustain. Each of these parameters is edited in a similar fashion.

CAUTION

GarageBand can only edit existing controller data. You can't insert a controller event on a track that doesn't already have one.

(a) (b)

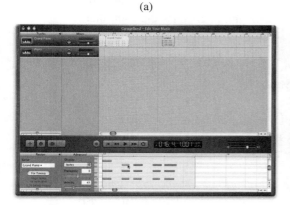 

FIGURE 8-14   Although GarageBand doesn't have an insert-note feature, you can copy one note and move it around. Here, we've selected one note (a); by OPTION-dragging the note, we can create a new note, which we can move anywhere we want in the editor (b).

Pitch Bend

One of the coolest things about instruments like guitar and saxophone is their ability to bend a note, to push it to a new pitch without changing fingering. A traditional keyboard instrument can't do that, but the people who developed the MIDI synthesizer created a command that would give the keyboardist a chance to get the bends.

(a) (b)

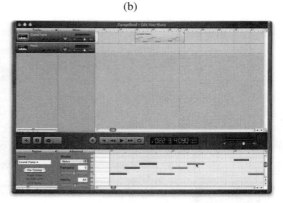

FIGURE 8-15   We've selected a group of notes (a) and OPTION-dragged them to create a new phrase (b).

To use pitch bend, you'll need a controller with a pitch wheel. Fortunately, that would qualify just about any controller on the market. To raise pitch, push the controller up; to lower it, pull it back.

 *Usually, pitch bend covers a range of two half-steps. But some instruments can be set to a pitch range of one octave or more.*

To edit pitch bend, select Pitch Bend in the Display pop-up menu. You will see the pitch bend envelope (see Figure 8-16). Click anywhere in the envelope with the mouse to set a new edit node and drag the node to a new position.

CAUTION *When editing pitch bend, it's usually a good idea to make sure that you have some point where the parameter returns to zero. Otherwise, the music you're editing can sound out of tune with the rest of the track.*

Edit Modulation

Modulation is one of the most expressive controllers available to the electronic musician. It can be used for a lot of things, depending on the instrument you're working with. For example, you might use the "mod wheel" to control a filter sweep, or to add a vibrato-like effect, or even to change the level of an effect like reverb. With some of the more advanced Software Instruments on the market, you can choose what parameter the modulation control affects.

To edit modulation data, choose Modulation in the Display pop-up (see Figure 8-17). Like pitch bend, modulation shows an envelope, which you can drag to the appropriate

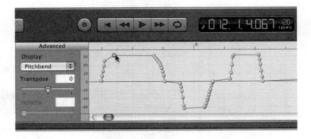

FIGURE 8-16   The pitch bend envelope. Note that the center position is zero-pitch bend, where the note remains unchanged. You lower the note's pitch by dragging the envelope below the center line. Raise the pitch by dragging the envelope above it.

FIGURE 8-17   To edit modulation, grab a node in the envelope (a), and drag it to a new position (b).

The Power of Editing

Programs like GarageBand are great tools because they let you compose by improvising. Because of the way you can move things around, make edits after the fact, and create different versions of your song, it's easy to get your ideas down without having to worry about how all the pieces will eventually fit together.

Take, for example, GarageBand's capabilities for editing Software Instrument tracks. This type of editing has been available in high-end sequencer programs for years, and is a key element in a composer's tool kit. When you have to create music on a deadline—say, for a commercial—it really helps to be able to go in and delete or move any wrong notes, fix the timing of the overall track, change the tempo, and try the same part with different instrument sounds. Just switching from, say, an acoustic piano to an electric piano can completely change the mood of a piece of music. I had instances where I accidentally had an instrument set to play that was completely different than one I intended, and it ended up sounding even better. You just never know.

But not only does a program like GarageBand allow you to edit Software Instruments freely, you can also edit audio loops and the audio tracks you've recorded—and do so without destroying the originals. Being able to move a verse around, copy a chorus and repeat it, or even take one word that a singer sang and put it in a different spot, opens up a whole world of possibilities. It means, for example, that you can take the best sections from multiple takes of a lead vocalist, and easily "comp" them together to assemble the best possible performance. I've even corrected recorded guitar parts after the fact by copying a single chord from one spot and using it to replace a wrong chord from another. The creative options are virtually endless.

—In addition to being a senior editor at Electronic Musician *magazine,*
Mike Levine is a guitarist and commercial composer who's written
music for numerous commercials and television programs.

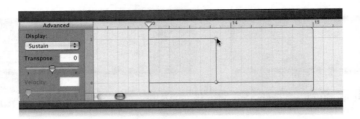

FIGURE 8-18   The sustain editor

position. But in this case, the parameter's value runs from 0 to 127. A zero value is no modulation; 127 is intense modulation.

Edit Sustain

An acoustic piano's sustain pedal lets the instrument's strings resonate even after you've released the keys—an important part of any pianist's repertoire. Most keyboard controllers let you attach a sustain pedal, which you can use to impart a sound that's similar to a piano's natural sustain (I say similar because this is one of the most difficult elements of the piano sound to reproduce with a digital instrument).

To edit sustain, select Sustain in the Display pop-up (see Figure 8-18). This envelope has two positions: on and off.

Work with Real Instruments

Real Instrument tracks may not let you edit with the exacting detail you can achieve when working with Software Instrument tracks, but there's still plenty you can do in the editors. Here, you can focus in on a Real Instrument region and split it in very precise detail. You can then remove, copy, and rearrange the pieces as you see fit. This applies to Real Instrument tracks created with Apple Loops as well as to Real Instrument recordings—the tracks you record yourself.

> NOTE *You can transpose Real Instrument regions, but you cannot transpose Real Instrument recordings you've made yourself.*

Read the Region

As we saw in the Software Instrument section, the Real Instrument editor window follows a grid that's similar to the timeline. But there are some key differences.

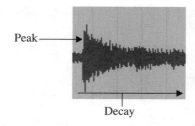

Peak

Decay

FIGURE 8-19   The Real Instrument editor shows a waveform display.

Instead of pitch and time, you see amplitude, or loudness, and time. You can't edit a waveform's amplitude in GarageBand (though we will learn how to do so with some third-party applications in Chapter 10).

However, the Real Instrument editor's "waveform" display (see Figure 8-19) offers a lot of information about each beat of the music. The high point of the wave shows the attack—the place where the note starts and is at its loudest.

Select Some Audio

In the Real Instrument editor, the cursor will change depending on its position in relation to the waveform. For the most part, it works the same way as the pointer in the timeline: put the cursor in the upper right-hand edge of the region, and the loop pointer appears; the lower-right edge will give you the trim pointer; the left edge also gives you a trim pointer. However, when you click in the body of the region, you won't see the typical arrow cursor that appears in the timeline. Instead, a crosshair cursor appears.

To select some audio, drag the crosshair cursor over the waveform. As with most editing functions in GarageBand, the resolution of the cursor depends on the grid setting.

TIP   *If you check Automatic in the Grid Setting pop up, GarageBand will base the grid resolution on the current zoom setting.*

Although you can select any part of the waveform, most edits work best when you select audio from "peak to peak." This should give you the cleanest sound. Figure 8-20 shows a typical selection.

Once you've selected some audio, there are several things you can do. You can split the selection from the rest of the region to create two or more smaller regions;

8

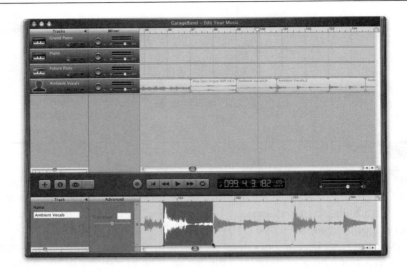

FIGURE 8-20   We've selected audio in the instrument editor by starting at the peak of the first note, and moving to just before the next one.

you can loop the selection, you can remove the selection, and you can copy and paste the selection.

Split a Region in the Track Editor

To split a region in the track editor, select the passage you want separated with the crosshairs cursor. Click the selected area. You'll see the boundaries of the new region, both in the editor and in the timeline. Figure 8-21 shows an example.

As you can see, GarageBand automatically names each of the new regions. You can loop, trim, move, and transpose (assuming that the region is from an Apple Loop) the new regions individually.

Loop and Trim a Region in the Track Editor

As mentioned above, you can both loop and/or trim a region in the track editor. This is handy because you can zoom in on a region in the track editor, while letting the timeline serve as an overview. When you drag the edge of a region, it's transparent—you can see the audio it's covering (see Figure 8-22). Once you release the cursor, the region becomes solid once again.

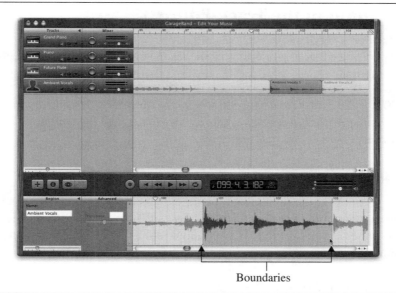

Boundaries

FIGURE 8-21 Here, we split a region to create three new pieces. Note the borders, which indicate the new regions' boundaries.

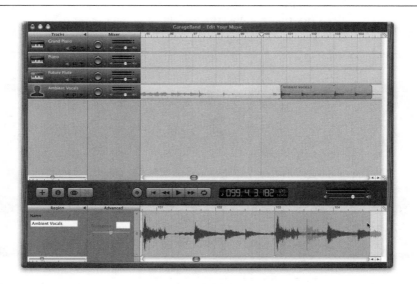

FIGURE 8-22 You can loop a region in the track editor. Note the "transparent" view.

8

Delete Audio in the Track Editor

The track editor is very handy if you want to remove a section of audio quickly. Simply select the part of the region you want to remove, and press the DELETE key. Figure 8-23 shows an example.

The track editor is very useful when you want to delete unwanted noises from your Real Instrument recordings—for example, headphone bleed or breaths between phrases on a vocal track.

Cut, Copy, and Paste in the Track Editor

One way the track editor varies from the timeline is that you can't just drag regions around with the mouse very easily (though, as we'll see, it is possible). However, you can use the track editor to toss your audio into a new musical salad in a couple of different ways:

- Select the audio.

- Use the Edit Cut (COMMAND-X) or Copy (COMMAND-C) commands to bring the selection into the clipboard.

- Move the Playhead to the position at which you want to insert the audio. Your ability to move the Playhead will be tied to the grid resolution.

(a) (b)

FIGURE 8-23 We've selected some audio (a), and removed it with the DELETE key (b).

You can move the Playhead from within the track editor, or in the timeline.

■ Paste the audio from the clipboard (COMMAND-V).

Drag Audio with the Cursor

In the timeline, it's easy to move a region with the mouse: simply click it and drag it around. In the track editor, however, you won't see the arrow cursor, but if you click in the upper portion of the region, you will see a "move" cursor. You can use it to select some audio from one or more adjacent regions and drag it. One of the cool things about this feature is that you can drag regions that are separated by silence, as shown in Figure 8-24.

The Split and Join commands do not work within the track editor.

(a) (b)

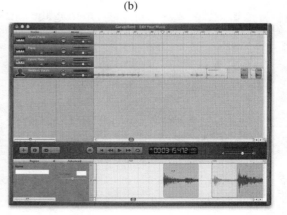

FIGURE 8-24   Here, we've selected two regions (a). We can drag them to a new position together (b).

Assemble a Take

GarageBand's new Duplicate Track feature makes it easy to create a number of alternative versions of a track (the command works equally well on Software and Real Instrument tracks).

> **NOTE** *Duplicate Track copies track settings such as instrument type and effects, but does not copy any of the material in the timeline, nor does it copy any settings you've made to mute, solo, volume, or pan position.*

In this example, we're working with a Real Instrument recording, but it works equally well with Software Instruments. Before we start, let's assume you've already created a Track and set its effects the way you want. (We went over the first half of this exercise in Chapter 6.)

1. Select the track you wish to duplicate.

2. Mute the track (you don't want to hear it while you're playing the alternative track).

3. Choose Track | Duplicate Track (or use COMMAND-D).

4. Record the new track.

5. Repeat as necessary, muting the earlier version of the take each time, as shown here:

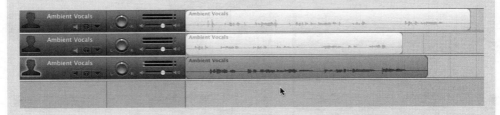

Now that you've got a bunch of takes to choose from, you can audition each in turn by:

- Unmuting them one at a time

- Unmuting *all* of them, and soloing each of the tracks in turn

> **TIP** *If you choose the "solo" method, be sure to solo any additional tracks you want to hear in the background. For example, if you want to hear the vocal against the piano track, solo both the vocal track and the piano track.*

If one of the takes is perfect, you won't have much left to do. But you may find that there are parts of each track that work better than others. In this case, you'll need to assemble the regions in the various tracks to create a perfect take.

First, use Duplicate Track one more time, to create a blank track. This will be your assembly area. Next, use whichever editing method is most appropriate to create a separate region for each of the pieces you wish to assemble, as shown here:

> **TIP** *If you're having trouble selecting exactly the region boundaries you want, disable Snap to Grid in the Control menu (or with COMMAND-G).*

Place the regions in the new track. You can simply drag the regions from their previous location, or you can copy them to the new track by OPTION-dragging. Finally, name the new track (we called ours "Assembled Vocals") and mute all of the earlier takes, as shown here. You have the option of deleting the old takes, or keeping them around for future reference. Either way, your newly assembled track should now contain an ideal performance!

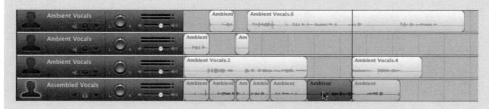

8

Moving On

Audio and MIDI (Software Instrument) editing is an art unto itself. Careful use of GarageBand's editing features can make your music sound tight, or it can open doors that simply aren't possible in human performance. However, overuse can make your music sound mechanical, and can also drive you a little nuts. (Take it from someone who wasted more than one night moving various drum samples around by fractions of a second; in the end, I was better off re-recording the part!) As with any musical endeavor, editing takes practice. The good news is that GarageBand is nondestructive: you can edit away without actually ruining the original data. If you want to experiment, use the Save As feature to create a backup version of your song; edit on one, and keep the other for reference.

With a program like GarageBand, editing is not only about fixing a bad performance. It is also the first step of the mixing processes, a way to fine-tune the dynamics of a Software Instrument part and to remove unwanted noise from a Real Instrument recording. We'll be referring to the editors as we build our mix in Chapter 9.

Chapter 9

Mix Your Song and Prepare a Finished Master

How to...

- Set a track's volume
- Set a track's position in the stereo field
- Automate volume settings
- Add audio effects to individual tracks
- Add audio effects to multiple tracks
- Apply different types of effects
- Use the master track
- Create and save a custom effect
- Export your song to iTunes

Recording and editing are two big slices of the production pie. The third—mixing—may well be the most elusive. After all, it's pretty easy to tell if you've played a part right. If there are mistakes, you have the option of editing the part to correct them or replaying it until it's perfect.

But mixing is different: there's no "right" way to mix a song. Sure, some styles of music may point you in a sonic direction, like pumping the bass and kick drum for a dance tune or keeping the guitar bright and clean for a country song. But there are also many variations within a given musical style. Should the drums be loud and reverberant, or quiet and "dry?" Should the vocal be up front, or buried in the mix? Should the background vocals be panned to the left and right, or should they sit right down the middle? The answer to these questions is "yes." Anything goes in mixing as long as it sounds good.

A good mix has three things going for it. First, it should be clear, so that every instrument can be distinctly heard. Second, it should help convey the mood of the song; if you're writing a death-metal tune, a mix with the vocals way up front and the guitars buried would make the head-bangers want to bang you on the head. Finally, the mix should add some interest, so that your song unfolds over time. In this way, mixing is the final part of the songwriting and arranging process.

We're going to save the "art" of mixing and arranging for Chapter 10. Before we can get into these creative details, we must first learn how to operate GarageBand's mixing controls.

E Pluribus Unum: The Basics of Mixing

E pluribus unum, which is Latin for "From many, one," perfectly describes the art of mixing. Your goal is to take many divergent musical parts and combine them into a cohesive whole.

Before we get to the "one," let's start with the many. Each track in GarageBand offers a wide array of controls that not only affect how that track sounds individually, but how well it blends with those around it. These include the volume and pan controls, the track effects, and the master effects.

Open the Track Mixer

In order to access GarageBand's mixing controls, you must open the Track Mixer, shown here. If the Track Mixer is not visible, click the triangular switch at the top of the track header.

NOTE *You can adjust a track's volume with the volume curves without opening the Track Mixer. We cover curves later in this chapter.*

Adjust the Volume of Individual Tracks

The most basic of all mix parameters is volume, which sets a track's loudness relative to those around it. In GarageBand, there are several ways to adjust a track's individual volume.

Use the Volume Slider

The volume slider (see Figure 9-1) is the most basic tool for adjusting volume. When you open a new track, the slider is set to 0dB, or decibels. The decibel is the unit used to measure a sound's loudness.

FIGURE 9-1   The volume slider

 *A setting of 0 does not mean that the track is silent. It simply means that the volume slider is neither making the track louder nor quieter.*

To raise the track's level, move the slider to the right. To lower its level, move the slider to the left.

Use the Volume Curve

You can also adjust a track's volume with the volume curve (see Figure 9-2). To reveal the volume curve, click the Show Volume Curve button (the triangle in the track header). To adjust overall volume with the volume curve, grab the control point at the beginning of the track. Pull the control point down to lower volume; raise it up to increase volume.

Use the Curves to Automate Volume

One of the most important features in a professional mixing studio is track *automation*. In the old days, people used to ride the mixer by hand. If you missed a fade, you had to redo the entire mix. Automation lets you make changes automatically. Not only does this free up your hands—making it possible to work with more than one track at a time—it also lets you adjust your volume changes until it's exactly where you want it, and saves the results so that they play back exactly as you want them to.

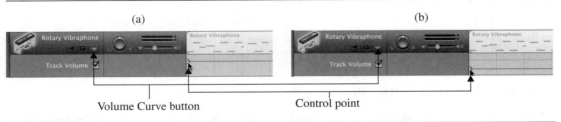

FIGURE 9-2   You can adjust the track's overall volume with the volume curve. You can grab the volume curve by the "control point" at the beginning of the track (a) and moving it (b).

9

> NOTE *GarageBand doesn't offer all the automation features of some of the higher-end audio programs (some of which let you automate every parameter known to man, and a few known only to machines), but it does let you automate volume with the volume curves.*

The volume curve is useful when you want to instruct GarageBand to automatically change volume over time. The most common uses for volume automation are to fade in and out on a track, and to make precise volume adjustments in a specific part of a track. You can toggle the volume curve on and off by checking the Track Volume box in the track header.

Create a Fade-out

A fade-out is one of the most common ways to automate volume changes. With a fade-out, your music gets gradually quieter until it can no longer be heard. You can use this technique on individual tracks, or on the entire mix by fading out on the master track:

1. Open the volume curve.

2. Set the volume to the desired starting point.

3. Move the cursor to the place in the song where you want the fade to begin.

4. Click in the volume curve to create a new control point (see Figure 9-3). The new point may appear larger than the other—this means that it is selected.

5. Move the cursor to the position where you want the fade to end, and create a new control point (see Figure 9-4).

6. Drag the new control point to the bottom of the track volume area. You should see something like Figure 9-5.

In the fade shown in Figure 9-5, the volume will decrease steadily between the control points. If you want a more abrupt fade, you can add control points in between the start and end of the fade. Figure 9-6 shows a slightly more complex fade; it starts slowly, then fades out faster toward the end.

FIGURE 9-3   This volume curve now has a new control point.

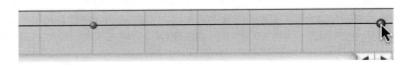

FIGURE 9-4   We've added another control point...

 *You can change the duration of the fade by dragging the control point in the timeline.*

Create a Fade-in

You can use a similar technique to create a fade-in (this time you start at silence, and move up), as shown in Figure 9-7.

A fade-in can be useful for a number of applications. You can use it to create a smooth transition between two similar parts that overlap (fade one out and fade the other in), as shown in Figure 9-8. You can also use a fade-in to soften the beginning of a part.

Raise and Lower Volume at Specific Places in a Song

Fades are useful, but there's more you can do with the volume curves. One of the most important is the ability to raise or lower a track when necessary. For example, let's say your song has a vocal track and a lead guitar track. You'd probably want the lead guitar to be quieter during the vocal lines, then raise its volume for the guitar solo. Figure 9-9 shows an example. Note how tight the fades are.

Use the Pan Control

 Loudness is only one factor in mixing. Another important element is stereo position—where the track sits in the left-right stereo field. The pan knob is used to control this ("pan" is short for "panorama").

FIGURE 9-5   ...and dragged it down to create a fade.

FIGURE 9-6   By adding another control point, we were able to control the speed and character of our fade.

FIGURE 9-7   A fade-in

9

FIGURE 9-8   Here are two similar tracks with overlapping parts. By fading the top track out and the bottom track in, we can create a smooth transition. This technique is known as crossfading.

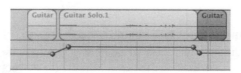

FIGURE 9-9   You can use the volume curve to create a quick change. Here, we raised the volume of a guitar solo. Note that during the solo, the curve is flat, then is quickly brought down after the solo ends.

We discussed the pan control in Chapter 3, but here's a quick refresher. When you're working with a one-channel, or *mono*, track, the pan control sets the track's position in the stereo field. Move the control all the way to the left, and the track will only be heard in the left speaker. Move it all the way to the right, and you will only hear sound in the right speaker. Put it in the middle, and you'll hear the sound equally in both speakers. With a stereo track, the pan control sets the balance between the left and right sides of the track.

Location, Location

If you panned everything dead center, you'd have a mono mix; there would be no variation at all between the left and right channels. This was the standard way of recording and mixing up until the 1960s, when stereo started to become the norm. It's interesting to listen to early stereo recordings; you can tell that people in the music business were still trying to figure out how to use this new technology. Often, you'd find songs where all the instruments would be on one side, and the vocals on another, or the bass on the left, the guitar on the right, and the vocals and drums in the middle. Ironically, one of the most important things about early stereo mixes was that they had to also sound good when played back on mono equipment, such as the car radios of the day.

Today, mono compatibility isn't that important: most people have stereos. And the idea of separating the vocals from the instruments is generally considered a little extreme. The pan control can be effective when used subtly. Figure 9-10 shows a possible panning scheme for a "typical" mix. (I know I said earlier there was no such thing as "typical." That's true, but bear with me anyway.)

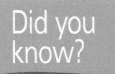

The Volume Effect

We haven't really discussed GarageBand's track effects yet, but this is a good place to point out that the volume slider and curves are not the only ways in which you can alter a track's loudness. Some GarageBand effects, such as EQ, compression, and Amp Simulation, can affect the volume of a track. If you're using third-party Audio Unit effects with GarageBand, you may find that some of them also have "gain" or "level" controls that let you adjust the volume (a common feature on a compressor plug-in, for example). With Software Instruments, you have even more control; you can adjust a note's velocity to make it louder or softer, and you can adjust the properties of the instrument itself to change its volume.

As you can see in Figure 9-10, the two backing vocal tracks are positioned all the way to the right and left, respectively. The lead guitar is slightly to the left, while the rhythm guitar is slightly to the right. The bass and vocals are dead center, and the stereo drum loop is equally distributed across left and right channels.

There are no rules about which instrument should be panned where, but in general, lead vocals are traditionally kept dead center. Bass is usually panned center, in part because low-frequency information is less directional, so there's little point in panning the bass. With a traditional drum kit, the kick and snare are usually panned center, while the toms and cymbals are distributed across the stereo field in a way that reflects their position on a drum set. Other instruments are fair game, but it's a good idea to separate similar sounds—for example, two guitar parts—by panning them across from each other.

Don't feel that you must pan an instrument all the way in one direction or another. You can create plenty of space for a track by panning it only slightly in one direction or another.

9

FIGURE 9-10   Here's an example of a mix with different instruments in various pan positions.

Use Effects

Volume and pan can help you get a basic mix, but the real flavor comes when you add effects. GarageBand comes with an impressive array of audio effects, and you can augment the standard effects by adding Apple's Jam Pack or with third-party Audio Units effects (see Chapter 13).

NOTE *In audio software, effects are often referred to as plug-ins. A* plug-in *is a piece of software that, when added to a host application, enhances its performance.*

Add Track Effects

Effects play an integral role in all GarageBand tracks, whether they're of the Real Instrument or Software Instrument variety. Each instrument in the GarageBand library has an accompanying effects preset, and, as you might expect, the preset's parameters are designed to suit that particular instrument; the effects offered in the Detailed Drums preset are very different from those in the Grunge (guitar) preset.

You can see an instrument's effects in the New Track Inspector (see Figure 9-11) any time you create a new track. With existing tracks, you can view the effects in

FIGURE 9-11   In the Track Info Inspector, you can click the Details triangle to get access to the effects.

Sound Stew

Whether you're an experienced musician or a newcomer to the world of music production (actually, you can be both), one of the most satisfying things is to be able to sound like yourself. Although GarageBand's sonic building blocks—its collection of Apple Loops—were designed by other people, your music doesn't have to sound secondhand.

GarageBand gives you plenty of ways to shape your music, from sound design to audio editing to Software Instrument editing. This chapter will offer a few tips to get you started.

NOTE

For these exercises, we used a system equipped with GarageBand 1.1 and Jam Pack. You don't need Jam Pack to do similar work, but the added resources the package offers are a big plus when it comes to sound shaping.

Cooking with the Amp Simulator

One of the cool things about GarageBand is that it's guitar friendly. Most loop-oriented software is so heavily focused on the dance scene that it ignores traditional guitar-based pop and rock musicians. But GarageBand's built-in Amp Simulator lets you create some great guitar sounds without having to mic up an amplifier.

The Guitar/Amp/Effects Trinity

Talk to an experienced guitarist about their favorite instrument, and it's likely that they'll rattle off a long list of gear, not just the name of their favorite guitar. The guitar may be the physical instrument, but the amplifier and effects it plugs into have as much—and some argue more—influence on the sound. Guitarists are as fanatical about their amps and "stompboxes" (guitar jargon for "effects") as they are about the instruments themselves.

But in truth, it's the relationship between these elements that makes the sound come to life. For example, a Gibson Les Paul, which is equipped with twin-coil "humbucking" pickups, will sound bold and fat when played through a typical British Marshall amplifier. The Les Paul/Marshall combination pretty much defined the sound of hard rock from the late 1960s on.

A Fender Stratocaster, which has thinner single-coil pickups, will sound a little brighter and funkier through the Marshall stack, and though it will still have a hard-rock edge, the Fender won't generate as much distortion, or overdrive (at least, not without the help of a separate distortion box). Play that same Strat through a Fender Twin Reverb amp, and the sound will be clean, clear, and percussive—perfect for surf music, country, and R&B rhythm.

Amps

The difference has to do with the interactive relationship between guitar and amp. The first guitar amps were built in the era when tubes—glass devices that look a bit like light bulbs—dominated audio technology. The tubes processed the audio signal and helped shape its tone. Their inefficiency—their tendency to reduce some frequencies while enhancing others, to distort, and to compress the signal—helped define the signature sound of modern music. Interestingly, as audio technology advanced, guitarists found that higher fidelity didn't suit them; the guitar sounded too bright, too clean, too clinical. They liked the sound of the old, inefficient, tube designs. Today, many guitar amps are still built with tubes. More important, the job of *any* amp designer, even one working on a digital simulator, is to re-create the sound of those early tube amps.

The most important characteristic of a tube amp is its *gain* characteristic: the way it boosts your guitar's quiet signal and makes it loud enough to drive a set of speakers. A low-gain amp is designed to sound clean: the guitar has a detailed percussive quality, even when the amp is turned up. Clean sounds are often used for rhythm guitar, but they're also the standard in country solos, jazz, and many pop styles.

A high-gain amp is designed to sound "dirty," or distorted. With these designs, the first part of the amp, called the *preamp*, will overload the tubes, causing "overdrive," a syrupy rich sound that gives the guitar a horn-like sustain and tone. You can vary the amount of drive to suit the music: a moderately driven, or "crunch," sound is good for power chords and bluesy solos; a more overdriven tone, with lots of sustain, is the foundation of the rock lead guitar sound.

MODEL BEHAVIOR

Most modeled amps are designed to emulate the classic tube amps of the 1960s and '70s. For legal reasons, most modelers use a generic term to describe each of the amps they are emulating. Generally speaking, here are the translations:

- **British Gain** Usually based on a Marshall Stack that overdrives easily. Amps used by Hendrix, Led Zeppelin, Van Halen, and other hard rockers. (See Figure 1.)

- **British Clean** A Vox amp, used by the Beatles and other British Invasion bands, Tom Petty, and U2 guitarist The Edge.

- **American Gain** Usually based on a high-gain Mesa amp. In the 1970s, Mesa revolutionized amp design by giving the player separate control over the preamp and power amp sections, which allowed for overdrive at low to moderate volumes. Their idea caught on and is now the standard in amp design. GarageBand's Amp Simulator has separate controls for preamp and master volume.

- **American Clean** Based on classic Fender amps of the past, these have a lush, rich sound with plenty of detail, and are widely used for country, blues, funk, and rock 'n' roll.

Figure 1: A classic Marshall stack defines the high-gain British amp sound. (Image courtesy of Marshall Amplification.)

Effects

Effects are another important part of the typical guitarist's arsenal. Their use became widespread in the Psychedelic '60s, and, as with amplifiers, most modern guitar effects are designed to emulate the sound of classic Fuzz tones, Cry Baby Wah Wah pedals, Uni-Vibes, Echoplexes, and many others. Most of these effects were designed to reside on the floor, so that the guitarist could operate them with his or her feet while playing—thus the name "stompbox." Today, there are hundreds of stompbox effects on the market, and dozens of digital modeling devices that are designed to emulate them.

In the old days, guitarists would place all of their effects in between the guitar and the amp. Today, most guitarists split their effects. Stompboxes, such as distortion pedals, compressors, and wah wahs, are placed before the amp. Spatial effects, such as chorus, delay, and reverb, are often placed after the amp's gain stage in a special circuit called an *effects loop*. The position of an effect relative to the amp can have a real impact on the tone.

The Virtual Rig

Of course, you can create your own guitar sounds by editing an existing sound in GarageBand, but it's also fun to build your own "rig" from scratch. A GarageBand guitar rig consists of an amp and effects.

Let's start by choosing an amp:

1. Plug your guitar into GarageBand and turn its volume control all the way up.

2. Open a Track Info window (or create a new track).

3. Set the track for mono input, and activate track monitor (see Figure 2).

4. Play the Guitar. You should hear some sound coming through GarageBand.

5. Open the first additional effect slot and choose Amp Simulation.

6. Open the Amp Simulation edit window (see Figure 3).

7. Choose a model and begin editing.

As you can see, the end of the list is only the beginning of the processes. From here, we have a lot of options, and the correct choices will depend on a number of factors:

- The musical style and the role of the guitar
- The type of guitar you're using
- Any additional effects you've added between the guitar and the computer

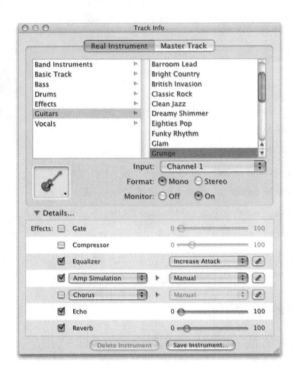

Figure 2. A Guitar track is set up and ready for tweaking.

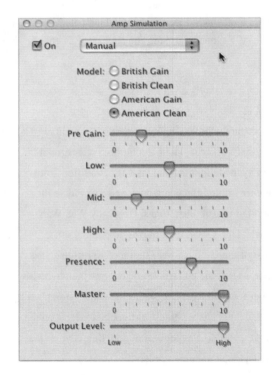

Figure 3. The Amp Simulator edit window

NOTE

For the sake of consistency, we're going to assume that you're plugging your guitar directly into your audio interface, and not using any physical effects or preamps in your signal path. However, if you *do* use external effects, such as compression or distortion, be sure to adjust your computer's audio inputs so that the added gain from the effects doesn't overload your track.

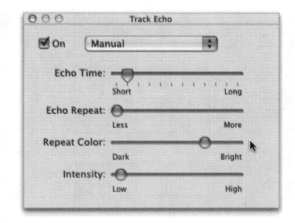

Figure 4. Track Echo screen

Nashville Sound

Country music is characterized by clean, twangy guitars. The prototypical country instrument is the Fender Telecaster, though models by Gretsch, Gibson, and others are also popular. Modern country guitarists often go for a rock sound when soloing, but we're going to focus here on the classic "chicken pickin'" sound.

Recommended Ingredients

- Single-coil guitar such as Fender Stratocaster or Telecaster
- Compressor
- American Clean amp
- Track Echo, or short delay
- Reverb

Herbs and Spices

- Tremolo (instead of Track Echo)
- EQ

People to Listen To

- Albert Lee
- The Hellecasters
- Johnny Hyland

Settings

- **Guitar**   Use pickup closest to the bridge.
- **Compressor**   On, turned up for heavy compression
- **Equalizer (Optional)**   Cut bass and mids, slight boost to highs.
- **Amp**   See Figure 5.
  - **Pre Gain**   4–5
  - **Low**   4–5
  - **Mid**   4–5 (lower if you're using a humbucker-equipped guitar)
  - **High**   7–8
  - **Presence**   8–10
  - **Master**   8
- **Track Echo**
  - **Time**   Short
  - **Repeat**   Less
  - **Color**   Bright
  - **Intensity**   Low
  - **Reverb**   Moderate

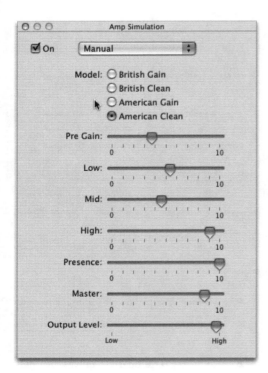

Figure 5. Amp settings for a classic country clean sound. Use the pickup closest to the guitar's bridge for a twangier sound.

Tips

- Although this sound is designed for single-coil guitars, you can get close with a humbucker-equipped model by cutting low midrange with the EQ.
- Use the pickup nearest the neck and replace Track Echo with Chorus for a nice pop rhythm sound.

Blues Guitar/Rock Rhythm

A great blues guitar sound should have a singing quality, but shouldn't be "fuzzed out." This sound hovers on the edge of distortion, and many blues guitarists will use the volume control on their guitar to go from a clean quiet sound to a more raucous overdrive. The overdriven sound is also great for rock rhythm guitar.

Recommended Ingredients

- Single-coil or humbucker-equipped electric guitar
- American Clean amp
- Reverb

Herbs and Spices

- Compressor
- Track Echo
- Tremolo (instead of Track Echo)
- EQ

People to Listen To

- Eric Clapton
- Buddy Guy
- Robert Cray
- Stevie Ray Vaughan

Settings

- **Guitar**   Use neck pickup for deeper sound, bridge pickup for stinging sound.
- **Compressor (Optional)**   Set to taste.
- **Equalizer (Optional)**   Boost lows and low midrange for a warmer sound, and to give a single-coil guitar a humbucker-like sound.
- **Amp**   See Figure 6.
    - **Pre Gain**   9–10
    - **Low**   6
    - **Mid**   7–10 (lower if you're using a humbucker-equipped guitar)
    - **High**   8
    - **Presence**   6–10 (depending on the characteristic sound of your guitar)
    - **Master**   8
- **Track Echo (Optional)**
    - **Time**   Short to medium

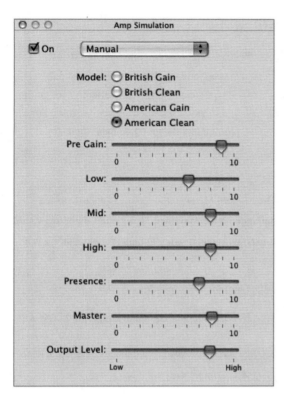

Figure 6. Amp settings for a clean blues sound. Use the guitar's volume control to go from clean to dirty.

- **Repeat** Less
- **Color** Bright
- **Intensity** Low
- **Reverb** Moderate

Tips

- Use the EQ to fatten up the midrange if you're playing power chords.

- With a three-pickup guitar like a Fender Stratocaster, the "middle positions" can deliver a funkier sound, a la Stevie Ray Vaughan.

Rock Lead

This sound is characterized by a smooth, overdriven sound and lush effects. It can work with single-coil and humbucking guitars but is usually created with the latter.

Recommended Ingredients

- Humbucker-equipped guitar, such as Gibson Les Paul
- Compressor
- British Gain or American Gain amp model
- Track Echo
- Reverb

Herbs and Spices

- Chorus, Phase, or Flanger
- EQ

People to Listen To

- Eddie Van Halen
- Jeff Beck
- Joe Satriani
- Carlos Santana

Settings

- **Guitar** Use the bridge pickup for a brighter sound, the neck for a smoother sound.
- **Compressor** On, turned up for moderate to heavy compression
- **Equalizer (Optional)** Boost mids when using a single-coil pickup.
- **Amp** See Figure 7.
  - **Pre Gain** 4–5 (higher with single-coil)
  - **Low** 6

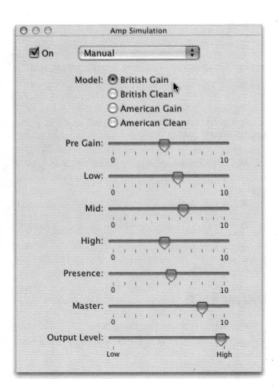

Figure 7. Amp settings for a rock lead sound. You can switch between British and American gain models for different sounds. The Brit model has more midrange, the American a little more top-end crunch.

Tips

- Switch between American and British models to create sonic variations.
- This sound is especially effective for getting a "legato" sound on slower passages. For a more precise sound on faster runs, try reducing the Pre Gain.

Heavy-Metal Meltdown

The Modern Metal sound features super-distorted guitars with the midrange "scooped." Often, this sound is used with seven-string guitars (the extra string is a low B).

Recommended Ingredients

- Humbucker-equipped guitar, preferably a seven-string, or a six-string that has been tuned down
- Compressor
- EQ
- American Gain amp model

- **Mid**   6–8
- **High**   5–6
- **Presence**   5–6
- **Master**   8
- **Track Echo**
  - **Time**   Medium
  - **Repeat**   Low-moderate
  - **Color**   Medium
  - **Intensity**   Low to moderate
  - **Reverb**   Moderate

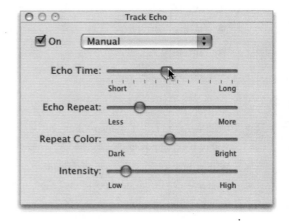

Figure 8. Track Echo screen

Herbs and Spices

- Any modulation or delay effect
- Graphic Equalizer

People to Listen To

- Dimebag Darrell
- Korn
- Metallica

Settings

- **Guitar**   Use either pickup.
- **Compressor**   On, turned up for heavy compression
- **Equalizer**   Boost bass; cut mids, boost highs
- **Amp**   See Figure 9.
  - **Pre Gain**   7–8
  - **Low**   6
  - **Mid**   1–4
  - **High**   7
  - **Presence**   To taste
  - **Master**   8

Tips

- If you have a graphic equalizer plug-in at your disposal, use it in place of the GarageBand EQ to create a "smile" curve, with the mids cut.
- This sound can be very effective when you "double-track" guitars. To do so, record a part on one track and pan it to the left. Make a new track and record the same part, panning it to the right.

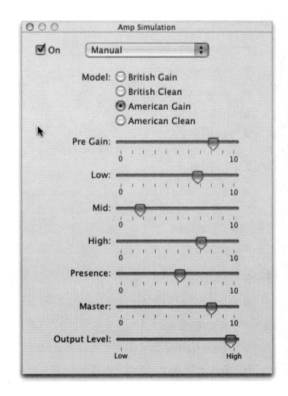

Figure 9. To get a thrash-metal "scooped" sound, boost highs and lows and cut midrange.

Take It to The Edge

U2 guitarist The Edge helped redefine the guitarist's role in pop music, and continues to be a sonic innovator. The Edge uses lots of effects to create his sound, but delay is the most important element of his tone. Other guitarists who are known for their sonic innovation include Adrian Belew, David Torn, and the pioneer of the psychedelic guitar, the late Jimi Hendrix.

Recommended Ingredients

- Fender Stratocaster
- Compressor
- British Clean amp
- Track Echo
- Reverb

Herbs and Spices

- Modulation Effect (If you use a modulation effect, you will need to feed the track to the master echo.)
- EQ

People to Listen To

- U2
- King Crimson
- Jimi Hendrix
- Robin Trower

Settings

- **Guitar**   Use any pickup.
- **Compressor**   On, turned up for moderate compression
- **Equalizer (Optional)**   To taste
- **Amp**   See Figure 10.
  - **Pre Gain**   6–8
  - **Low**   4–5
  - **Mid**   4–5 (lower if you're using a humbucker-equipped guitar)
  - **High**   7–8
  - **Presence**   6–8
  - **Master**   8

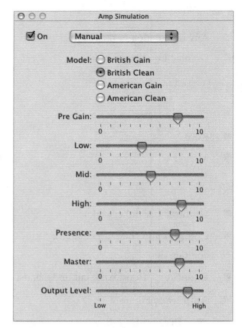

Figure 10. Amp settings for a modern pop sound. Use Pre Gain to take the sound from clean to overdrive.

- **Track Echo**
  - **Time**   Medium
  - **Repeat**   Medium
  - **Color**   Moderate
  - **Intensity**   Moderate
  - **Reverb**   Optional

Tips

- Use the guitar's volume control to create swells and other effects.
- Try and match the echo to the tempo of your music.
- Switch the order between the Amp Simulator and the Track Echo for different sounds.

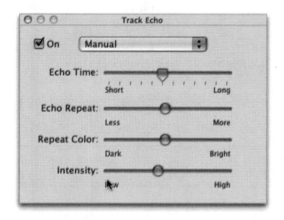

Figure 11. Track Echo screen

The Key to the Keys

S ynthesizers pose an interesting paradox. On one hand, most models come loaded with great sounds, so you don't need to be a programming expert to get a lot out of them. But this can also be a curse: most people are too intimidated by the technology to delve deeper and create their own unique sounds with their synths.

GarageBand's built-in synths not only sound good, they're easy to program. In fact, they serve as a good starting point for synth sound design. After you try a GarageBand synth, you might want to take a crack at a more complex hardware or software model.

My Generation

The first element in creating a keyboard sound is choosing a generator. GarageBand comes with lots of options, including sample-based players, analog synth emulators, and digital synths. Each creates sound in its own way. For example, the sample players use short digital recordings, known as samples, to generate a realistic sound, while the analog generators imitate, or model, the sound of a vintage synthesizer, and the digital generators are designed to sound like modern digital synths.

The cool part about creating your own sounds is that there are no rules. You can use an Organ generator, for example, to create a bass sound, or an Analog generator to create a pseudo brass sound. The number of choices is nearly limitless. Chapter 10 includes some information about working with GarageBand software instruments, but here, we'll get our hands dirty and create a few custom sounds. Once you go through these exercises, experiment with other generators and effects.

The Organ Bass

GarageBand's Tonewheel Organ generator is designed to sound like a classic Hammond B-3 organ, which was one of the most popular keyboards in the 1960s and '70s. It's a versatile instrument, and is especially effective as an alternative to a standard bass.

Recommended Ingredients

- ■ Tonewheel Organ generator
- ■ Equalizer

Herbs and Spices

- ■ Tremolo
- ■ Bit reduction (for an outrageous distorted sound)
- ■ Amp Simulation

Settings

- ■ **Tonewheel Organ**   See Figure 12.
  - ■ **Drawbars**   More (all the way left)
  - ■ **Percussion Level**   Second

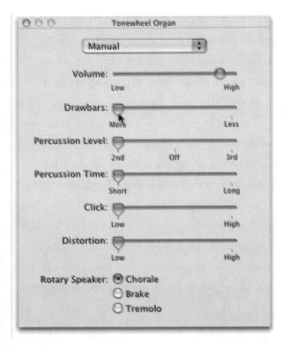

Figure 12. You can create a nice bass sound with the Tonewheel Organ.

- ■ **Percussion Time**   Short
- ■ **Click**   Low; edge it up for a more forceful sound.
- ■ **Distortion**   Any setting
- ■ **Rotary Speaker**   Chorale

Tips

- ■ Insert Amp Simulation as an added effect to give the sound a rock 'n' roll edge.
- ■ Insert Bitcrusher as an added effect to create a very aggressive distortion.
- ■ Insert Tremolo as an added effect to create a dreamer sound.

Steppin' Out

An *Arpeggio* (Italian for "broken chord") is a chord played one note at a time. Automatic arpeggiators are popular in dance music and electronica, and are often

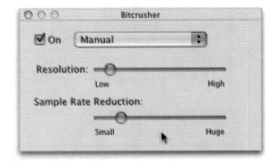

Figure 13. Bitcrusher screen

found on modern synthesizers and sequencers. GarageBand doesn't have an arpeggiator function, but you can get something close with the Digital Stepper generator, a powerful digital synth that can do everything from icy pads to gurgling machine music. Playing the stepper as we've set it here is almost like playing instant music. Just hold a chord and go. The instrument does the rest.

Recommended Ingredients

- ■ Digital Stepper
- ■ Track Echo (or a liberal amount of master Echo)
- ■ Reverb

Herbs and Spices

- ■ Tremolo
- ■ Flanger
- ■ Automatic Filter

Settings

- ■ **Digital Stepper**   See Figure 14.
  - ■ **Balance**   Set slider about halfway.
  - ■ **Modulation**   Slightly toward Low
  - ■ **Harmonics**   Vary this to taste. We like it best in the middle.
  - ■ **Harmonic Steps**   See above.

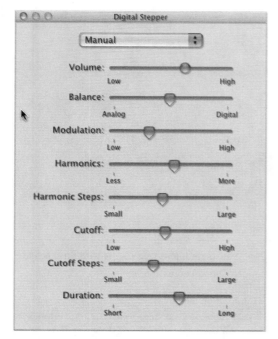

Figure 14. The Digital Stepper can create some gurgling sounds that are like instant music.

- ■ **Cutoff** Dead center
- ■ **Cutoff Steps** Small to medium
- ■ **Duration** Medium to long
- ■ **Track Echo**
  - ■ **Time** Medium to long
  - ■ **Repeat** Medium to more
  - ■ **Color** Dark
  - ■ **Intensity** Moderate

Tips

- ■ If you use the Automatic Filter as an added effect, set the Stepper's filter higher.
- ■ Try Tremolo at slow speed, high intensity, with auto pan activated—freaky!
- ■ Hold a chord, then change one note at a time to create an undulating chord progression.

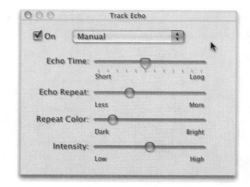

Figure 15. Track Echo settings for a dreamy synth sound

Brass Pad

Not all exotic sounds are originated by synthesizers. You can use sample-based generators to create some otherworldly timbres, as well. In this example, we've started with a brass sound, but by adjusting attack time and adding effects, we've created a pad worthy of a late-night sci-fi movie.

Recommended Ingredients

- ■ Horns generator
- ■ Compressor
- ■ Flanger
- ■ Automatic Filter
- ■ Echo
- ■ Reverb

Herbs and Spices

- ■ Replace Flanger with Phaser.

Settings

- ■ **Horns** See Figure 16.
  - ■ **Cutoff** High
  - ■ **Attack** Slightly slow; even a subtle move of the slider, as shown, should do

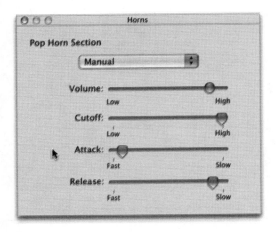

Figure 16. You can use brass or another sampled instrument to create some eerie, unnatural sounds.

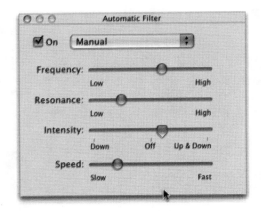

Figure 17. Automatic Filter screen

the trick; you can exaggerate the effect by making the attack even slower.

- **Release** Slow. The longer the release, the longer the sample will sustain after you release the keys.

■ **Flanger**

- **Intensity** About 75% toward High
- **Speed** About 75% toward Slow
- **Feedback** Start low, and experiment by adding more. Too much feedback will make the sound unmusical—but very spacey.

■ **Automatic Filter** See Figure 17.

- **Frequency** Moderate
- **Resonance** Low to moderate
- **Intensity** Just to the right of Off, as shown
- **Speed** Slow to moderate

Tips

- Replace brass with the Voice generator for a scary choir sound (you'll need to adjust attack time when you swap the generator). You can

also get interesting results with Strings and Tuned Percussion.

- Use plenty of Echo and Reverb.
- Increase resonance to add more overtones to the sound.

Mixed Nuts

A s we discuss in Chapters 9 and 10, mixing is an art unto itself. Although GarageBand's mixer isn't as elaborate as that found in a program like Apple/Emagic's Logic series, you can combine GarageBand's mixing and editing features to create some very interesting sounds and effects.

The Drum Split

In professional recording studios, the drums are usually tracked so that each drum is on a separate track. This way the mix engineer can use the audio processing that best suits each individual drum. For example, it's common practice to keep the kick drum dry, while adding reverb to the snare drum. That's not so easy to do in GarageBand, but there is a way to separate drums and process them so they each sound their best. First you'll need to create two identical Software Instrument tracks, which you can do with GarageBand 1.1's new "Duplicate Track" command (see Figure 18).

The Drum Edit

Next, choose a drum loop and drag it into the first track. Drag the *same loop* into the second track, as shown in Figure 19. (You can OPTION-drag the first loop to the new track to copy it.)

Next, open the track editor for the first track. From here, locate and select all snare drums, as shown in Figure 20. Snare drum is on the D1 key.

Delete the snare drums. The loop should now look like Figure 21.

> **TIP**
>
> Duplicate Track is located in the Track menu, and can also be performed with COMMAND-D.

Now, select the duplicate track. This time, we're going to select everything *except* the snare drum. Your new region should look like Figure 22.

If you play the track, you'll hear the complete drum pattern. The only difference from the original version is

> **TIP**
>
> Use COMMAND-A (Select All) to select all the drums on the region, then SHIFT-click on the snare drum to de-select it.

Figure 18. The new Duplicate Track command lets you copy a track's audio parameters.

Figure 19. Two tracks, with the same drum loop.

that the snare is now on its own track, where we can process it differently.

> **TIP**
>
> It might be useful at this point to rename the separate tracks and regions. We've called our new tracks/regions "Kick and Hi-Hat" and "Snare," respectively.

Process the Snare

Once you split the snare, you can add effect to each track separately. First, set up the cycle so that GarageBand repeats the drum regions, and start playback.

Open Track info for the track containing the Snare region, and add some reverb. You'll immediately hear the snare stand out from the rest of the drums. Figure 23 shows the difference between the processing used on the two tracks.

Figure 20. We've selected the snare drums in this loop...

Figure 21. ...and deleted them from the loop.

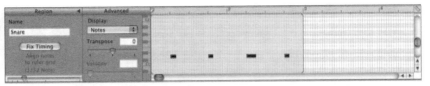

Figure 22. Our second drum track contains only snare hits.

Stretch the Loop

Once you're done editing the snare, you can keep the two tracks as they are, or you can create another track and split the kick and cymbals for even more sonic flexibility. Once you're done splitting and setting up tracks, you can stretch the regions, as you would with any other Apple Loops.

Last Licks

T hese are just a few of the creative tracks you can do with GarageBand. You'll learn more about the various tools and techniques to perform them throughout the rest of this book. With a little experimentation, you should have no problem coming up with a few techniques of your own.

CAUTION

Save your work! We hope that, as you've worked through these exercises, you've modified the ideas shown here to fit your own tastes. Before you move on, save your new creations with the Save instrument button in the Track Info inspector. This way, they'll be available to every GarageBand project you open.

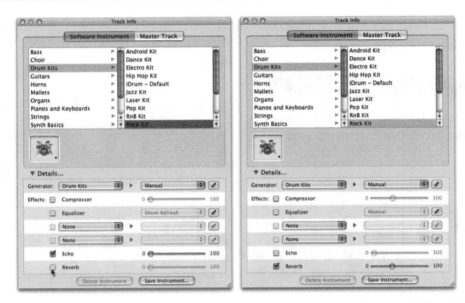

Figure 23. The Kick and Hi-Hat tracks on the left sound tight and dry, while the Snare (on the right) sounds big and lush, thanks to the reverb we've added.

the Track Info Inspector. Either way, you'll need to expand the inspector to show the effects' details, as shown in Figure 9-12.

As you can see, the Track Inspector has a number of sliders, pop-up menus, check boxes, and switches. Figure 9-12 gives us a closer look. Each track has two "additional effect" insert slots—each of which lets you add an effect of your choice—and edit buttons that let you access some of the effects' hidden parameters.

Most of these controls are self-explanatory. The sliders adjust the amount or intensity of the effect; the check boxes let you choose whether an effect is on or *bypassed* (off). The preset pop-ups let you choose a ready-made effects setting, and the edit buttons give you access to an effect's complete set of controls.

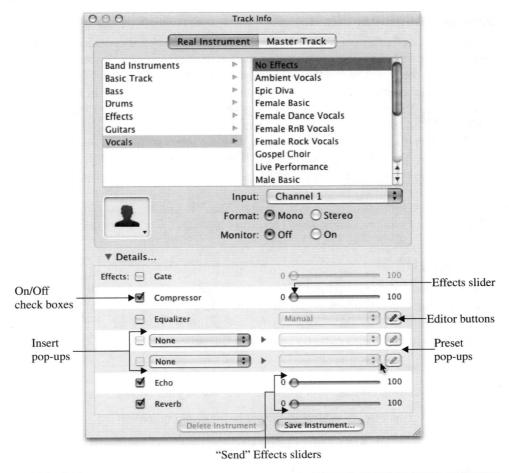

FIGURE 9-12   In the Track Info Inspector, you can turn individual effects on and off and adjust their sound.

The Signal Path

Professional engineers are fond of talking about the "signal path," a fancy way of saying "the order in which everything is hooked together." Although GarageBand is a "virtual" studio that's based in software, it too has a signal path.

The effects in each track follow a particular order: gate, compressor, equalizer, and two "insert" effects—slots where you can put any Audio Units effects processor available on your system. The echo and reverb effects are a little different in that they're not part of the track's signal path, but are what's known as *send-and-return* effects, which are available to all tracks. Sound confusing? No worries: we'll clear all this up later, in "Send and Return." But first, let's take a step back and look at what role various processors play in audio production.

Add an Additional Effect

The additional effects slots (we'll them call inserts for the sake of convenience, and because that's what their equivalents are called in other music software) are the wild card in the signal path. Here's where you can add any GarageBand or AU effect that's installed on your Mac. This is one of the most powerful features in the program because it gives you very precise control over your sound. To access these effects, click on the additional effects pop-up menu (see Figure 9-13).

To add an effect, scroll through the list with the mouse. The effect will load into the slot. From there, you have the option of editing the effect manually, or choosing an effect's preset from the pop-up menu (see Figure 9-14).

 TIP   *There's nothing wrong with using presets, but GarageBand's effects are very easy to edit manually. Don't be afraid to grab a few sliders and experiment!*

Effects 101

There are many different types of effect processors, and each has a different role in shaping your sound. The main categories include

- Dynamics effects, which control audio level

- EQ, which controls tone

- Modulation effects, which add some color to your sound

- Distortion effects, which add crunch, fuzz, and noise

- Delay, which adds distinct echoes

- Reverb, which adds ambience

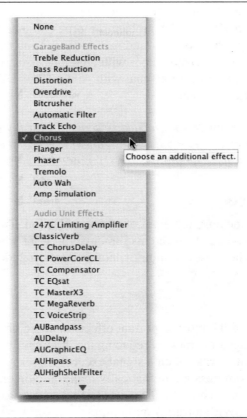

FIGURE 9-13   The Insert pop-up gives you access to all the plug-ins installed on your system.

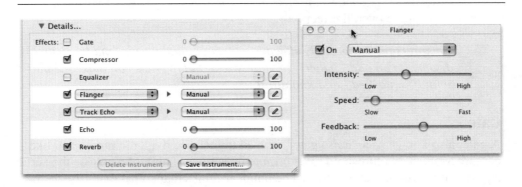

FIGURE 9-14   We've loaded the Flanger into the first Additional Effect slot. The preset pop-up allows quick access to a number of different Flanger sounds.

In addition to these "typical" effects, you'll find some unusual processors that do things like automatically fix pitch problems; morph one sound to another; degrade a signal to give it a funky, "lo-fi" sound; give acoustic instruments a synth-like character; and more. GarageBand comes with an impressive array of built-in effects, and it's easy to add more to your arsenal with Audio Units (AU) plug-ins, which we'll discuss further in Chapter 13.

As you're working on your mix, keep some of your favorite recordings close at hand (for example, loaded into iTunes). Every once in a while, A/B your work against these recordings for reference.

Dynamic Effects

Dynamic effects are the unsung heroes of audio production. They're used to control audio level, so that you can hear the instruments you want when you want, without hearing distortion. The most common dynamic effects include compression, gate, and limiter.

Compressor

Compression is one of the most important effects in audio production. It's used to limit the dynamic range of a track by reducing the difference between quiet and loud signals. Here's how it works: when a signal exceeds a user-selectable level—called the *threshold*—the compressor automatically makes it quieter. Signal that's below the threshold is left alone. This way, the quieter signal appears to be boosted in relation to the louder signal. With a traditional compressor (and many third-party AU compressors), you have control over parameters like threshold, gain, ratio (which controls the amount the signal gets reduced), and the speed at which the compressor goes into effect. GarageBand's built-in compressor is much simpler, and offers a single slider to control the overall effect.

Compression is especially effective on bass, guitar, vocals, and (sometimes) drums. It can add "punch" to your tracks, but overuse can make the music sound "squashed" and unnatural.

Gate

A gate, also known as a "noise gate," is used to increase dynamic range, and like compression, uses a threshold to determine its actions. Think of a gate as the audio equivalent of a nightclub bouncer. The bouncer thinks that signal that's above the threshold is "cool" so it opens the gate and the audio gets into the mix. Any signal that's below the threshold is kept out. As with compression, GarageBand's gate is a one-slider operation. But you will find some gate plug-ins that offer control over threshold, the amount that signals below the threshold will be reduced, and the speed at which the effect will work.

 *A gate can be used to eliminate unwanted noises (like breaths on a vocal track, or "bleed" from other instruments on a drum or guitar track), and can also be used to create some special effects, such as gated reverb, where the reverb's decay is cut off abruptly.*

Limiting

A limiter is similar to a compressor, but instead of reducing the signal based on a ratio, it simply prevents the audio from getting louder than a user-selectable threshold. Limiters are very useful for mastering because they let you pump your mix up loud without causing clipping. GarageBand does not come with a built-in limiter, but there are plenty of AU limiters available, including Apple's AU Peak Limiter

 *Use a limiter as a final effect on your master track. It's also effective on bass and drums as an alternative to a compressor.*

Equalization

An equalizer, or EQ, is used to control the tone by adjusting the balance between low, midrange, and high frequencies. GarageBand's built-in EQ has three "bands," which means that it can work on three different frequency ranges at once, and includes low and high shelving bands, with a semiparametric midrange. Say what? Read on to get to know some basic EQ terms.

Shelving EQ

Shelving EQ affects frequencies above or below a user-selected point. For example, with a high shelving EQ set to 4 kHz, the EQ would work on frequencies above 4 kHz, and its effect would increase as the frequencies get higher (see Figure 9-15).

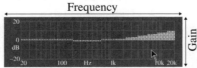

FIGURE 9-15   A shelving EQ

Parametric EQ

Parametric EQ is a little more complex. It lets you set the center frequency of each band, as well as the range (or "Q") that the EQ will affect and the boost or cut of the band. A parametric EQ boosts or cuts frequencies around the center point in what's known as a "bell curve" (see Figure 9-16).

 A semiparametric EQ is similar to a parametric EQ in that it lets you set the frequency and gain, but does not let you adjust the Q.

Graphic EQ

A graphic EQ has fixed curves on predetermined frequencies, but offers more bands than a typical shelving or parametric EQ. Figure 9-17 shows an AU graphic EQ, which has a whopping 31 bands.

High-Pass and Low-Pass Filters

High- and low-pass filters are used to let only a certain frequency range through. A high-pass filter will let only frequencies above the hinge point through; a low-pass filter lets only signals below the hinge through. A high-pass filter is good for reducing bass rumble; a low-pass filter can reduce hiss and can isolate a low sound, like a kick drum, from high sounds, like cymbals.

 *Instead of boosting a frequency range you want to hear more prominently, try cutting the frequencies around it. This may yield cleaner results.*

Modulation Effects

We could write a whole book on modulation effects. Suffice it to say that they're among the more creative utensils in your audio toolbox. The term *modulate* means "to change over time," and most modulation effects do just that, sweeping and swishing and trembling. There are many variations of modulation effects, and modulation characteristics can also be found on some delay and reverb effects. So with that caveat in mind, let's look at some of the most common mod effects.

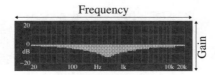

FIGURE 9-16   A parametric EQ's bell curve

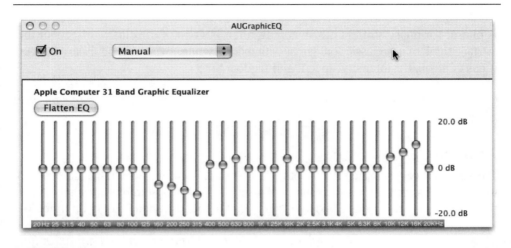

FIGURE 9-17   A graphic EQ. The "Flatten EQ" button resets all the sliders back to 0 dB.

Chorus

Chorus is designed to make one instrument sound like two by creating a slight delay and pitch change. The amount of the change is controlled by the *intensity* setting. A speed, or *frequency,* control adjusts how fast the chorus cycles through the entire range. You can create a very subtle effect with a low speed and a low intensity. A moderate intensity and a faster speed will create a vibrato-like effect. High speed, high intensity creates an "underwater" effect.

Chorus is a very popular effect on guitar, electric piano, and synthesizer. It can also be effective on vocals.

Flanger

A flanger is similar to a chorus, but has a more intense, metallic sound. It uses a series of very short delays to create a sweeping effect. The feedback control, which adds a little bit of the output back to the input, can intensify the flange sound, giving your track the sound of a psychedelic jet in midtakeoff.

Flanger is effective on guitar, drums, and—if you're looking for a dose of flower power—an entire mix.

Phaser

A phaser (or phase shifter) is a sweeping filter. It's one of the classic effects of the 1970s—think of any classic soul guitar with that pulsating, swishy sound. Like a flanger, it has controls for intensity, speed, and feedback.

 *Phaser is great on guitar and keyboards, and can also be effective on bass.*

Tremolo

Tremolo is a very simple effect—but it's a classic. Tremolo, which has controls for intensity and speed, affects the volume of a signal to create a shimmering sound that's pure "lounge." The James Bond and "surf" guitar sounds relied heavily on tremolo.

 *Tremolo is especially effective on electric piano, organ, and guitar. In fact, it's built into many a classic vintage guitar amp.*

Automatic Filter

Filter effects are sort of a cross between EQ and modulation—or more accurately, they are EQs that modulate. The classic wah wah sound is a type of filter that's controlled by a foot pedal. With an autofilter, you set the speed and intensity of the filter's sweep, as you do with chorus and other mod effects, and set the frequency as you would with an EQ. Another parameter is called resonance, which adds a little more grit and dimension to the sound.

 *Filters are the basis of many analog synth-type sounds and are popular in all types of electronic music—especially dance styles. You can use an autofilter on anything from keyboards to drums to electric and synth bass. Resonance can add a chirpy, metallic edge to the sound.*

Distortion and Gain Effects

In normal audio settings, distortion is not considered to be a good thing: the noise, the crackling, the crunch—any engineer worth his or her lab coat will tell you that these are to be avoided at all costs. Of course, rock 'n' roll was never much of a venue for the lab coat set, and rock guitarists discovered early on that a distorted sound made their axes sing. Distortion—also known as fuzz, overdrive, and crunch—has been a mainstay in the pop sound ever since, and can be applied to everything from electric guitar and bass to synth, organ, vocals, and even drums.

GarageBand has two built-in gain effects. The relatively basic distortion offers controls for drive (the amount of distortion), tone (or EQ), and loudness. You can use it to create some subtle crunch or a blizzard of fuzz.

 Gain effects like distortion can make the signal louder. If you add a lot of drive, you may want to compensate by reducing the loudness. Otherwise, your mix may be plagued by the bad kind of distortion—digital clipping.

Amp Simulation

Okay, maybe I'm biased because I'm a guitar player, but GarageBand's Amp Simulation is my favorite feature in the whole program. It is designed to emulate the behavior of a real guitar amp. Its controls are like that of a real amp: Pre Gain (which sets up the distortion) bass, middle, treble, and "presence" tone controls (presence adds a little more high end to the sound), a master volume control, and a separate output control.

In a way, the Amp Simulator (see Figure 9-18) is a little like a software instrument in that it models the sound of real hardware amplifiers. There are four basic models to choose from, covering the four most popular clean and overdriven sounds in modern music.

Like a real amp, the proper setting depends on the song, the characteristics of your guitar, and your own playing style. There are plenty of presets to choose from, but I advise you to open the plug-in manually and have at the controls.

TIP *Although it's designed for guitar, Amp Simulation is also effective on bass, synths, and even vocals and drums. Heck, I'd even use it on Xylophone, but then, as I said, I am a guitarist.*

Echo

Echo, which is also known as delay, is one of the most popular effects in audio production, and traces its roots back to the old analog recording studios of the 1950s. Back in those days, engineers found a way to manipulate a tape recorder so that it would record a sound and then play it back a fraction of a second later. This kind of "tape" echo can be heard on early Elvis Presley recordings and countless others.

Digital delay is far more complex and controllable than those early tape echoes, but the principle is similar: take a signal and delay it by a set amount. By mixing the delayed signal back with the original dry signal, you create a repeating echo effect. With a digital delay, you can control not only the amount of time between the original and delayed signals—known as delay time—but also the number of repeats and, typically, the volume of the delayed signal.

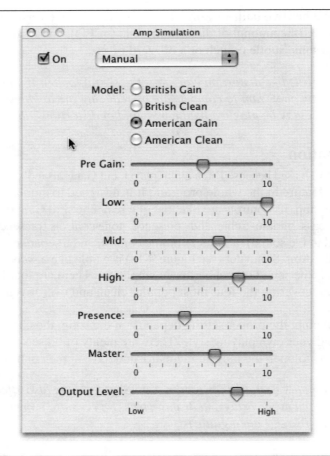

FIGURE 9-18   The Amp Simulation is designed to function and sound like a "real" guitar amp.

The parameter that controls the number of repeats is often referred to as feedback, because the delayed signal is fed back into the delay to create more echoes.

GarageBand actually has two separate echoes available for any given track. The standard echo, found at the bottom of the Track Inspector, feeds the track to the master delay, which is a send-and-return effect that is shared by *all* the tracks in the song (see Figure 9-19). With this echo, you use a slider to determine how strongly the track will feed the delay, but the actual settings of the delay are determined by the master track.

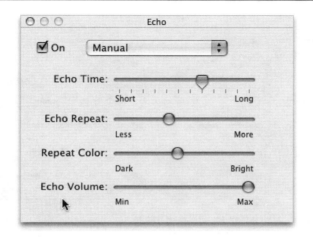

FIGURE 9-19   The main Echo slider is used to feed the track's signal to the master delay.

NEW IN 1.1   With version 1.1, GarageBand adds another delay to your bag of tricks: Track Echo (see Figure 9-20). Track Echo is available as an insert effect (see above on how to add an insert effect), and is useful because it lets you set up an independent delay for a specific track. With Track Echo, for example, you can create a fast, rhythmic echo for a drum loop and still use the master echo to create a long delay for a vocal track.

Echo Parameters

A typical echo/delay effect lets you control delay time (the amount of time between the original signal and the first echo), feedback (the number of repeats), and the mix between the "dry" (or original) signal and the "wet" (or affected) signal. GarageBand's echo effect has controls for Echo Time, Echo Repeat, Intensity (mix), and Repeat Color—an EQ that lets you decide if the repeats will be bright and trebly or dark and bassy.

 *In this discussion, the word "echo" is synonymous with delay; I use the term "delay" to describe the effect in general because it's more common in audio, and is what you'll see in most plug-ins.*

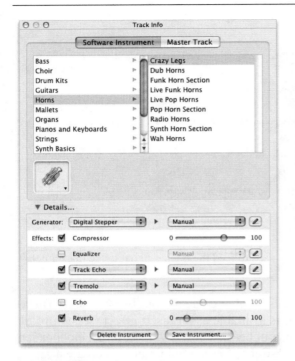

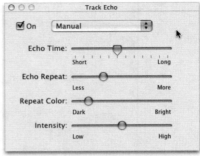

FIGURE 9-20   Track Echo is an important new addition to GarageBand 1.1.

> TIP
>
> *Echo can be very effective on many different sources. U2's guitarist The Edge has made a career of playing through a complex array of echo devices. For a 1950s rockabilly type sound, try a very short echo time. For a rhythmic delay, play a percussive track and adjust the echo slider as the music plays until the echo "syncs up" with the original signal. Longer echoes are good for dramatic effects on vocals, lead guitar, or any other featured instrument. It's also useful if you want to create a sound effect for falling into the Grand Canyon.*

Reverb

Reverb, which is short for reverberation, is probably the effect you'll use most often in GarageBand. Like Echo, it's an ambient, time-based effect. But where Echo offers up distinct individual repeats, Reverb has a much more diffuse sound, more like the sound you'd get when walking into a concert hall, church, or tiled bathroom. In fact, that's Reverb's job: to imitate the sound of real acoustical spaces.

In GarageBand, Reverb is a send-and-return effect, which means that one Reverb setting will be available to all the tracks. There are, however, plenty of third-party AU reverbs on the market, and these can be added to an individual track via one of the insert slots.

 *Reverb tends to use a lot of processing power, so it's best to use as few reverb instances as possible in a mix. That's one reason why Apple kept it as a send-and-return effect in GarageBand.*

You add reverb to a track with the reverb slider in the Track Inspector. As with the master echo effect, the actual reverb settings are made in the Master Track Inspector. You can access the master track's effects at any time by clicking the Master Track tab in the Track Inspector.

Reverb Parameters

GarageBand's reverb effect (see Figure 9-21) is pretty basic. Its parameters include Reverb Time (which controls how long the reverb lasts, or *decays*), Reverb Color (as with echo, this is an EQ that affects the reverb's tone), and Reverb Volume (which controls the amount of "wet," or affected, signal that will be added into the mix).

As I mentioned above, there are plenty of plug-in reverbs available, and these can be added to individual tracks and to the master track via an insert slot. Figure 9-22 shows the Apple AU Matrix Reverb. As you can see, it sports a few more parameters than the GarageBand reverb.

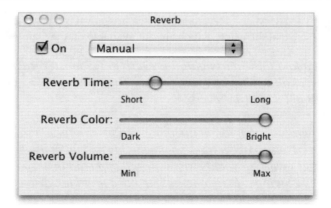

FIGURE 9-21 The GarageBand reverb effect is pretty basic by software reverb standards, but it gets the job done.

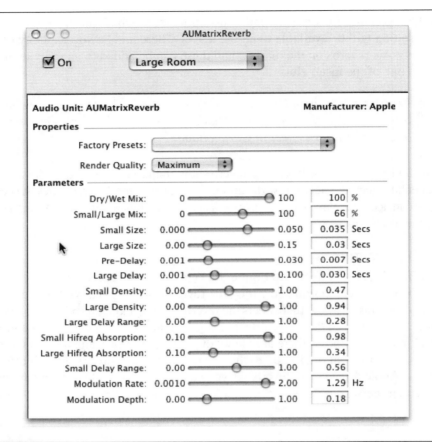

FIGURE 9-22   The AU Matrix Reverb lets you control advanced parameters such as room size and diffusion, which are not available on the GarageBand reverb.

NOTE   *You can add a third-party plug-in reverb to the master track, but this effect is not accessible with the reverb slider. The slider only accesses GarageBand's built-in reverb.*

TIP   *Reverb works on just about anything, but be careful not to overuse it: too much reverb can make a track sound muddy and unfocused. Many producers like to add reverb to vocals, snare drum, and lead instruments like guitar, horns, and strings. Instruments like bass and kick drum are usually left "dry."*

Voices from the Community

Beauty Is in the Ear of the Beholder

A great mix is subjective, but to me, it has to have punch and variety and, above all, it has to make me sit up and take notice. I like to hear guitars—lots of them, different kinds, different voicings, acoustic, electric—but not necessarily all going at once. Bring up an electric rhythm here, pull it down while gradually adding in another there, just to keep things moving.

To prevent the guitars from clashing, I try to give them as much space as possible in the mix. Assuming it's an electric song, I'll pan two electric guitars fairly hard left and hard right, with an acoustic rhythm going down the middle or slightly off-center. I'll typically put a limiter on the acoustic guitar to give it the feel and edge of the electric guitars, and to keep the acoustic's lower overtones in check.

With drums, I like to hear the bass-drum beater up front and fairly percussive. I like a good, crisp snare sound dead center (and on occasion I may muffle the drum head slightly to get the right tone) and pan rack toms and floor tom slightly (but faithful to the physical layout of the drums). I also like the whole set good and compressed, including cymbals (to get that nice elongated wash).

Finally, I think vocals should be as up-front as possible, double-tracked in places for added effect, and always recorded with compressor or limiter. If there's echo involved, I want there to be a fair amount of pre-delay to the signal to keep it from sounding too "wet." Though I prefer "live" echo (chamber, plate), when using a digital reverb I'll take some time and tweak EQ, decay and pre-delay so I can have a few dedicated pre-sets that sound a bit closer to the real thing.

—David Simons is the author of Studio Stories: How the Great Records of New York Were Made *(Backbeat Books). He just finished building a live echo chamber off his basement studio.*

Send and Return (Master) Effects

GarageBand's master Echo and Reverb effects are what are known in audio circles as "send-and-return" effects. This term has nothing to do with the effects themselves, but rather refers to how sound is routed from a track to the effects processors, and from the processors back to your mix.

When it comes to adding a signal processor (the industry term for audio effect) into a signal chain, there are two types of connections: *series* (or inline); and *parallel* (or send-and-return).

Series Connections

A series connection puts all the parts of the signal chain in a row, as shown in Figure 9-23.

As you can see, a signal passes from one part of the chain directly to the next part—sort of like a relay racer's baton—before reaching the output. The effects work within the chain, but won't be applied to any other tracks (in other words, the relay racers stay in their own lane; the other teams must be content to pass their own batons). GarageBand's track effects (except for echo and reverb) are in series. They work on one track at a time. Each individual track can have its own series of effects, each with its own settings.

Parallel Connection

A parallel effects chain is a little different. Here, more than one signal can feed the effect's input at the same time. This is done with a special output called a "send," which is available on each track. The send takes signal from the track without interrupting the track's signal flow to the main output—imagine the track is donating blood—and routes that signal to the effect's input. The effect's output is then routed, or "returned" to the main output, where it blends with output of the individual tracks. Because both the tracks *and* the effects return are going to the same output, they are said to running in parallel (see Figure 9-24).

How to Use a Send

In GarageBand, sends are really easy to use (in fact, you've probably been using them already, and are only reading this part because you simply hunger for information). As you raise the level of reverb in a guitar track, for example, you're increasing the

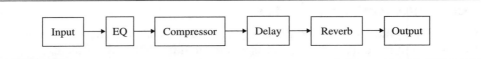

FIGURE 9-23 In a series signal chain, each component feeds the next directly.

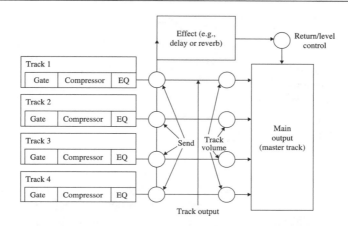

FIGURE 9-24   Sends are used to take a signal from a track or tracks and route it to effects without interrupting the track's signal flow.

amount of the guitar track's signal that will feed the reverb. You're not changing how the reverb affects any of the other channels. However, if you go into the Master Track Inspector (see Figure 9-25), you can change the reverb's sound. Settings you make here will affect every track that's being "sent" to the reverb.

The Master Track

In a hardware mixer, the final stage that the signal passes through before going out to a mixdown deck or speakers is called the *master section*. Whereas each instrument track's controls are designed to set the relative tone and balance, the master track governs the final level of the mix, and lets you add effects that change the sound of all instrument tracks.

Like the instrument tracks, the master track has a volume curve, which lets you automate the loudness of the entire mix.

> TIP   *Use the master volume curve to create a fade-out of your entire mix.*

The Master Track Inspector shows the effects available in the master track. These include Echo and Reverb—the send-and-return effects discussed above—as well as Equalizer, Compressor, and one additional effect insert slot.

Note that, unlike the instrument tracks, EQ and Compression are *last* in the signal chain.

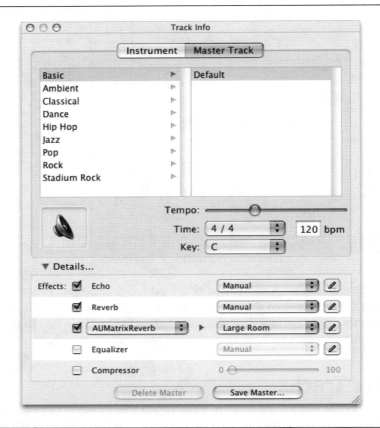

FIGURE 9-25 The Master Track Inspector lets you makes echo and reverb available to all the tracks in your song.

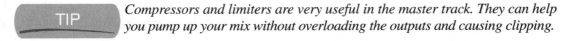

Compressors and limiters are very useful in the master track. They can help you pump up your mix without overloading the outputs and causing clipping.

As with the instrument tracks, you can manually choose from preset effects, or manually edit the effects to your liking. When you have a master setting that you like, you can save it as a preset.

Export Your Mix to iTunes

Once you have all your instruments edited, your track level, pan, and effects set, and your master track in order, you're ready to export your mix as an AIFF audio file into iTunes. From there, it can be converted into MP3, burned onto a CD, or shared with other music software.

CAUTION   *After you've added effects and made all your mix settings, give a final check to see if the song is clipping—generating digital distortion—by playing it back and carefully checking the output meters. If you're overloaded—you'll see GarageBand's meters fire red, or may even hear the distortion in your speakers or headphones—try reducing the master track's volume or using the compressor to prevent overloads.*

Fortunately, this is probably one of the easier operations you'll ever do with your computer. To export the entire song, with all the tracks heard, choose File | Export to iTunes and … well, that's all, actually. GarageBand does the rest (see Figure 9-26).

TIP   *Be sure to delete or mute any unwanted tracks before you export the mix to iTunes.*

Congratulations! You created a finished master—a song you can share with family and friends. The resulting file will show up in your iTunes library automatically, and will bear the name of your song file.

9

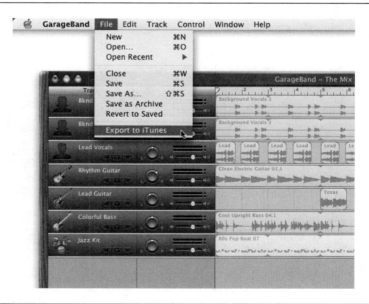

FIGURE 9-26   Exporting your mix to iTunes is as easy as going into the File menu and giving the command.

Save a Preset

When you adjust effects on a track, GarageBand remembers your settings and stores them with the song. Every time you open the song, the effects will be as you left them. But there are times when you might also want to save a particular effect for use in other songs. You can do this two ways. If you save the instrument track, it will store all of the effects in the track at their current settings. This is the best way to go if you want to create a multieffect chain for use in other songs. However, you may also want to save the settings of an effect individually.

Save an Instrument Track

Adjust the instruments effects to your liking. Select the instrument category into which you want to store the effect. Here, we've selected "Bass." Click the Save Instrument button (at the bottom of the Track Info Inspector) and type in the name for the new instrument preset.

Save an Individual Effect

Open the effect's editor and adjust its parameters. Open the reset pop-up, and select Make Preset at the top of the window. Type the new effect's name in the preset field, shown here:

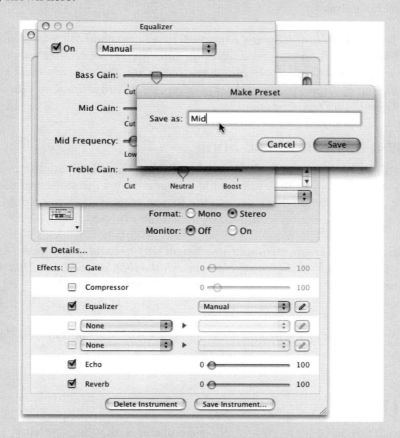

The next time you look in that effect's preset menu, you'll see your new effect.

TIP *You can organize your own presets by naming them with a prefix, such as My EQ—Mid Cut; My EQ—Bass Boost, and so on. Because effects are sorted alphabetically in the menus, these effects will appear together.*

Export Individual Tracks

You don't have to export a complete mix to iTunes. You can solo one or more tracks and GarageBand will exclude all others when exporting to iTunes. This technique is commonly referred to as bouncing. The "bounced" file can then be imported back into GarageBand.

You can use GarageBand's Export to iTunes command to create a new audio file out of a loop you've edited in the timeline. It can also let you combine, or bounce, several tracks into a new audio file. You can then drag the new file out of iTunes (or the Finder) directly into GarageBand, or edit it in the Loop Utility (see Chapter 13).

Export a Section of the Song

You can also export only a limited section of your song. Activate the cycle (COMMAND-C) and adjust the cycle region so that it covers the section of the song you want to export. When that's set, use the Export command as you would for the whole song; only the region within the cycle will be exported.

Exporting a small section is an efficient way to build a new audio file out of an edited loop. Set the cycle to match the loop boundaries. This way, the new file will line up exactly with the loop, with no "dead space" on either end of it.

See Chapter 11 for details on how to work with your master and share your music with the world at large.

Moving On

We've gone through a lot of parameters and controls in this chapter, but in a way, we haven't scratched the surface of mixing, which is all about careful listening and experimentation. GarageBand gives you the opportunity to experiment with effects and volume curves, and combines these sonic manipulations with the editing techniques described in Chapter 8 to create a spicy musical brew. Next chapter, we'll look at some of the more creative aspects of making music with GarageBand.

Chapter 10

Think Like a Producer

How to...

- Get to know basic song structure
- Develop an arrangement
- Blend different instruments
- Use effects effectively
- Design your own sounds with software instruments

Music software affords us technology that was simply unavailable a decade ago outside the realm of the recording studio. In many ways, a even a modest iBook equipped with GarageBand is more powerful than the recorders and mixers the Beatles used when they made their landmark album *Sgt. Pepper's Lonely Hearts Club Band*. After all, that album was recorded onto a four-track recorder, and was made before the wide availability of synthesizers, the existence of samplers, or the advent of digital recording. But if you listen to that—or any other—classic album, it won't take you long to figure out that the technology was only a small part of the puzzle. Yes, the music business is reliant on high-tech audio gear, expensive microphones, and finely tuned acoustical spaces. But great music starts in the heart and in the brain. Before technology can make it easier to execute your great ideas, the ideas need to be there in the first place.

The Beatles were amazing songwriters, but they were also fortunate enough to work with a great producer in George Martin. He helped them realize the potential in their songs and guided them as they moved into new musical and sonic territory. But most GarageBand users will be working, if not alone, then in a home environment with little or no professional help. You have ultimate creative freedom, but creative freedom can be overwhelming.

So now that you know a bit about what GarageBand can do, it's time to peek in between the lines at some of the techniques that you won't find in the Help menu.

NOTE   *One mistake that many beginners seem to make is in not developing their ideas to full potential. A drag, drop, and stretch program like GarageBand makes it easy to simply lay out a few loops, play a melody, and have done with it. There's nothing wrong with that, but you don't have to stop there.*

Get to Know Basic Song Structure

Although there's no such thing as a "correct" song structure, most pieces of music do follow some sort of form in which a song can be broken down into components. These components are often identified by letters A, B, C, and so on. The letters have nothing to do with note names; they simply indicate a part of the song.

The most basic elements of a song are the verse (often referred to as the A section) and the chorus (B). In a pop song that has lyrics, the verses usually tell the story or give the details, while the chorus states the theme of the song. Verses tend to have different lyrics from one to the next, but the chorus *usually* repeats the same—or similar—material over and over. The chorus should be the catchiest, most memorable part of the song.

> **TIP**   *If you were thinking of music in terms of a joke, the verse is the setup, the chorus is the punch line. This is not always the case, but it serves as a general rule.*

If every song had only one or two parts, people would lose interest after only about 90 seconds. Songwriters build around the A and B sections with additional, transitional parts. For example, a *prechorus* section that sets up the chorus, helps the song build, and tips the listener off that there's about to be a payoff. A quiet section in the middle of an upbeat tune lets the listener reflect and sets up for a big ending. Those are just two examples of a C section, or *bridge,* which, as the name implies, ties the various parts of the song together. A bridge can also be high energy, while taking the song in a different harmonic and/or rhythmic direction. Then there are instrumental breaks, solos, riffs, and other short, transitional sections. Even silence, when used correctly, can be an effective attention grabber.

10

Map Your Song

When an experienced songwriter works on a song, it will often develop a natural structure of its own. But that's not always the case. I know songwriters with notebooks and cassette tapes full of orphaned verses and catchy choruses that have nothing around them. The stuff in those notebooks probably came at a moment of inspiration. The craft of songwriting, though, has as much to do with perspiration, of forging the elements until they fit together. GarageBand is a great tool for this because it lets you move sections of music around and see how they work together.

As you do, you can develop a map of your song. Let's say, for example, that you have three parts: verse, chorus, and bridge (A, B, and C). There are many ways to put them together. For example, you could start with a simple verse, chorus, verse, chorus structure and add the bridge before the final chorus (A B A B C B). Or, you could build slowly to the choruses (A A B A B A B C B), or you could start and end with the chorus and not bother with the bridge (B A B A B B). Notice that the chorus repeats: that's a common technique in pop songs.

Variations on a Theme

Thus far, we've used two or three parts to build our song, but you could have as many or as few as you like. One good technique is to create a variation on one of the core parts and use it as an introduction or as a short interlude in the middle of the song. For example, if the verse is normally eight bars long, you could create a variation that's two bars long and use it for an instrumental break.

You can use GarageBand to record and develop separate ideas, and then assemble them later. First, save each idea into its own song. Arrange and mix the songs, then export the mixes to iTunes. Next, open a new GarageBand song file, and import the audio files from iTunes into your new project (this works best if the component songs are of the same key and tempo). From there, you can assemble and edit them in the GarageBand's timeline.

Build Up and Down

There's no rule that says that you have to use different chords for the A, B, and C sections of your song, but most songwriters do try to give each section its own chord progression or rhythmic pattern. For example, you may use the chords C, F, and G for the verse, then switch to an F–G progression for the chorus.

But chord progressions are only one way to create variation. You can change the rhythmic pattern for a chorus by using a different drum part, or going from a slow and steady bass part to one that's faster and funkier.

Another popular technique is called modulation, in which the entire *song* changes to a new key at a strategic moment. The Who's "My Generation" is a good example. (Who songwriter Pete Townsend's songs are also noteworthy for their bridges, which typically stand in sharp contrast to the verses and choruses—e.g., *Goin' Mobile* on *Who's Next.*) In GarageBand, you can select all of the nondrum parts and transpose them to create harmonic modulation as shown in Figure 10-1.

This is harmonic modulation, as opposed to the electronic modulation effect we discussed in the last chapter.

FIGURE 10-1   You can use the transpose command to create modulation.

If you have a repeating chorus at the end of the song, try raising the later repeats by one full step for an extra dose of intensity.

Let the Sound Evolve

Song structure isn't the only way for a song to develop over time. A good producer knows how to introduce new sounds and to change existing sounds so that a piece of music continues to sound fresh as it plays, often building in intensity and interest. This is especially important in musical styles that are relatively static—such as dance music. With dance music, you can't do too much to change the beat or bass line—that would interrupt the dancers' momentum. Instead, dance producers like to introduce many little details, such as short fills, sonic changes, effects, and new textures.

But you don't have to be a dance producer to use some of these techniques. Adding a new part to a chorus—for example, introducing a power-chord guitar—can add impact to that part of the song. For the next chorus, you could bring in a second guitar. Figure 10-2 shows how a song might evolve over time.

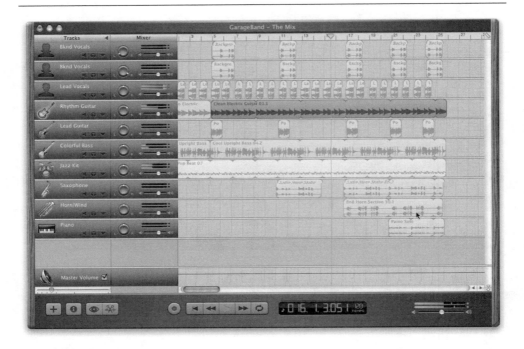

FIGURE 10-2   Here's an arrangement that develops over time.

 The power guitar (on the Lead Guitar track) comes in for the choruses, and each chorus adds one more part. At the end of the song, we introduce a piano solo.

Be a "Comp-rang-ducer"

One of the interesting things about a program like GarageBand is that it blurs the lines between composing, arranging, and producing. You can come to it with a song already written, and use GarageBand to record and produce the song; or you can open it up as a blank slate, grab an inspiring loop or software instrument, and begin writing.

Write and Record in Sections

If you're starting a new tune, one of the most effective techniques is to break it down and take a section at a time. You can use GarageBand's Cycle feature to create a one-verse loop (see Figure 10-3).

FIGURE 10-3   We've created an eight-bar loop, which we've decided is equivalent to one verse.

From there, you can play or drag in a basic rhythmic bed, play a few chords, or add a melody. Some songwriters like to create the complete backing track before adding melody lines; others like to start with a melody and then figure out what fits around it.

Once you have a section in place, move the cycle to the next eight bars and start the next verse or chorus (see Figure 10-4). You can copy elements from the first part of the song to give you a head start.

Let the Sound Do the Work

Sometimes, I like to imagine what it must have been like back in the days of Tin Pan Alley, when professional songwriters sat in dingy offices with their pianos, notebooks, and used coffee cups, writing songs for the singers of the day. In those days, the songwriter would create a basic tune, then hand it off to an arranger, who'd write the parts for the bands or orchestras that would play behind the singer.

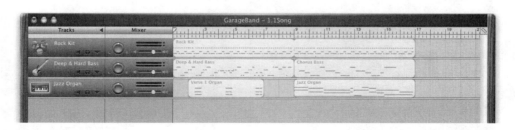

FIGURE 10-4   Once you have part of the song in place, move to the next section.

10

Nowadays, a songwriter is not restricted to a single instrument and sound. Just as important, the role of arranger is now part of the songwriting job. GarageBand is a great tool for exploring your inner arranger.

Same Part, New Instrument

One technique is to start by playing something relatively basic—such as a chord or chord progression—and quickly switch through a range of instruments. A simple C-minor chord conveys a different mood on electric piano than it does on an analog synth or brass sample.

You can record a passage of music and loop it, as in Figure 10-5, then assign different instruments to the track and see where they can take you.

Add an Effect

Effects can also be a source of inspiration. Echo is especially powerful because it can actually change the rhythmic structure of a piece. Try adding a medium to long echo to a simple drum or percussion loop. Set the mix to around 50 percent wet, so that the delayed signal is about equal to the original signal. Your simple pattern is now a cascading, pulsating loop.

FIGURE 10-5 Try looping a simple part, then see how it sounds with different instruments.

TIP *GarageBand's Echo effect cannot automatically synchronize delay time to your song's tempo, nor does it tell the exact length of the echo. But most third-party delay and echo effects do let you know how long a delay is— the measurement is usually in milliseconds. You can calculate a delay time that's in sync with your song with the following formula: 60/tempo (BPM) × 1,000 = Milliseconds for 1 beat. If you don't fancy doing the math yourself, you can download a delay calculator, such as the freeware DelayCalculator by Dirk Rockendorf, shown here.*

Collaborate with Others

Music is a collaborative art form. In fact, the concept of being able to do it all yourself is very new. A lot of composers fall into the trap of feeling like just because they *can* create a complete arrangement by themselves that they don't need to work with other musicians. But GarageBand is actually a good program for collaboration. In fact, every time you use one of the Apple Loops that come with it, you're collaborating with the people who composed and played on those loops. Same goes for commercial loop libraries. Their energy is part of your music.

Obviously, the most immediate way to collaborate is to invite other musicians into your studio and work with them personally (or, if you have a laptop, take your studio to them). But you can also collaborate remotely. You can export a song into iTunes, make an MP3 from the resulting audio file, and e-mail it to a collaborator. He or she can then import the MP3 into their own music software, add some tracks of their own, and send you the audio files of the new tracks. This way, you can work with people from around the world.

CAUTION *MP3, though convenient for Internet sharing and e-mailing, doesn't offer the sound quality of AIFF files. You can, however, share AIFF files over an FTP or .Mac account, or copy them onto a CD-ROM and use the good old U.S. Postal Service to send them to your collaborators.*

Create a Blend

So far, we've discussed several techniques for building an arrangement, but if you simply throw together a bunch of sounds, you're just as likely to create a muddy mess as a masterpiece. One of a producer's most important jobs is to blend sounds so that they live in harmony.

A great-sounding song is a combination of an interesting structure, where song itself unfolds over time; a good arrangement, where the instruments convey the feeling of the song and help it build toward an appropriate climax; and a good mix, where the levels and effects let the instruments "speak" without sounding cluttered.

Mixing is an art, and some of the music business's top producers and engineers specialize in mixing. But while there's no set way to mix a song, there are a few techniques you can use as a starting point in your own work.

Pick Instruments that Work Together

Although there are always exceptions to any rule—especially in the arts—most songs sound best when they have a good balance between low, midrange, and high sounds.

The Low End

Bass and drums are the foundation of most pop styles. As a composer/producer, you have plenty of leeway when choosing which drum and bass sounds work together. Don't be afraid to use an upright bass sound with an electronic drum kit, or vice versa.

You're not restricted to using a bass guitar to cover your bottom end. The low notes of an organ, synthesizer, or even piano can make a refreshing substitute for a bass guitar.

CAUTION   *Try to avoid having too many parts playing low notes at the same time. If, for example, you have organ, piano, and bass in the same song, you may end up with three instruments playing in the same octave (the bass and the left-hand parts for the piano and organ). That can sound very muddy.*

The bass drum, or "kick," is another key factor in creating a solid foundation. The kick sound should match the mood of the music—don't, for example, use a feathery jazz kick for a dance tune, unless you're going to set the pulse with another instrument.

TIP   *The pattern of the kick should work with that of the bass. They don't have to be an exact match, but when bass and kick fire at the same time, it will give your song more impact and cohesion.*

Midrange

With most songs, midrange instruments form the densest part of the mix. Guitars, vocals, keyboards, snare drum and tom-toms, brass, synthesizers, percussion—all compete for a slice of the midrange pie at least some of the time. In the next section, we'll discuss ways you can use EQ and effects to create room for these important voices.

For example, let's say your song has parts for rhythm and lead guitar, keyboards, and vocals. If you use an overdriven rhythm guitar and, say, an organ, the parts may compete with one another. But a clean rhythm guitar or an acoustic guitar will stand out against the thicker sound of the organ. In the same way, a lead guitar will work well filling the spaces around the vocal part, but can get in the way if you play it while the singer sings.

Another technique is to create parts that complement one another. For example, if you want to play the same rhythmic figure on both piano and guitar, voice them an octave apart. If you want multiple instruments to play a chord, play only a few notes of the chord on each instrument. You'll be amazed at how quickly your mix will open up.

TIP *When you're working with Software Instrument Apple Loops, you can use the track editor to remove some notes from a part, thereby creating harmonic space for other instruments.*

10

The High End

High-end instruments include the high notes of strings, horns, keyboards, cymbals, high-pitched percussion like shakers, cabasas, and tambourines, and some vocal parts. You can open up your arrangement effectively by using the high register for solos and featured parts—the sound will stand out and won't compete with the masses in the midrange.

The trick is to have enough high end to provide detail, but not so much that the music will sound tinny or shrill. Cymbals add a splash of excitement to any mix, but are often overused—and overloud—on home mixes (this is especially true with hi-hat).

TIP *You can create an interesting drum part by removing the cymbals and hi-hat, and replacing their parts with another sound or instrument.*

Create Layers

The techniques we've just described involve the judicious use of a few carefully chosen parts. And while there's nothing wrong with minimalism, it's not the only way to create exciting music. In fact, the exact opposite approach can also be effective. But if you pile on the instruments, be ready to work harder on your mix.

One effective technique is called *layering,* where two different sounding instruments play identical parts. One of the most popular examples is the combination of piano and strings. To create a layer in GarageBand, you need two tracks. Copy the same part to both, and assign each to a different instrument, as shown in Figure 10-6.

Doubling

Doubling is a technique where the same instrument plays the same part on two different tracks. If you pan the tracks opposite one another, you can create a big, wide sound. Doubling is commonly used on vocals and guitars.

 *Simply copying the same part to two tracks isn't as effective a doubling technique as actually playing or singing the part separately on each track. The subtle timing differences between the two parts enhance the effect.*

Call and Response

Want to make two similar instruments work together? How about letting them take turns. With the call and response technique, you set up alternating patterns between instruments. Figure 10-7 shows a simple call and response pattern between guitar and saxophone. The guitar plays, the sax is silent. The guitar stops, and the sax takes over.

FIGURE 10-6   We've copied a region from the Piano track to the Strings track to create a layer.

FIGURE 10-7 Call and response is an effective way to blend similar sounding instruments.

Overlapping Parts

A call-and-response technique such as that outlined above need not be a strict either/or proposition. You can create a little more drama by overlapping the parts. In Figure 10-8, the sax plays a couple of notes as the guitar is finishing up.

The ideas outlined here are only a few of the production techniques you can explore with GarageBand. If you have an understanding of harmony and arranging, you already have a head start. But even if you're new to music and don't know a C chord from an umbilical cord, you can use the program to open new musical doors. Remember, if you don't like what you hear, there's always the trusty Undo command (COMMAND-Z).

Use Effects Effectively

While compelling song structure and careful arranging are important elements in your finished song, you can't overlook the importance of audio processing. Effects can enhance an arrangement by letting each instrument stand out, or they can transform your song into something unrecognizable. They can help or they can hurt, so use them wisely.

One of the first things an aspiring composer and arranger must learn is the sound of various instruments. For the mixer, it's the same with effects; you need to take the time to listen to have various effects work on different instruments and in different

FIGURE 10-8 Overlapping parts can create a sense of excitement and cohesion.

10

applications before you can really master them. But while there's no substitute for trial and triumph (sounds so much better than trial and error, doesn't it?), there are a few things you can do to get started.

Create Space with EQ

An equalizer is a powerful tool because it can transform the tonal character of an instrument. But some of the most effective uses of EQ are more subtle. When you have two instruments that play in similar ranges, you can use EQ to prevent them from competing. For example, you can use an EQ to enhance the sound of the bass—not by boosting the bass's low end, but by removing some of the lower frequencies of other tracks, such as guitar.

Figure 10-9 shows an EQ set to a high-pass filter (or low roll-off), which makes the signal below a certain frequency quieter. By applying it to the guitar at around 120 Hz, you probably won't take away from the guitar's character, but you will remove some of the lower midrange frequencies that can obscure the bass.

Some engineers will apply a low roll-off to every instrument except bass and kick drum.

Use Different Amounts of Reverb to Create Ambience

Reverb always seems to make everything sound better, so it's tempting to apply reverb to all your tracks. But if you use an equal amount of reverb on every track, your mix may sound congested. One technique is to apply more reverb to some tracks and little

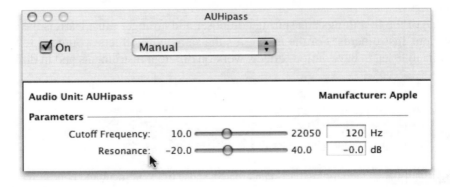

FIGURE 10-9   To enhance the bass guitar, use an EQ to reduce the lower frequencies of other instruments.

or none to others. This will give your mix some dimension because you'll have a sense of being closer to some instruments, further away from others. The more reverb you put on something, the further away it sounds. So, reverb and delay can help add front-to-back dimension to your mixes.

> **TIP** *Lead vocals sound great with lots of reverb, but too much 'verb can make you sound like you're singing in the Grand Canyon. Instead of burying your voice in reverb, try keeping it relatively dry, and use more reverb on tracks like background vocals and snare drum.*

Replace Reverb with Echo

Reverb and echo are both time-based effects, and though they sound quite different, each can add dimension to a particular part. Echo, for example, can be effective on vocals, guitar, and other lead instruments. You can combine echo and reverb, but if you use echo alone on, say, lead vocals, you can give the sound some space without making it seem too far away.

Use Compression to Control Dynamic Range

Talk to a professional engineer about his or her favorite effects, and most likely a compressor is at or near the top of the list. Compressors aren't as glamorous as reverbs, delays, and modulation effects, but they are essential in mixing, where quiet parts can get buried and loud parts can cause overload. Some engineers apply a separate compressor to every track in a mix. You don't need to do that, but tracks like vocals, bass, and guitar can benefit from compression.

10

> **NOTE** *For more details on compression and other audio effects, refer to Chapter 9.*

Spice Up Your Mix with Modulation

Modulation effects are great for adding a little flavor to a mix. If you have two or more parts playing similar sounds, use an effect like chorus or phaser on one of the parts to make it stand out. You can also use modulation to enhance another effect, such as echo/delay. In GarageBand's additional effects insert slots, place an echo in the first slot and a chorus in the second to give the delay repeats a swirling sound.

Don't use two modulation effects on the same track—they're likely to fight one another sonically and waste processing power to boot.

You can create a chain of effects and save it as an instrument that you can recall at any time. If your effects chain is appropriate for a wide range of instruments, you might want to store it under the Basic Track category. See the section "Store Your Work" later in this chapter for more on how to save an instrument.

Add and Edit Effects in the Master Track

The master track is the last stage in GarageBand's audio signal path. Here, you can add effects and make adjustments that affect the whole mix. In general, subtle moves are best, but don't be afraid to experiment with EQ, compression, and effects. The master track is also where you can adjust the global echo and reverb effects that are available to the individual tracks. To view the master track, choose Show Master Track in the Track menu (or use the keyboard shortcut COMMAND-B and open its inspector as you would any other track).

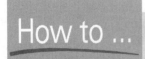 **Use Volume Curves to Make a Part Stand Out**

We discussed the use of volume curves in Chapter 9. Volume automation is an extremely effective mixing tool. You can use a curve to raise guitar for a solo and duck it during a vocal part. If you want to get more detailed, you can use the curve to adjust volume on a more precise basis. For example, say you have a vocal track, and every time the singer goes into her lower register, her voice gets quiet. A compressor can help, but she objects to the "squashed" sound it imparts on the tone. Instead of compressing here, zoom in tightly on the song and use the volume curves to bring up only the low notes. Figure 10-10 shows an example.

You can "read" the waveform display to find the quieter notes in a passage. The lower the waveform, the quieter the sound.

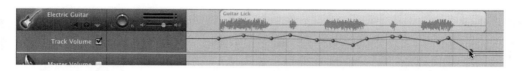

FIGURE 10-10 You can use the volume curves to adjust a performance on a note-by-note basis.

Design Your Own Software Instrument Sounds

GarageBand comes loaded with great-sounding software instruments, and you can augment those with Jam Pack and with the many Audio Units–compatible plug-ins on the market. With hundreds of presets to choose from, you're unlikely to run out of sounds that can work in your projects.

But you don't need to rely on presets. You can edit GarageBand's software instruments to create unique sounds that fit your song and arrangement perfectly. Better yet, it's pretty easy. Let's start by opening a Track Inspector for a Software Instrument (see Figure 10-11).

You can start by loading an existing instrument and preset, or you can build an instrument from scratch.

Access the Instrument Generators

GarageBand software instruments are created with different instrument generators, which fall into two categories: sampled instruments (such as horns, woodwinds, strings, pianos, and drums) and modeled instruments (such as analog and digital synthesizers, electric piano, drawbar organ, and clavinet). The instruments are derived from those used in Apple's popular Logic program.

Sampled instruments use less computer processing power than modeled instruments.

You can access the generators via a pop-up menu in the inspector (see Figure 10-12). This will show all GarageBand instruments, as well as any third-party plug-ins you have added to your system.

You'll see some generators labeled "Mono." A mono-voiced synthesizer can only play one note at a time. Although this seems like a limitation, mono synths can be very effective on bass and lead parts.

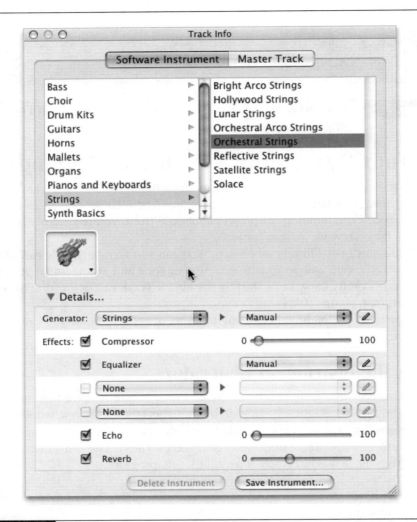

FIGURE 10-11   To create a Software Instrument, start by opening the Track Inspector.

Whether it's modeled or sample-based, each generator offers its own sound and has its own set of parameters. You can access the parameters by clicking the Edit button (see Figure 10-13).

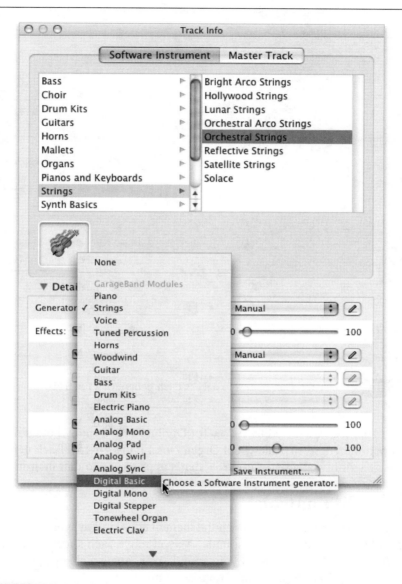

FIGURE 10-12 The Generator pop-up menu shows all the software instruments available on your system.

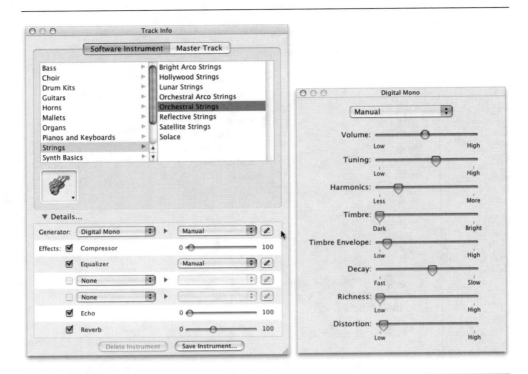

FIGURE 10-13 Use the Edit button to access each generator's controls.

Figure 10-14 shows the edit window for Digital Basic Synth—note how it offers different parameters from Tonewheel Organ (see Figure 10-15). Each generator's edit window will reveal a set of controls that's appropriate to that instrument.

Use the Edit Controls

Once you choose a generator and open the manual edit window, you're ready to start moving sliders and making some sounds. As you move each slider, you can play along to hear what effect it has on your sound. You can also change generators as the music plays to hear how the different generators compare.

TIP *To free up your hands while designing your instrument, record an appropriate passage of music (or import an Apple Loop) to the track you're editing and cycle the part so that it plays back continuously.*

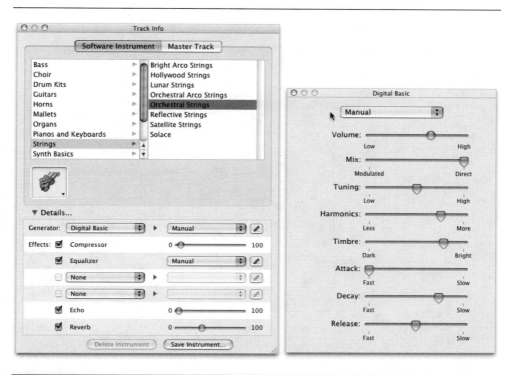

FIGURE 10-14 Here, we see how Digital Basic Synth differs...

Common Parameters

We don't have room in this book to go through every parameter of every software instrument generator, but there are some common parameters that are available on most instruments.

Attack Time

Attack time determines how quickly the sound begins after a note is played on the controller. A short attack time will give the sound a punchy, percussive quality. A longer attack time will cause the sound to swell up slowly.

Decay Time

Decay time determines how long a note will sustain. A short decay time yields a staccato sound—think of a plucked violin. A longer decay lets a sound continue for as long as you hold the note.

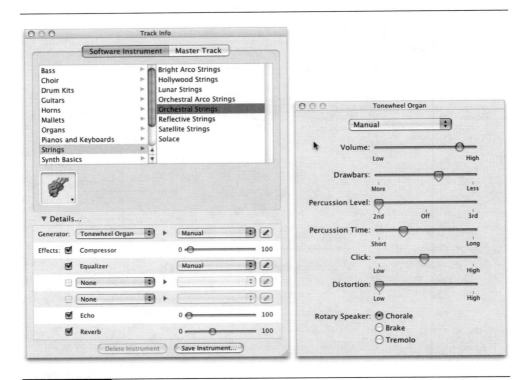

FIGURE 10-15 ... from Tonewheel Organ

Release Time

Release time determines how long the sound can be heard after you stop playing the note. With a short release time, the note will stop immediately after you stop playing. Most real-world instruments resonate a little bit, even after a note is played. You can use release time to imitate that resonance. A long release time will create a similar effect to that of a piano's sustain pedal.

Timbre and Cutoff

Timbre (on the digital synth models) and cutoff (on the analog models) control the tone by filtering out higher frequencies. Put the slider all the way to the right for a brighter sound.

Add Effects

As you tweak your generator, don't forget that there's still plenty to do. You can add effects that complement the settings you make with the generator editor. For example, use an autofilter plug-in to give an analog synth a sweeping sound, or use distortion to give a clean digital synth some edge, or add phaser to a clavinet for a classic '70s funk sound.

Store Your Work

Once you have your instrument (or master track) the way you want it, be sure to store your work. This will make the new instrument available in all of your GarageBand projects. To store your sound, click in the Track Inspector's Instrument column and choose the instrument category under which you want it stored. Then click the Save Instrument button ("Save Master" if you're working in the master track) on the bottom right of the inspector. Type a name into the Save As field (shown next) in the Save Instrument window, click the Save button, and you're done. (The same process works for both Real and Software Instruments and the master track.)

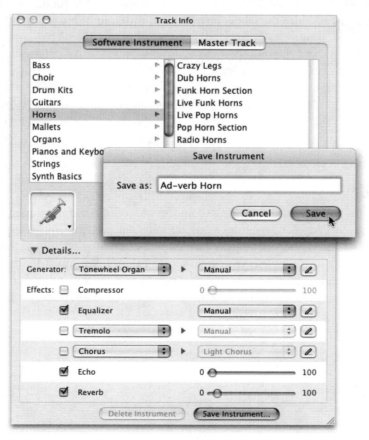

Less Is More

One thing I see a lot of new producers doing is putting too much "stuff" in the music. I think it was David Gilmour of Pink Floyd who said, "It's not what you play but what you *don't* play." In GarageBand, it's very easy to overplay. Because it's loop-based, you have a tendency to pile things on, and that's not how music is typically written. It's not just about putting things in; taking things out and leaving space is just as important.

Another thing about working with a program like GarageBand is that you have to realize that your "collaborators" are just musicians like yourself, and that their opinions and perceptions are subjective. For example, take the loop browser tags: One person's idea of "relaxed" might not be yours. Don't skip over loops just because the labels on them don't fit your criteria. Don't be afraid to listen at random.

For a songwriter, the loops should be a very quick way of getting inspiration, not a quick way of writing music. There's nothing like grabbing a mic, plugging it in, and making music. The nice thing about GarageBand is that it lets you do both.

—*Will Edwards, multi-platinum–winning producer/engineer at Sprockets Music*

Moving On

The art of producing can take as long to master as any musical instrument. The most important thing to do is to listen to as much music as possible and compare your work with your favorite recordings. Learn to pick out how parts fit together in a good mix, and apply those ideas to your own work. Finally, you must learn to listen objectively. Be honest with yourself about which parts work and which don't, and don't be afraid to go back and fix things if necessary. GarageBand gives you many opportunities to get the music right.

Chapter 11

Distribute
Your Music

How to...

- Export your songs to iTunes
- Tag your files fully
- Create an MP3 from an AIFF
- Share files over the Internet
- Burn your songs to CD
- Put your songs on your iPod
- Work with audio formats
- Use your songs with the other iLife applications

Thus far, we've gone through the whole process of creating music in GarageBand. We've imported and massaged loops, played and primped Software Instrument tracks, recorded through your Mac's audio inputs, mixed, edited, added effects—all in the name of creating that most precious of recorded commodities: the finished master. So the next question is: now what?

Hopefully, you're writing tunes that you like enough to share with the outside world. One of the cool things about working in a computer environment is the ease with which it lets you prepare your music to share with others. You can burn CDs or create MP3s and other electronic files for Internet distribution, and even use your own songs to create a soundtrack for an iMovie.

Export Your Songs to iTunes

The first step in distributing your music is to export each song from GarageBand to iTunes. We touched on this in Chapter 9—it's the last stage in the mixing process— and it could hardly be easier. Here's we'll discuss the tag information that GarageBand adds to your audio file.

Check the Information in Export Preferences

As you saw in Chapter 3, GarageBand uses the information in Export preferences (see Figure 11-1) to tag the songs you export and assign them to a playlist. So if you haven't already entered suitable information, choose GarageBand | Preferences (or press COMMAND-comma), click Export, and enter the appropriate information:

- ■ **iTunes Playlist**   Enter the playlist to which you want iTunes to assign the songs. If this playlist doesn't already exist, GarageBand will prompt iTunes to create it. You can assign the songs to other playlists manually after exporting them, but putting them in a playlist on export helps prevent them from getting lost in your music library.

- ■ **Composer Name**   iTunes assigns this name to both the Composer tag and to the Artist tag, and uses this name for the artist folder in which the file is stored. You can change either name in iTunes.

- ■ **Album Name**   iTunes assigns this name to the Album tag, and uses this name for the album folder in which the file is stored.

Click the Close button or press COMMAND-W to close the Preferences window after entering your information.

Prepare to Export

As we discussed in Chapters 9 and 10, you can export a song at any time and in any state—it does not need to be "complete." But usually you'll want to get a song into a more-or-less finished state before distributing it to the world at large. The song doesn't have to be totally finished—you might want to export several different mixes

FIGURE 11-1   Check the playlist, composer, and album information in Export preferences before exporting songs.

of a song so that you can listen to them on a variety of audio equipment and decide which mix to go with or what further work each mix required.

Check the overall volume of the song before you export it. You'll typically want it to be as loud as possible without clipping occurring. Play the song and drag the master volume slider to a suitable position.

 *Whether you've finished the song or merely got it to an intermediate stage, save the song before exporting it. If you plan on creating different versions of the mix, use Save As to create a different song file for each mix.*

GarageBand's default setting is to export the entire song—from the first measure to the end of the final region. If you want to export only part of a song, click the Cycle button to display the cycle region, and then drag the cycle region's boundaries to define the part of the song you want to export.

 *Cycle must be active for this to work; if the cycle region is hidden, GarageBand will export the entire song regardless of the length of the cycle region.*

If iTunes is already running, close any open windows or open dialog boxes, because these may prevent GarageBand from exporting the song.

Export a Song

To export the song, choose File | Export To iTunes. You'll see a panel showing GarageBand's progress as it exports the song (shown here). The export is a silent process; you will not hear audio playback.

When GarageBand has finished exporting the song, it automatically switches to iTunes and displays the playlist containing the song. Double-click the song to start it playing.

 *Exporting a song from GarageBand 1.0 sometimes causes an older version of iTunes to open in Classic instead of your current version of iTunes on Mac OS X. To fix this problem, update to GarageBand 1.1 or a later version.*

About the Audio File

When GarageBand exports a song, it creates a CD-quality 16-bit AIFF file with a sample rate of 44.1 kHz, (the same specs as a CD audio file).

When GarageBand generates the AIFF file, it names it after the song. For example, if you export a song named "Industrial Decay," GarageBand and iTunes create the file Industrial Decay.aif. If a file with that name already exists in the folder, GarageBand

and iTunes add a sequential number to each subsequent file: Industrial Decay 1.aif, Industrial Decay 2.aif, and so on.

GarageBand will store the song within the folder you specify in your iTunes preferences. It automatically creates a subfolder for your audio files, so that they're easy to find amidst the other files in your iTunes collection.

The easiest way to access the song file directly is to CONTROL-*click it in iTunes and choose Show Song File from the shortcut menu. iTunes opens a Finder window to the folder that contains the song file.*

Organize Your iTunes Library

Apple has made iTunes so user-friendly that you can perform all its essential functions— importing CD tracks and converting them to compressed files, playing music at mind-altering volume, and melting your credit cards at the iTunes Music Store— without cracking open the Help file. But to get the most out of iTunes, you must keep your music library organized so that you don't lose songs. To keep your library organized, you need to tag your songs correctly—not coincidentally, exactly what you need to do to help your intended audience enjoy your music files to the full.

Tag Your Files Fully

As you saw a moment ago, GarageBand applies basic tag information to each file you export. But if you're planning to distribute your songs, you should tag them fully. iTunes enables you to add the basic tags (such as Name, Artist, Album, Composer, Comments, and Genre), but if you want to add a full set of tags (including lyrics), you need another application.

Basic Tagging with iTunes

You can adjust individual tags by working in the main window in iTunes: Click the entry you want to change, pause, click it again to display an edit box, type the new text, and press RETURN. This works fine for editing one tag at a time, but you'll get better results faster by using the Song Information dialog box:

1. Select the song or songs whose tags you want to change.

    CONTROL-click and choose Get Info from the shortcut menu, or press COMMAND-I, to display the Song Information dialog box (for a single song) or the Multiple Song Information dialog box (if you selected multiple songs). Figure 11-2 shows the Info tab of the Song Information dialog box

FIGURE 11-2   Use the Song Information dialog box to edit the tags for a single song.

(whose title bears the name of the song you're examining), and Figure 11-3 shows the Multiple Song Information dialog box.

2. On the Info tab of the Song Information dialog box, or in the Multiple Song dialog box, enter the tag information for the song: type in the text fields, and use the pop-up menus and check boxes as appropriate.

3. Click OK to close dialog box. (In the Song Information dialog box, you also have the option of clicking the Previous button or the Next button to move to another song without closing the dialog box.)

More Advanced Tagging

For more advanced tagging than iTunes can manage, you need a custom tagging application. One of the more powerful tagging applications is MP3 Rage ($24.95), which is a suite of applets for tagging, managing, and generally working with MP3 files. Figure 11-4 shows the QuickEdit feature of MP3 Rage, which lets you quickly change the tags on either a single file or on multiple files at once. You can add

Multiple Song Information

Artist

Acme Power Trio

Album

APT Enough

Grouping

Composer

Acme Power Trio

Comments

Check out our tour schedule at http://
www.acmepowertrio.com!|

Genre

Metal

Volume Adjustment

-100%   None   +100%

Year

2004

Track Number

of

Disc Number

of

BPM

Artwork

Part of a Compilation   My Rating

No

Equalizer Preset

None

Cancel   OK

FIGURE 11-3   Use the Multiple Song Information dialog box to edit the tags for two or more songs at once.

lyrics and artwork, both of which can greatly increase a song's appeal to its potential audience.

TIP   *For specialized tagging needs, visit Doug's AppleScripts For iTunes site (www.malcolmadams.com/itunes/scrxcont.php). This site contains free scripts for performing many operations with iTunes, including intricate retagging operations.*

Add Artwork to a Song

In the old days, creating an album cover, or even an insert card for a cassette, took either considerable effort on your part or the services of a professional artist—and usually a fair amount of time. These days, you can add a compelling image to a song instantly using a digital camera and a modicum of effort.

This is great—but as you may suspect, there's a catch. ID3 tags are in what might be termed euphemistically "a state of flux," and information you enter in one tag editor may not carry through to all MP3 players (or even to another tag editor). So when adding artwork to a song, be sure to test your results with other MP3 players.

11

FIGURE 11-4   MP3 Rage offers powerful tagging features, including the ability to add lyrics and artwork to songs.

You can add a picture to a song in iTunes. Click the Show or Hide Song Artwork button (fourth from the left in the lower-left corner of the iTunes window) to display the artwork pane, and drag a picture from a Finder window (or from iPhoto) to it (the fact that it says "Drag Album Artwork Here" is a hint).

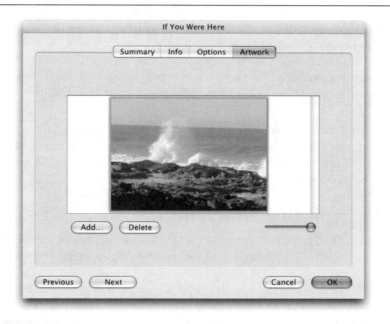

FIGURE 11-5   You can add one or more pictures to a song by using the Artwork tab of the Song Information dialog box.

You can also add one or more pictures by using the controls on the Artwork tab of the Song Info dialog box (see Figure 11-5) or with the Artwork box in the Multiple Song Information dialog box. But you may find that pictures you add in this way may not be readable for other MP3 players.

In most cases, you can get better results by using a tag editor such as MP3 Rage to add the pictures to the MP3 files. But even when you do so, the images aren't always readable by other MP3 players, so you should check your files using a variety of players before distributing the files.

Create an MP3 from an AIFF

As you learned earlier in this chapter, GarageBand exports songs as AIFF files. AIFF files have superior audio quality because they're uncompressed, but if you want to be able to distribute your songs easily over the Internet, you'll probably want to create space-saving compressed files from them. iTunes enables you to create compressed files in several different formats, including the widely used MP3 format. MP3 is *lossy* compression—it discards some of the data in order to compress the file as a whole—so there's a trade-off of degrading the audio quality in order to reduce the file size. (For discussion of the other audio formats iTunes can handle, see "Understand Other Audio Formats" at the end of this chapter.)

Lossy compression is a form of data compression; this is different from the audio compression signal processing we discussed in Chapters 9 and 10.

Not all MP3 files are created equal, and various factors affect the sound quality, size, and compatibility of the file. Before you convert an AIFF file to MP3 with iTunes, you can use iTunes importing preferences to set the specifications of MP3 files you'll be generating.

Set Your Importing Preferences

Choose iTunes | Preferences (or press COMMAND-comma) to open the Preferences dialog box, and then click Importing to display the Importing preferences (see Figure 11-6).

Select MP3 Encoder in the Import Using pop-up, and then use the Setting pop-up to specify the quality. iTunes offers three presets: Good Quality (128 Kbps), High Quality (160 Kbps), and Higher Quality (192 Kbps). These presets provide good

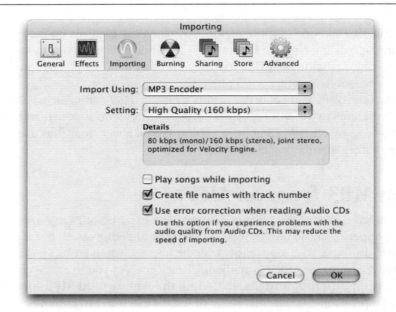

FIGURE 11-6 Use the Importing preferences to specify which encoder to use.

basic settings for people wanting to import (rip and encode) their CDs to relatively high-quality MP3 files. Higher-quality files are larger.

Choose the Bit Rate

For creating MP3 files from songs you've created in GarageBand, you'll probably want to experiment with the Custom setting that iTunes offers. You may be able to get better results than the three presets will give you.

Open the Setting pop-up and click Custom to display the MP3 Encoder dialog box (see Figure 11-7). Then, use its controls (discussed next) to specify parameters for encoding MP3 files.

Start by choosing the appropriate bit rate in the Stereo Bit Rate pop-up:

- iTunes offers bit rates from 16 Kbps to 320 Kbps.

- The higher the bit rate, the more information is retained and the higher the audio quality. On the other hand, a higher bit rate means a larger file—and a potentially slower download for people who are trying to access your music over a dial-up connection.

- The more information, the greater the file size. Uncompressed audio requires around 10MB per minute (with a stereo file); 128-Kbps audio requires around 1MB per minute; and 320-Kbps audio requires around 2.5MB per minute.

11

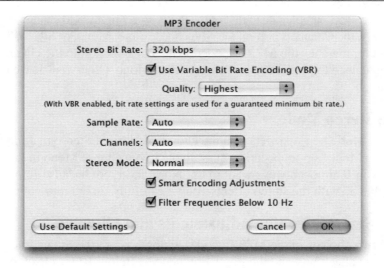

FIGURE 11-7 For best results, use the MP3 Encoder dialog box to specify exactly the bit rate and other encoding options for your MP3 files.

■   Treat 128 Kbps as a practical minimum for music files. Bit rates below this are okay for spoken audio or for radio broadcasts, but you need at least 128 Kbps to do justice to the tracks you've composed.

■   iTunes uses the stereo bit rate as the exact bit rate for encoding constant bit rate (CBR) files and the minimum bit rate for encoding variable bit rate (VBR) files.

Choose Between CBR and VBR

Next, decide whether to use CBR or VBR. CBR encodes every part of the audio at the exact bit rate you specify, so that a second of silence takes up as much disk space as a second of full-on instruments and vocals. CBR is wasteful of space, but is compatible with even the oldest MP3 players (both hardware and software players). By contrast, VBR allocates space as needed, so it stores more data for a complex passage than for a simple passage. As a result, VBR files tend to sound better than CBR files, but some older players can't play them.

Choose Sample Rate and Channels

The next settings you can change in the MP3 Encoder dialog box are ones you probably won't want to change: sample rate and channels. The *sample rate* is the number of times per second the encoder samples the music it's encoding. CD-quality audio uses a sample rate of 44.1 kHz, and this is the sample rate that GarageBand uses when you export AIFFs. iTunes' default setting, Auto, automatically matches the MP3 Encoder's sample rate to that of the input, so it's best not to change this setting.

Similarly, the Channels pop-up lets you choose Auto, Mono, or Stereo. The default setting, Auto, matches the MP3 Encoder's channel selection to the channels in the input. If you need to produce mono tracks, select Mono. Otherwise, leave Channels set to Auto.

Choose Stereo Mode

The Stereo Mode pop-up offers you the choice of Normal Stereo or Joint Stereo. (The Stereo Mode pop-up becomes unavailable if you choose Mono in the Channels pop-up.) You'll almost always want to use Normal Stereo, because Joint Stereo will play havoc with the stereo effects you've carefully mixed into your songs.

Choose Smart Encoding Adjustments and Filtering

The final two choices in the MP3 Encoder dialog box are the Smart Encoding Adjustments check box and the Filter Frequencies Below 10 Hz check box. Smart

Encoding Adjustments allows iTunes to override any settings you've chosen that will result in an unsuitable combination. Filter Frequencies Below 10 Hz removes frequencies below 10 Hz from the MP3 file. The "normal" range of human hearing is thought to be 15–20 Hz (depending on the researcher) or 20 kHz, with frequencies below human hearing range being considered *infrasound* ("below sound") and frequencies above 20 kHz being considered *ultrasound* ("beyond sound").

Neither infrasound nor ultrasound is entirely useless—infrasound annoys elephants (who can hear it) and has been shown to produce disquieting feelings in people (who can't), and ultrasound stimulates injured tissue, annoys dogs, and helps bats keep out of your hair. But you'll probably agree there's little point in including infrasound in songs you're trying to compress for easy distribution. (iTunes doesn't offer you the choice of including ultrasound in your MP3 files.)

After you finish making choices in the MP3 Encoder dialog box, click the OK button to close it. iTunes returns you to the Importing preferences sheet, which is updated to show your choices. Click the OK button to close the Importing preferences pane.

Create the MP3 File

After you've specified the details of the MP3 encoding, all you need do to create an MP3 file is select the source AIFF in the library and choose Advanced | Convert Selection to MP3 (or CONTROL-click on the song in the library or playlist window and choose Convert Selection to MP3). iTunes performs the conversion, and the MP3 file appears in your music library.

If your iTunes encoder is set to AIFF, this menu selection will read Convert to AIFF.

iTunes applies the same tag information to the MP3 file as was in the original file, and saves the MP3 file in the same folder as the original. In the iTunes interface, the MP3 file appears to have the same information as the original. The easiest way to tell the difference immediately is to check the Date Added column, in which the later date or time will show you which is the newer file. Alternatively, you can tell which file is which by CONTROL-clicking the audio file, choosing Get Info, and checking the Kind readout on the Summary tab of the information dialog box. An AIFF file appears as AIFF Audio File, while an MP3 file appears as MPEG Audio File.

As you can see, once you've chosen the encoder settings, the conversion process could hardly be simpler. But iTunes offers a couple of variations that you may want to use from time to time: removing the beginning or end (or both) of a song from the files you convert, and sewing multiple songs together into a single song file.

Edit the Audio File in iTunes

The AIFF file you create in GarageBand (and the MP3s you create from it) may not be entirely ready for distribution. Various factors, including the start and end of the file, its audio level, and overall tone, may need adjustment. In professional musical circles, this process is called *mastering,* and is a very specialized part of the production process. iTunes can perform some basic editing and mastering tasks; for more elaborate work on your files, you may want to consider an audio editing application such as BIAS Peak (see Chapter 13). Here, we'll focus on what you can do with iTunes.

Remove the Beginning or End from a Song

iTunes can trim a portion of an audio file's beginning or end. You can use this feature to remove unwanted silence at the beginning or end of a song, or to create an excerpt of a song for online distribution.

To remove the beginning or end of a song in iTunes:

1. Select the song you want to affect.

2. Choose File | Get Info or press COMMAND-I to display the Information dialog box for the song.

3. Click the Options tab button (see Figure 11-8).

4. Type the start time (in minutes:seconds format—for example, 0:03 to start three seconds into the track) in the Start Time text box. iTunes selects the Start Time check box for you automatically when you adjust the contents of the text box.

5. To trim the end of the song as well, enter the time in the Stop Time text box.

6. Click OK to close the Song Information dialog box. (Alternatively, click Previous or Next to move to another track you want to change.)

> **TIP** *For more precise musical control, you might consider trimming the song's boundaries in GarageBand before you export it. When Snap to Grid is enabled, you can set the cycle to cover a specific range of music, as described earlier in this chapter and in Chapter 9.*

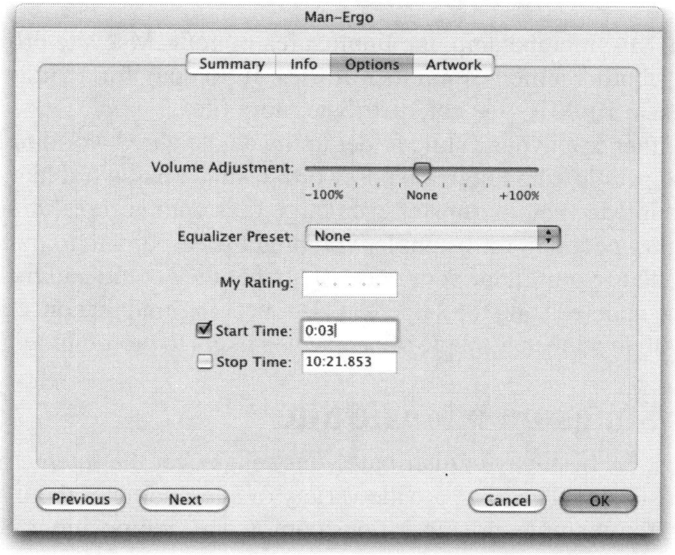

FIGURE 11-8   The controls on the Options tab of a song's Information dialog box let you trim its beginning or end, adjust its volume, rate it, or apply an equalizer preset to it.

Share Files over the Internet

So, you've produced some fine-sounding songs and created high-quality MP3 files of them. Now you need to get them to your audience via the Internet. This section advises you on your options for doing so.

Send Files via E-mail

The most direct method of sharing a file over the Internet is to attach it to an e-mail message. The advantages of this method are that you can direct the files to specific recipients and that it is quick and easy: chances are that both you and your audience have e-mail, and even dial-up connections can handle moderate-sized attachments, even if it takes them a few minutes.

The disadvantages of this method are that many ISPs block attachments larger than a few megabytes to protect their mail servers from being swamped, making e-mail viable for sending only compressed files of relatively short songs. For example, if you send a 3MB file (such as an MP3 file of a three-minute song compressed at 128 Kbps), it'll probably get through. If you send the same song as a 27MB AIFF file, many mail servers would likely refuse it.

Put Your Files on Your .Mac Site

If you have a .Mac membership, the Public area of your .Mac site provides an easy means of distributing a modest number of files. If you pay for additional space beyond the basic 100MB, you can distribute more files.

You can either open your Public folder to the whole wired world or limit access to your site to people who know the password. Using a password like this enables you to use your .Mac site to transfer even large files with acceptable security to one or two other people—for example, you might use your site to transfer a partly completed song to your guitarist or vocalist so that they could add their part and then return the updated song the same way. But bear in mind that once you've shared a password with more than a couple of people, it's likely to be compromised very soon.

Put Your Songs on a Music Site

In many cases, the best way to distribute your songs over the Internet is to put them on a music site. There are a wide variety of sites, some of them specific to GarageBand (for example, iCompositions.com, www.icompositions.com) and others that host music composed and recorded in any way (for example, GarageBand.com, www.garageband.com). If you pick a popular site, your songs will be able to benefit from the people visiting the site and looking for new music.

You'll probably also want to direct your audience to that site to access your songs. For example, if you send out an e-mail newsletter about your music, you could include details of the songs you've posted and links to them. If you play concerts, you could hand out flyers with information about accessing the songs.

When evaluating music sites, get input from your musical friends, but also be sure to consider the following key criteria:

- Which rights to your songs are you granting to the site? You'll always be granting permission to reproduce your music and distribute it—without that permission, the site couldn't put the music up for streaming or download— but you should make sure this is on a nonexclusive basis so that you can distribute your songs yourself as well. Are you granting the site the right to distribute the songs on the Internet only, or can they also burn them to CDs for promotional or other purposes? Make sure you retain ownership of your songs and that you can remove them from the site when you no longer want them there.

- How much space does the site give you? At this writing, sites such as iCompositions.com offer 150MB for free and 350MB for a modest yearly fee. Other sites require you to put in some effort (for example, by reviewing other people's songs) before you can upload your songs.

- Does the site give you the space and tools to create a satisfactory artist area to provide the information you want to share with your audience?

- Does the site only provide songs for free streaming or download, or does it have a mechanism for selling songs as well? Can you sell CDs of your songs?

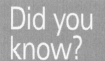

You should only distribute songs to which you own the copyright—or have legal permission to use. Distributing a cover of another artist's song—no matter how distinctive from the original version—is illegal without permission.

Run Your Own Site Using Hosted Space

If you don't want to cede the distribution rights to your songs to the company that runs a music site, you can run your own site using hosted space or your own computer and Internet connection. Using hosted space is almost always a better idea, because that way you don't have to worry about keeping your computer and Internet connection

Did you know?

Why You Should Use Hosted Space Rather Than Running Your Own Site

Most ISPs don't allow you to run a server on a standard residential agreement (check your fine print to find out what limitations you agreed to) and don't provide enough upstream bandwidth for you to do so effectively. This means that running a server gives you the worst of all worlds:

- Anyone downloading a song from your site will get a slow download rate. If more than a couple of people try to download at once, the download rates will be truly miserable—perhaps slow enough to make some people give up.

- If your site gets a lot of traffic, your ISP will probably notice and "encourage" you to upgrade to a service that allows you to run a server.

- If your site doesn't get a lot of traffic, you're pretty much wasting your time anyway.

- You have to keep your computer up and running the whole time and either maintain a static IP address or use a DNS updating service to ensure that people can find your site.

running all the time. You also don't have to worry about violating your ISP agreement (see the preceding "Did You Know" sidebar).

Release Your Files on P2P Networks

Another option to consider is releasing your songs for free distribution on P2P networks such as Kazaa and Grokster. Peer-to-peer (P2P) networks have deservedly gotten a bad reputation because of the millions of copyrighted files that are shared on them without authorization, but these networks are just as effective at distributing files that their copyright holders have decided to share freely. And despite the vigorous efforts of the RIAA and its lawyers, millions of people are still actively using P2P networks for sharing music.

If you use a P2P network yourself, you can "release" your songs by putting them in your shared folder. Your challenge then becomes encouraging other people to download them and to share them with others. Consider leveraging your audience by actively encouraging them to share your songs freely via the P2P networks they use.

Burn Your Songs to CD

Despite the rapid rise to prominence of MP3 as a means for sharing music, the humble old audio CD is still the most widely used medium for distributing and playing music. Recordable CDs are cheap, ubiquitous, and can sound very good.

Understand the Different Types of CDs You Can Burn

iTunes makes it easy to burn your songs to audio CDs that are compliant with the Red Book standard (which got its name from the red binder in which it was published). More practically, these audio CDs will play on any standard CD player or on a CD-ROM or DVD drive (for example, the optical drive on your Mac).

iTunes also lets you create CDs that contain music in MP3 files. The advantage of an MP3 CD is that you can fit on it much more music than fits on a standard audio CD. You can also put playlists on an MP3 CD to specify the order in which the songs play. The disadvantages are that the audio quality is lower than CD quality—how much lower depends on the bit rate you use—and that most standard CD players can't play MP3 CDs: instead, you need an MP3-capable CD drive or a CD-ROM drive. These limitations mean that MP3 CDs are most useful for distributing large numbers of files to people who have computers.

Beyond audio CDs and MP3 CDs, iTunes also lets you create data CDs—CDs that contain audio files in any compressed or uncompressed format that iTunes can handle. Data CDs are good for backing up your playlists and music library. Even better for backing up are data DVDs, which can contain up to 4.7GB of data and which you can create using iTunes if you have a SuperDrive or other compatible DVD burner.

Prepare for Burning

Before you burn a disc, you must tell iTunes which kind of CD (or DVD) you want to burn, how fast to burn, and (in some cases) which burner to use. You also need to create a playlist that contains the songs you want to burn.

Tell iTunes Which Kind of CD to Create

To tell iTunes which kind of CD to create, choose iTunes | Preferences (or press COMMAND-comma). In the Preferences dialog box, click the Burning button to display the Burning preferences (see Figure 11-9).

If your Mac has two or more burners, select the appropriate burner in the CD Burner pop-up.

In the Preferred Speed pop-up, choose a specific speed if necessary. Otherwise, leave Maximum Possible, the default setting, selected. Usually you'll need to change the speed only if you find that full-steam-ahead burning doesn't work properly—for example, it might produce errors on the discs.

In the Disc Format area, select the Audio CD option button, the MP3 CD option button, or the Data CD or DVD option button as appropriate. (If your burner can't handle DVDs, or if iTunes doesn't support burning DVDs with your burner, the data option is called Data CD.)

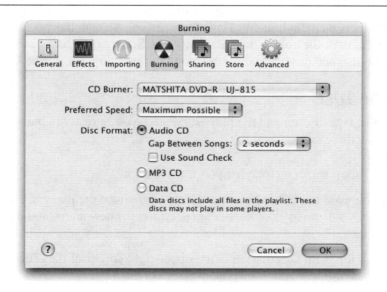

11

FIGURE 11-9   Specify what kind of disc you want iTunes to burn.

To create an audio CD, select the Audio CD option button. In the Gap Between Songs pop-up, choose the number of seconds' gap to use between tracks: none, 1, 2, 3, 4, or 5 seconds. The default is 2 seconds.

For an audio CD, select the Sound Check check box if you want iTunes to normalize the volume of each track on the CD. If you're burning a variety of songs created by other people to CD, using Sound Check is usually a good idea, because it helps you avoid uncomfortable variations in volume caused by the songs having been output at different levels. But if you're burning a CD of your own songs that you've carefully mixed and exported at exactly the right volumes, you'll probably want to leave Sound Check off so that it doesn't interfere with the relative volumes you've set on your tracks.

After choosing burning preferences, click the OK button to close the Preferences dialog box.

Create a Playlist

Next, create a playlist that contains the songs you want to burn to the disc.

If you've already exported all your compositions to the same playlist, all you need do is select that playlist in the Source pane so that its contents are displayed, and then drag the songs into the play order you want for the CD.

If your songs are currently residing in various iTunes playlists—or if you want to add other songs from you music library—create a new playlist by choosing File | New Playlist or pressing COMMAND-N. iTunes adds the new playlist to the Source pane and selects its default name. Type the name you want and press ENTER. Click the Library item or the appropriate playlist in the Source pane, drag each song to the new playlist, and arrange the songs into the order you want for the CD.

Burn the Disc

With the disc type chosen and the playlist created, you're ready to burn the CD. To do so, follow these steps:

1. In iTunes, select the playlist you want to burn.

2. If you want the CD to have a different name from the playlist, change the playlist's name by double-clicking it, typing the new name, and then pressing RETURN.

3. Click the Burn Disc button in the upper-right corner of the iTunes window. iTunes prompts you to insert a blank CD.

How to ... **Get Your CDs Mass-Produced**

Individual CDs that you burn yourself might be fine for bandmates, friends, and family. But if you want to reach a wider audience, you may want to have your CDs mass-produced. Although CD duplication machines are available, most users will probably opt to go to a professional duplication house. The services offered by these companies can range from the very basic—making copies of an audio CD that you provide—to the more elaborate—mastering and sequencing the CD, creating the art work, and manufacturing the complete package. Often, you can provide these duplicators with artwork you generate yourself, or create a CD jacket design based on one of their templates. Not only will these CDs be potentially more time- and cost-effective than creating your own, the overall package can be more professional.

Although the range of service costs can vary widely, there are a few things to keep in mind as you choose a duplication service:

- **Can I get a test pressing?**   You should have a chance to listen to the master CD before they start pressing 1,000 copies. Listen carefully to the sequence, transitions between tracks, and tone and volume of the individual tracks.

- **Can I proof artwork?**   As with audio, you'll want to take a careful look at printed material that will accompany the CD: the J-card, booklet, and the printing on the CD itself.

- **Do I need mastering?**   Although you can master your own work, it's often advisable to have a fresh, objective, and experienced set of ears on your work. Mastering can get pricey, but it can be money well spent if you plan to distribute your CD to radio stations, media, and retail outlets.

Finally, some duplicators offer extras, such as including one of your songs on a compilation, or free membership to a music-sales site such as CD Baby (www.cdbaby.com)—to make their services more appealing. Shop carefully. Two of the better-known companies are Disc Makers (www.discmakers.com) and Oasis CD Manufacturing (www.oasiscd.com)

11

4. Insert the CD. iTunes checks the disc and then prompts you to click the Burn Disc button to start the burn:

NOTE   *If you've chosen too many songs to fit on one CD, iTunes warns you of the problem. If you've chosen to create an audio CD, iTunes offers you the choice of creating multiple CDs with the playlist split across them or canceling the burn so that you can remove songs from the playlist to make it fit on a single CD. iTunes offers the same choices if you're creating a data disc. If you're creating an MP3 CD, iTunes lets you choose whether to burn one CD containing all the songs that'll fit or cancel the burn, but it doesn't offer you the option of creating multiple MP3 CDs.*

5. Click the Burn Disc button. iTunes starts burning the CD:

When iTunes has finished burning, it plays a notification sound. CONTROL-click the disc's icon on your desktop and choose the Eject command from the shortcut menu to eject the disc. Alternatively, drag the disc's icon to the Trash.

Put Your Songs on Your iPod

If you want to take your songs with you so that you can listen to them and work on them in your mind, the iPod makes the process easy. Simply export your songs from GarageBand to iTunes, and then synchronize your iPod (or iPod mini) with iTunes to load the songs on the iPod:

■ If you've chosen to use automatic synchronization (the default), connect your iPod to your Mac via the FireWire cable triggers synchronization.

■ If you've chosen to synchronize only selected iTunes playlists with your iPod, click the Display iPod Options button to display the iPod Preferences dialog box, select the playlist in the Automatically Update Selected Playlists Only list box, and then click the OK button.

FIGURE 11-10   If you've chosen to manage your iPod manually, drag the songs (or a playlist) to the iPod. Otherwise, synchronize your entire library or the appropriate playlists to add your songs to your iPod.

If you've chosen to manage songs and playlists manually, connect your iPod and then drag each song, or a playlist containing your songs, to the iPod's item in the Source pane to add the songs to the iPod (see Figure 11-10).

 *See* How to Do Everything with Your iPod & iPod Mini *(McGraw-Hill/ Osborne, 2004) for instructions on just about anything you may want to do with your iPod or iPod mini.*

Work with Other Audio Formats

Audio CDs are the best means of sharing your songs directly with other people in the physical world, and MP3 files are the most popular means of sharing your songs via the Internet. But sometimes you may prefer to use the other audio formats that iTunes offers: AIFF, AAC, WAV, and Apple Lossless Encoder. This section tells you what you need to know about these formats to use them effectively.

After selecting the format you want to use and choosing any options for it, you can convert one or more selected songs to that format by opening the Advanced menu and choosing the appropriate command: Convert Selection to AAC, Convert Selection to AIFF, Convert Selection to Apple Lossless, or Convert Selection to WAV.

Advanced Audio Coding (AAC)

Advanced Audio Coding (AAC) is the default codec (coder/decoder) for importing music into iTunes. Like MP3, AAC is lossy compression, so you lose audio quality when you convert one of your songs from AIFF to AAC. This quality loss is almost negligible if you use a high bit rate.

AAC provides higher music quality than MP3 at the same file size, or roughly equivalent music quality at a smaller file size. For example, most listeners reckon that 128-Kbps AAC files sound as good as, if not better than, 160-Kbps MP3 files. So if you know your audience can listen to AAC files, they're a better choice than MP3 files. But at this writing, iTunes (for both Mac OS X and Windows) is the only mainstream player that can handle AAC files with aplomb.

 *Unlike MP3, AAC offers the option of building protection into audio files. For example, Apple's iTunes Music Store sells AAC files that will play only on computers authorized to play them. At this writing, iTunes doesn't enable you to create protected AAC files yourself, only unprotected AAC files.*

AIFF

AIFF is the format in which GarageBand exports songs to iTunes, so you won't need to convert them unless you need to resample them at a lower quality or change them from stereo to mono. If you need to do so, display the Importing preferences sheet, select AIFF Encoder in the Import Using pop-up, choose Custom in the Setting pop-up, and then use the controls in the AIFF Encoder dialog box (shown here) to specify your needs.

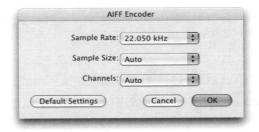

AIFF is the default format for uncompressed audio on the Mac, so it's a good choice for distributing full-quality, uncompressed songs. Because such files take up 10MB per minute, the files of normal-length songs are large enough to make most people think twice about transferring them over even the sturdiest broadband Internet connection. If all your file transfers are over a local area network, AIFFs are quite viable—but if you know your audience has iTunes, the Apple Lossless Encoder format (discussed next) may be a better choice.

Apple Lossless Encoder

Until April 2004, most digital audiophiles faced the tough choice between compressing their music (and so losing audio quality) or enjoying full-quality audio but having to deal with the huge size of uncompressed files. In most cases, compression won the day—faced with the choice of being able to pack 10,000 compressed songs on an iPod or having to settle for a mere thousand uncompressed songs, most people decided the slight loss in audio quality was worth the trade-off.

In April 2004, Apple released iTunes 4.5, which incorporated the Apple Lossless Encoder, a new encoder that compresses digital audio down to around half its size without losing audio quality. This capability makes the Apple Lossless Encoder great for distributing high-quality audio files to anyone who has iTunes (on either Mac OS X or Windows). Apple Lossless Encoder files will play on iPods (and the iPod mini) updated with versions of the iPod Software Updater released after iTunes 4.5, but not on most other portable digital audio players.

> NOTE   *Different generations of regular-size iPods use different versions of the iPod Software Updater, and the iPod mini uses yet another version. For best results, get the latest version of the iPod Software Updater available for your model of iPod.*

To use Apple Lossless Encoder, display the Importing preferences sheet, select Apple Lossless Encoder in the Import Using pop-up, and click the OK button. (The Apple Lossless Encoder has no configuration settings.)

WAV

If you want to share full-quality music files with Windows users, your best bet is to use the WAV format. Like AIFF, WAV contains uncompressed PCM audio, but it has a different header than AIFF. WAV files are used on Windows in much the same way as AIFF files are used on the Mac. Windows PCs that have iTunes installed can play AIFF files, but unless you're sure your audience has iTunes (or some other AIFF-friendly application) installed, WAV is a better bet for Windows users.

As with AIFF, the disadvantage to distributing WAV files is their large file size, which makes sending them across the Internet inadvisable for any but the fastest Internet connection.

To use the WAV Encoder, display the Importing preferences sheet, select WAV Encoder in the Import Using pop-up, and then choose Automatic or Custom in the Setting pop-up. The WAV Encoder dialog box (shown here) offers the same options as the AIFF Encoder dialog box: you can change the sample rate, the sample size, or the channels used, but in most cases you'll do best to stick with the default settings.

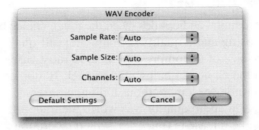

Use Your Songs with the Other iLife Applications

Once you've exported your songs from GarageBand to iTunes, you can use them freely in iPhoto, iMovie, and iDVD.

To make your songs easy to access in these three applications, add them to an iTunes playlist (as GarageBand almost forces you to do) rather than leaving them at large in your iTunes music library.

Use Your Songs in an iPhoto Slideshow

To use your songs in an iPhoto slideshow:

1. Select the slides (or album) and click the Slideshow button to display the Slideshow dialog box.

2. Click the Music tab to display it (see Figure 11-11).

3. Select the Play Music During Slideshow check box.

4. Select the playlist in the Source pop-up.

5. To play just one song, select it in the list box. Otherwise, leave the list with no songs selected to play the entire playlist.

6. Click the Play button to start the slideshow playing.

FIGURE 11-11 You can use your songs to accompany a slideshow in iPhoto.

Import Your Songs into iMovie

If you create movies with iMovie, you'll most likely want to compose some of your own soundtracks in GarageBand—after all, what better source of royalty-free music tailored to your movie's needs could there be?

To import a song into the open movie project in iMovie:

1. Export the song from GarageBand to iTunes as discussed earlier in this chapter.

2. Switch to iMovie.

3. If the timeline isn't displayed, click the Timeline button to display it.

4. On the timeline, position the playhead where you want the song to start.

5. Click the Audio button to display the Audio pane (see Figure 11-12).

6. In the Select An Audio Source pop-up menu at the top of the pane, select the playlist that contains the song.

7. In the list box, select the song.

8. Click the Place at Playhead button to place the song starting at the playhead's position. iMovie imports the song into the timeline's audio track.

9. Click the song to select it in the timeline.

10. Select the Edit Volume check box if it's currently cleared.

11. Click the volume line on the song to create control points, and then drag the control points to create the volume curve you want for the song.

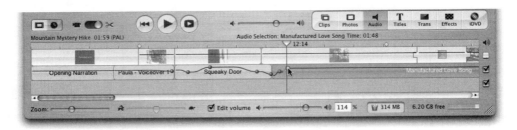

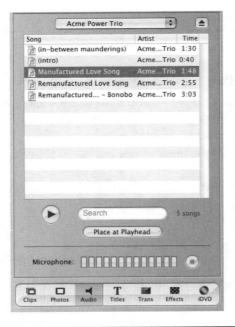

FIGURE 11-12   To import a song into iMovie, choose a playlist in the Select An Audio Source pop-up, choose a song, then click the Place at Playhead button to put it into the timeline.

Use Your Songs in iDVD

You can also use your songs in various areas in iDVD. To do so, follow these steps:

1. If the Customize drawer isn't displayed, click the Customize button to display it.

2. Click the Media tab to display the Media pane.

3. Select Audio in the pop-up menu to display the iTunes music library and your playlists in the upper list box (see Figure 11-13).

4. Select the playlist to display its contents in the lower list box.

5. Drag the song to where you want to place it.

11

FIGURE 11-13   Use the Media pane in iDVD's Customize drawer to access your songs.

Did you know?

The State of Independence

If you're serious about getting your music heard, you've probably just realized one of the music business' uncomfortable truths: that the actual making of the music (fun part) is only part of the job. The business end—making the contacts, getting the press kit together, getting the gigs, airplay, distribution, etc.—can be less of a joyride.

There's no question that the last decade has seen some fundamental changes in the music business. Today, the concept of the monolithic major label is constantly being eroded by Internet sharing, direct distribution of CDs, Internet radio, and other factors. For artists, this is both good news and bad news. The good news is that you have more control over your music than ever before, and are no longer dependent on the resources of a major label in order to be heard. The bad news is that you're in competition with millions of other independent musicians world-wide for the limited attention span of the audience, and you don't have a record label's promotional resources to open the door and to cover your back. (Then again, the label won't be there to take a substantial cut of your earnings, either.)

Fortunately, there are many resources available to the indie musician. Internet radio stations, music sharing sites, and online distributors (such as CD Baby) can get your music into the hands of potential fans. The independent press (both print and online) are often open to reviewing new music. Finally, small radio stations (the ones near the bottom of the FM dial) are often willing to play new artists on the air, especially if they're performing in the area. The Internet is a great research tool to find these resources. There are many books on the subject, including *The Indie Music Bible* by David Wimble (Music Sales Corporation) and *All You Need to Know About the Music Business* by Donald S. Passman (FreePress). On the Web, check out GetSigned.com, (www.getsigned.com), Indie-Music.com (www.indiemusic.com), Songwriter101.com, and the aforementioned GarageBand.com—no relation to the software—(www.garageband.com). For an expanded list of sources, see Appendix A.

Moving On

Now that you've created a finished master and used it to set the world ablaze, you have several options. You can bask in the glory, while sending your personal security team out with lemonade for the adoring fans who are camped out on your estate; you can change your name to a symbol and make it difficult for journalists to refer to you in print; or you can continue reading and learn about some of the hardware and software you can add to your setup to make GarageBand an even more powerful tool.

Part IV

Take GarageBand Beyond Its Horizons

Chapter 12

Add Peripheral Hardware

How to…

- Choose a MIDI interface
- Choose a MIDI controller
- Choose an audio interface
- Choose a monitoring system
- Use a physical mixer
- Use outboard signal processors
- Set up your studio

A computer loaded with GarageBand is a self-contained music production environment. But while you don't necessarily *need* to add lots of extra gear in order to make music with GarageBand, there are a number of elements that can enhance your experience and add to the capabilities of your musical studio.

When evaluating external hardware to use with GarageBand, think of yourself—and your Mac—as the center of the studio. All the other gear you buy should make it easier to get your music happening with your Mac. If that sounds obvious, then you've probably never put together a recording studio. The gear can take over your life faster than you can say "parameter." But don't be intimidated: If you take your time and do some research, you can put together a nice system that suits your production goals and stays out of your music's way.

Choose a MIDI Interface and Controller

A MIDI interface is used to route MIDI signals to and from your computer. Unless you plan to use your mouse to play the GarageBand keyboard, or have a utility like Midi Keys (which lets you play MIDI notes on your computer's keyboard) installed on your Mac, you'll need a MIDI interface in order to play software instruments in GarageBand.

Most MIDI interfaces use a USB port to connect to your computer, though there are a growing number of devices that use a FireWire connection for both MIDI and audio, and some PCI audio devices also include MIDI connections.

Interfaces come in three varieties: controller/interfaces, stand-alone interfaces, and audio/MIDI interfaces.

How to ... Right-Click on Your Mac

PC users have one advantage over Mac users—the two-button mouse. This allows them to right-click and access menu items and additional features. In OS X, you can CONTROL-click to get similar results, but that's a two-handed operation. However, a multibutton mouse or trackball, such as the Kensington Turbo Mouse Pro, lets you assign buttons to various functions, including CONTROL-clicking, key commands, and more. A wireless trackball like the Turbo Mouse Pro is also useful because it allows you to move away from the computer and operate GarageBand (or other software) from a distance, potentially eliminating one source of noise—the computer itself.

Controller/Interfaces

When it comes to convenience and portability, nothing beats a controller that can interface directly with the computer. These devices, such as the M-Audio Oxygen 8 and Edirol PCR-1 (see Figure 12-1), offer a quick and easy way to connect to your computer. When choosing a controller interface, the features you'll need to consider are as follows.

Number of Keys

On a piano keyboard, an octave (C to C) is 13 keys. Typically, controllers range from 25 (two octaves) to 88 keys. A smaller keyboard is fine for triggering samples, playing in simple parts, and drum programming. If you're a concert pianist (or even a serious amateur piano player), you'll probably want something larger.

MIDI Control Message Features

MIDI control messages are used to add expressive touches to your music. In addition to transmitting notes, a good MIDI controller should be able to send various control messages to your computer. GarageBand is compatible with *pitchbend,* which changes pitch in real time; *modulation,* which alters the sound of a software instrument in various ways (how depends on the instrument and its programming); and *sustain,* which is similar to the behavior of a piano's sustain pedal.

12

FIGURE 12-1   The Edirol PCR-1 is a portable MIDI controller and interface with audio ins and outs.

> **TIP**   *GarageBand uses MIDI velocity to control how loud or soft note a note plays in a software instrument. The majority of MIDI controllers available on the market offer velocity sensitivity, and some feature adjustable velocity settings, which let you match the keyboard's responsiveness to your style of playing.*

A control keyboard uses wheels and joysticks for pitch bend and modulation; sustain is typically handled with a pedal, which connects to the controller through a special jack.

The MIDI specification provides for many other control messages, and even though they're not currently supported in GarageBand, many of them are supported by software like Propellerhead Reason and Ableton Live, which can be used with GarageBand through ReWire (see Chapter 13). The most useful of these controllers is *volume,* which controls the loudness of a MIDI channel, and *aftertouch,* which is most often used to add a vibrato-like quality to a MIDI note.

Zones

Although GarageBand can only work with one MIDI channel at a time, there are controllers that can split into zones, with each zone sending out a different MIDI channel. This can be useful if you plan to use other MIDI software that supports multiple MIDI channels.

Stand-Alone Interfaces

If you already have a MIDI controller, you may want to consider a stand-alone interface. A stand-alone interface's sole job is to send MIDI signals to and from the computer. It offers no controller capabilities of its own.

You'll find stand-alone interfaces in a variety of sizes. Simple one-port interfaces, such as the Edirol UM-1SX, are portable and can be powered by the USB bus. These are fine for use with GarageBand. (A single cable can transmit up to 16 MIDI channels.)

If, however, you plan to use additional MIDI hardware and software with your computer, you may want to consider a multiport MIDI interface, such as the Emagic MT4 (see Figure 12-2).

A multiport interface is especially useful if you want to use more than one controller: For example, you could connect both a keyboard and a drum controller to GarageBand and have both available at all times.

Audio/MIDI Interfaces

Many of the latest generation of interfaces include audio and MIDI in one device. The obvious advantage of an audio/MIDI interface is that all of your connections are on one device. The disadvantage is that many of these all-in-ones have fewer connections than some of their stand-alone counterparts. Units like the TASCAM US-122 (see Figure 12-3) are compact and capable of handling both audio and MIDI I/O for your computer via USB. TASCAM, and other manufacturers, also offer larger USB Audio/MIDI devices that include more elaborate controls.

Audio/MIDI/Controllers

If you can live with a compact keyboard as your main controller, you might want a single device to handle audio, MIDI, and control functions. The M-Audio Ozone

FIGURE 12-2   Multiport MIDI interfaces like the Emagic let you connect several MIDI devices to your computer.

FIGURE 12-3   The TASCAM US-122 MIDI/audio interface

(see Figure 12-4), which the company has dubbed a "mobile workstation," does it all: 25-key MIDI controller; eight control knobs, and a two-in/two-out 24-bit 96-kHz audio interface, all in a package that weighs about four pounds.

Choose a MIDI Controller

Technically, a controller is any device that sends a MIDI message that is used to operate another device. Even if you have two MIDI keyboards cabled together, if you're triggering sounds in keyboard A by playing the keys on keyboard B, keyboard B would be considered to be the controller.

FIGURE 12-4   The M-Audio Ozone can handle all of GarageBand's audio/MIDI needs in a portable package.

If you already own a MIDI keyboard, such as a synthesizer or workstation, then that device will probably be more than suitable as a controller for GarageBand. If it can transmit MIDI note, pitch bend, modulation, and sustain messages, it can do everything GarageBand needs.

If you're starting from scratch, however, you'll have to do some homework before buying a controller.

In addition to the features discussed in the section "Controllers/Interfaces" in this chapter, you should ask yourself the following questions.

What Kind of Action Do I Need?

Controllers come in three types of action:

- *Piano weighted,* or "hammer action," keyboards are designed to emulate the feel of an acoustic piano. If you're a pianist who thrives on the feel of the real thing, this is probably your best bet, as long as you can find one that suits your playing style. In keeping with the piano theme, many weighted-action keyboards are large, offering 88 keys. Examples include the M-Audio Keystation Pro 88 and the Studiologic SL-880 Pro.

- *Semiweighted* keyboards offer a little more "feel" than a nonweighted keyboard, but are not as heavy as a weighted-action keyboard. Models come in a variety of sizes, but most are 61 keys or more. Examples include the Roland A-37 and the Studio Logic TMK-88.

- *Nonweighted keyboards* (also known as "synth action" keyboards) offer fast action, and are fine for those who started on electronic keyboards or organ. Most controllers fall into this category.

Do I Need Full-Sized Keys?

If you're looking at a compact controller, make sure you check that you can cope with the size of the keys. A compact device that offers full-sized keys might offer fewer keys, but they may be easier to play than a device with minikeys.

Do I Need Internal Sounds?

We've said this before, but it bears repeating: Although you can produce a lot of music with GarageBand, it's likely that you'll also want to use other devices when creating your music. An all-in-one keyboard workstation can offer sounds, a keyboard

12

controller, and a sequencer that might be part of a larger audio studio. While you won't be able to use the workstation's sounds or sequencer with GarageBand, it can be a valuable centerpiece for your studio. If you already have a workstation, there's no reason why you can't add GarageBand to your arsenal.

MIDI Controllers for Non-Keyboardists

Sometimes it seems that MIDI should be called KODI (keyboardists only digital interface). But in reality, there are many other devices that can be used as controllers.

- *Guitar controllers* can read the pitch and loudness of a guitar string and translate that info into MIDI messages. Roland makes a number of guitar synthesizers that also offer guitar-to-MIDI conversion via a special pickup. Like the Roland devices, the Axon's AX-100 can be retrofitted on a guitar and provides guitar-to-MIDI conversion. Brian Moore Guitars' iGuitar (see Figure 12-5) and the Fender Roland-Ready Strat each have a built-in interface that lets you plug it directly into a Roland-compatible device.

- *Drum controllers* use pads to send MIDI messages. In a typical drum controller configuration, each drum in an acoustic kit is represented by a pad, and each pad sends one MIDI note. Yamaha and Roland offer a number of individual pads or complete electronic drum sets. Compact units like Roland SPD-20 can be used in a table-top configuration, and played with sticks like any "real" drum. Akai's MPD16 USB MIDI Pad control unit has drum-machine-like pads that you can play with your fingers.

- *Wind and other controllers* are also available. Wind controllers let wind players get into the MIDI party. Devices like the Akai EWI3020 and Yamaha WX5 can play the notes and also turn breath into MIDI control messages. Other devices include foot controllers (similar to the pedals of an organ) and other MIDI-equipped devices such as acoustic pianos, accordions, and acoustic drums retrofitted with MIDI triggers.

Choose an Audio Interface

We've discussed audio interfaces throughout this book, so you already know that GarageBand can work with a variety of audio interfaces. Which interface is the ideal addition to your system depends on a lot of factors, and not all of these are related to GarageBand.

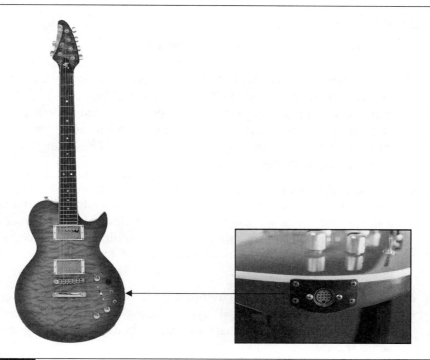

FIGURE 12-5   The Brian Moore iGuitar can be used with a Roland-compatible device to function as a MIDI controller.

Compatibility

GarageBand is a Core Audio application, so it goes without saying that your interface should be Core Audio–compatible too. But not all "compatible" devices are created equal. Some devices offer only basic Core Audio support, while others allow for better integration with OS X. As OS X evolves, your interface's driver software must evolve with it. Devices that are compatible with OS X 10.2 may not work with OS X 10.3 or later. Not only that, but even a subrelease of the OS can have an effect on the compatibility of an audio interface. For a list of officially supported devices, go to www.apple.com/ilife/garageband/compatibility.html.

NOTE   *Some devices that are not officially supported can work with GarageBand. If you already own a device that's not on the list, consult your manufacturer for details.*

Type of Connection

You'll find three types of audio interface connection:

- *USB* devices are generally affordable and are often portable. As we saw in the previous section, many USB interfaces combine audio with MIDI and even controller functions. USB interfaces can be used with both laptop and desktop computers. The problem with USB is that it can be prone to system traffic: with so much data running through the USB bus, things can get a bit clogged, and audio can suffer.

- *FireWire* interfaces are similar to USB devices, but take advantage of the faster FireWire connection speed, and are therefore preferred for multichannel audio. Devices like the Yamaha 01x and Digidesign 002 offer multichannel audio, MIDI, and control surface functions, while units such as the MOTU 828MKII focus on multichannel audio (though the MKII does have a MIDI port, as well).

- *PCI* devices, which reside in user-accessible slots inside a desktop computer, have the advantage of being always on and available. The high speed of your Mac's PCI slot also means that these interfaces can handle many channels of audio at once.

NOTE   *Multichannel audio is not an issue if you're restricting your computer music-making to GarageBand, but can be important with other applications.*

Number of Channels

GarageBand only needs two channels of audio into and out of the computer in order to work, so it's unlikely that you'll want a multichannel interface if you plan on staying in the "Garage." However, if you're looking to use a multichannel interface with another application, you can take advantage of some of its features in GarageBand as well. For example, you can plug a different audio source into each of the interface's inputs, and switch among them as you set up each new track in GarageBand—this will save you the hassle of patching in each instrument every time.

Monitoring Features

We've discussed latency—the time it takes for a signal going into GarageBand to be heard at its output—throughout this book. Although GarageBand's low latency mode works well, it can use up system resources, especially a G3- or G4-equipped computer. Some audio interfaces offer direct monitoring: the ability to hear any source plugged into them without putting that sound through the software.

Phantom in the Machine

Phantom power is an electrical signal that runs through a microphone cable. It's used to provide power to condenser microphones and other devices directly from the mixer or preamp.

CAUTION *If you use direct monitoring, you won't be able to hear the GarageBand effects you've added to the track as you record it. After the track has been recorded, however, you will be able to hear the effect.*

Most interfaces offer connection for both headphones and speakers. The ability to switch between the two is especially handy if you plan to record acoustic instruments and vocals with live microphones; turn off the speakers and use headphones when doing these kinds of tracks.

Audio Connections

An audio interface can have many different types of audio connections, and we went over some of them in Chapter 7. When you're shopping for an interface, it's important to consider what other types of gear you'll be connecting to it. If, for example, you plan to add a digital mixer to your system, you'll probably want an audio interface with both analog and digital connections. If you're going to use the interface with high-end outboard audio gear, such as microphone preamps, then the interface should have balanced analog connections and should be able to handle the high-level signal these devices put out. If you plan to plug a microphone directly into the interface, it should obviously have a microphone input—preferably with *phantom power,* which is necessary if you're going to use a condenser microphone.

Beyond the Computer

The idea of a computer-only studio is very attractive for many reasons. It's neat, it's powerful, and it's organized (GarageBand will remember where you last set your effects and software instrument controls, even if you don't). But even with all its power, GarageBand is probably not going to be the only thing you use to make music. The following section offers a brief look at some of the accessories you might add to your studio as time goes on.

12

Choose a Set of Audio Monitors

Although the art of recording involves many skills, probably the most important is listening. You need to be able to hear what's going in a song in order to create a good-sounding mix. Unfortunately, your Mac's internal speakers just don't cut it for musical applications.

There are plenty of affordable speakers on the market that are designed specifically for computer users. Many of these systems include two small speakers, which can be placed on your desk, and a larger unit called a *subwoofer,* which is dedicated to producing bass frequencies. Some of these "consumer" speaker systems sound good, though hardcore audio folks would say they're not "accurate" enough—they change the sound of music coming in, so it's hard to know how to adjust your mix.

Studio pros use the word "monitors" to describe their speaker systems because the speaker's job is to accurately portray what's going on inside the mix. Monitors come in many sizes, and are designed for many different functions. For GarageBand, it's most likely that you'll want a pair of small speakers that will be mounted close to your listening position. These are known in the trade as *nearfield monitors.*

Nearfield Monitors

Nearfield monitors are usually compact speakers. They're designed to sit within 3–6 feet of your listening position. The theory behind the near-field concept is that if the speakers are close, their sound won't be influenced by the acoustics of the room and therefore will be more accurate. The speakers are designed to project their sound in a focused direction, so that someone sitting in the "sweet spot" will hear them in all their glory. In reality, this "acoustical isolation" is only partly true: unless the room is acoustically treated and the speakers are positioned perfectly, the room's acoustics will come into play.

However, used correctly, near-field monitors work well. Figure 12-6 shows a typical near-field listening position. The speaker should be placed so that the high-frequency driver, or "tweeter," is at about ear level to the listener. Ideally, the distance between the speakers and between the speakers and the listeners, should be equal, so that you and the speakers form three points on an equilateral triangle.

NOTE   *When shopping for speakers, be aware that not all small speakers are near-field monitors. Bookshelf speakers that are designed for consumers' use will disperse the audio differently than a proper near-field speaker.*

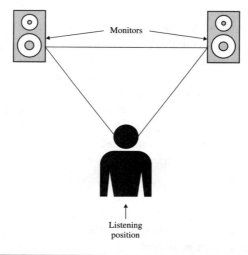

FIGURE 12-6   In the ideal near-field listening position, the monitors are at ear level and are equidistant from the listener.

Active and Passive Monitors

When it comes to monitors, the words "active" and "passive" have nothing to do with the speakers' personalities, but instead refer to the way the speakers are powered.

- *Active monitors* have built-in power amps, which means that all you need to do is plug your interface or mixer directly into the monitor and turn it on. The advantage of an active monitor is that the power amp is designed specifically for the speaker, so that the drivers are always receiving the proper amount of power. Some active monitors have separate power amps to run the upper and lower drivers. These models are said to be bi-amped.

- *Passive monitors* require a separate power amp to run. These monitors are generally less expensive than active models, and if you have a good power amp (or even a home stereo amp), you can find some good "passive" models both new and used (one of the most popular, the Yamaha NS10m, is no longer made, but can be found secondhand).

All things being equal, however, active monitors are the better bet. Because the power is built-in, you have less gear to worry about, and the fact that the power section is tailor-made for the speakers improves the sound and reduces the possibility of speaker damage.

12

Subwoofers

One of the best things about a typical near-field monitor is its size. Small speakers are easy to find a home for. One of the main drawbacks of the typical near-field monitor is its size. Small speakers don't do a good job with low frequencies. One way to compensate for this is with a big ol' speaker that's dedicated to the low end—a subwoofer. If you decide to add a subwoofer, keep in mind that it should complement your other speakers; you may have to adjust the response of the speakers so that the sub and the monitor's built-in woofers don't overlap in the low midrange. Ideally, you'll want to buy the whole thing as a system and choose a subwoofer of the same brand and type as your table-top speakers.

Headphones

You've spent some bucks for you Mac, and perhaps for a few audio peripherals as well. No that it's time to make some music, it's probably not the best idea to grab the headphones that came with your Walkman. If you spend any serious time recording, you're likely to become very intimate with your headphones. A good set will give you accurate sound and won't wear out your ears. A bad set will give you a headache.

Sony, AKG, Sennheiser, Audio-Technica, and Beyerdynamic are among the better manufacturers of headphones. Although there are hundreds of models to choose from, there are two basic design types—*open-air,* in which some of the ambient sound spills into the headphones, and *closed,* in which the listener is more isolated from the world outside:

- Open-air headphones are good for singers because they can hear themselves more easily as they sing.

- *Closed headphones* are good when you need to focus only on the signal coming through the "cans"—DJs, live sound engineers, drummers trying to hear a click track in a dense mix, etc. I keep both types around and use them as the situation requires.

Use a Physical Mixer

A mixer (also known as a mixing console or mixing board) is used to route a number of audio signals and combine them into a final stereo mix. GarageBand's built-in mixer is an example: it combines all of GarageBand's tracks into a final stereo audio stream. A hardware audio mixer can do something similar, but it can also be useful for more specialized work. For example, you can use a hardware mixer to combine five or six mics on a drum set into a stereo output, then route that stereo signal into

Did you know?

Two (or More)–Headed Monster

One headphone out is fine if you're working alone. But what if you want to add one or more musicians to the party? You could use speakers, but that's no good if you have an open microphone in the same room—the speakers' output will "bleed" into your GarageBand tracks. Instead, you can use a headphone splitter to create two connections from one headphones output. These simple devices are available at music and audio retailers. Just be sure that the plug on the splitter matches that of your interface. Some splitters, such as the compact Boostaroo (www.boostaroo.com) both split and boost the signal.

If you want to offer separate level controls for each set of headphones, consider a headphone amplifier. These devices can offer four or more headphones outputs, each with its own level control. Manufacturers include Rane, Furman, ART, Behringer, Rolls, and others.

GarageBand. Similarly, you can connect a different source to each channel of the mixer—a bass to channel 1, a vocal mic to channel 2, a tuba mic to channel 3, and so on—and then feed each one in turn to GarageBand without having to unplug and replug the instruments every time. A mixer can also be used to add outboard effects to boost the signal of a microphone, to set monitoring levels for playback, and more.

There are hundreds of mixers available on the market, ranging from small analog models to complex digital devices. Features to look out for include the following.

Number of Inputs

Write down the number of inputs you'll need, and then add a few to the total. If you're going to use GarageBand and a few mics, a small mixer with 8 or 12 inputs should be fine. But beware: studios can grow on you, and before you know it, a small mixer might be too small.

Format

A mixer's format refers to the type of audio signal it can accept. Choices include analog, digital, and hybrid—which can handle both analog and digital signal. (Okay, we're being a bit technical. Almost all digital mixers that are available to consumers are hybrid devices that work on both analog and digital signals.)

Desktop mixers such as the hybrid Yamaha 01v96 (see Figure 12-7) are relatively affordable, yet are powerful enough to handle dozens of audio channels at a time.

 *If you're looking at a digital mixer, make sure that its digital audio connections are compatible with those of your digital audio interface.*

Types of Connections

Like audio interfaces, mixers come with many different types of connections. A good mixer will have a mixture of connections and should be able to handle line, mic, and instrument level signals. You might also want a mixer that can connect outboard effects, both to individual channels (via *inserts*) and to the overall mix (via effects *sends* and *returns*).

Auxiliary and Group Buses

Auxiliary and group buses are used to create special mixes that are separate from the main mix. These can be used for stage monitor mixes, for creating a two-channel submix (such as a mix of a drum kit), and for routing signal to effects.

FIGURE 12-7   The Yamaha 01v96 can handle analog and digital signals (image courtesy of Yamaha).

Built-in Effects

In addition to EQ knobs, which are found on almost all mixers, many of the mixers available today offer built-in audio effects. These can be both send-and-return effects, such as delay and reverb, and channel effects, such as compression, gating, and more. You can use a mixer's built-in effects to add flavor to the signal before you send it to GarageBand.

Other Features

Beyond the basics listed above, there are several useful features to look for. *Control capabilities* allow the mixer to act as a MIDI control surface. These features can be used by applications such as Reason, Logic, and others. *Rack-size format* is useful if you plan to take the mixer out to gigs, or simply want to store it in your studio's rack. Multiple *switchable monitor outputs* are great if you want to hear your music on several different speaker systems at once. A *talkback system* lets you communicate with other people in your recording studio through the monitors or their headphones.

About Microphones

Microphones are among the most important pieces of gear in any studio. Top-quality mics can cost thousands of dollars, but there are plenty of affordable mics that can deliver outstanding results. Various mics are designed for different applications. The most important factors to consider are type, polar pattern, and frequency response/sound pressure level ability.

Types of Microphones

All microphones are designed to transform sound waves into electrical energy. The device that is used to "capture" the sound waves is called the "element." There are three main types of mics on the market.

Condenser mics have an electrically charged element, usually a very light film-like material, called a diaphragm. Condensers tend to be very sensitive and responsive, and are often used for voices, acoustic instruments, and drum overheads (mics positioned above a drum kit). Condensers come in many varieties, but can be broken down into two main groups: large diaphragm condensers tend to have a broad frequency response and are popular for voice, electric guitar, drum overheads, and other featured instruments; small diaphragm condensers are generally brighter sounding, but are also "faster" to read a wave, which makes them good for acoustic guitar and percussion.

12

 *Condenser mics need a power source to run; most will run on phantom power, which is supplied by the mixer or preamp (or audio interface) via the mic cable itself.*

Dynamic mics are probably the most common mics on the market. A dynamic mic has been described as a "loudspeaker in reverse." Its diaphragm is coupled directly to a wire coil, which moves back and forth in the field of a magnet, and this creates electrical energy. Dynamic mics tend to be hardy—one reason why they're very common onstage—though they're usually less sensitive than condenser mics. You can use a dynamic mic on any sound source, but they're most commonly used on guitar amps, drums, vocals, and loud instruments such as horns.

NOTE   *Dynamic mics do not need phantom power.*

Ribbon mics are similar to dynamic mics, though the element—a thin metal ribbon—can offer the responsiveness normally associated with a condenser mic. Some classic mics of yesteryear were ribbon mics, and several newer models are available, and these are less fragile than their predecessors. Ribbon mics are often used for vocals and acoustic instruments.

Polar Pattern

When you record something with a microphone, you point the mic at the source, right? Well, you may not know that the area you can capture by pointing a mic will vary depending on the mic's polar (or pickup) pattern.

- *Cardioid* polar pattern mics are very directional, and tend to pick up an area right in front of the mic. These are the most common mics, and are useful because they can (at least to some degree) isolate the source you want to record from the background noise.

- *Hypercardioid* mics have a tighter pickup pattern in front, but they also pick up a small amount of signal behind.

- *Omnidirectional* mics pick up all signal around the mic equally. These work well for recording ambient sounds, and can also be useful for picking up an ensemble, such as a choir.

- *Figure-8* mics pick up sound in front and behind, but reject the sound on the side. These are good for recording two vocalists at once, but can also be used when you want to capture the sound of an instrument and the ambience of the room it's in with one mic (you can also use an omni mic for this purpose).

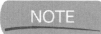 *Some mics have switchable polar patterns. These mics can be used in two or more modes.*

Frequency Response

Frequency response refers to a mic's ability to capture low-, middle-, and high-frequency sound waves. If a mic is "flat" across a part of the frequency range, that means that it picks up all sound waves equally. Most mics are not flat, however. Some frequencies will be louder than normal (this is called a "bump" because it looks like a bump on a frequency chart), while others will be quieter (called a dip, or a "roll off"). If you're recording a vocalist, for example, you might want a mic with a bump in the upper midrange, which can make the vocal sound stand out. If you're recording bass, you don't want a mic that rolls off steadily from the lower midrange frequencies down—it won't capture the bass's low end effectively.

Sensitivity and Sound Pressure Level

In addition to frequency response, a mic must be able to handle the source material well. For quiet signals, a mic must be sensitive enough to pick them up without your having to overboost the preamp or mixer (which can introduce noise). A sensitive mic is essential for quiet acoustic instruments. For louder signals, however, the mic must be able to handle high sound pressure levels, or SPL. Otherwise, the mic can overload and cause distortion. Some mics have switches, called *pads,* which let you compensate for high SPLs when necessary.

12

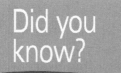 # Getting Closer: The Proximity Effect

A mic's frequency response can change depending on its position relative to the sound source. Most mics have what's called a "proximity effect," which describes how the mics response curve changes when the source gets very close to it. Usually, the proximity effect involves increased low midrange, which can make a voice sound deeper and fuller. That's one reason why many radio DJs like to "eat" the mic: it make them sound like, well, radio DJs.

 *Proximity effect is not an issue with omni mics, which can make them good for picking up acoustic guitars sounding too "boomy."*

Use a Preamp

A preamplifier—or preamp—is any device that boosts a low-level signal (like that of an electric guitar or microphone) to a level that can be used by other audio gear. In a studio environment, preamps can either be stand-alone devices or be part of another device, such as a mixer or audio interface. Professional engineers have long used outboard mic preamps, choosing different models for their specific sounds. Some of these pro preamps can cost more than your Mac, but there are also many affordable models available. If your audio interface does not have a mic input, you'll need a preamp to boost the mic (and possibly supply it with phantom power). Most mic preamps include built-in EQ, while some offer other features such as compression and even analog-to-digital conversion.

Even if your interface already has a mic input, you may want to consider an outboard preamp for its sonic qualities. But beware before plunking down your money on an outboard preamp that says it offers a million-dollar sound for $1.95. Some of these really do improve the sound of a microphone, but others are more hype than substance. Often, the mic preamps that are built into a decent mixer are as good or better than a low-cost outboard preamp.

Mics aren't the only devices that can benefit from the use of a preamp. There are dozens of models available for guitar and bass that allow you to get a sound similar to that of an amplifier when recording directly into your computer. Of course, GarageBand's Amp Simulation offers similar features, but if you're a hardcore guitarist, you may want to have an outboard device that you can also use in live performance.

Use an Outboard Signal Processor

GarageBand comes equipped with a comprehensive set of effects, and you can augment these with plug-ins. So, why would you want to use an outboard *signal processor,* or effects device? There are several reasons. You might like the special sound of a particular model. You might want to record a track with effects in place in order to free up GarageBand's system resources and place less strain on the computer's internal processor. You might use an external processor as a "front end" to improve the sound of your source before it reaches GarageBand.

But not all signal processors are used for noticeable sound coloring. Some professional engineers always use a signal processor such as a compressor or limiter when they record. Compressors and limiters help protect against distortion (by reducing the likelihood of a digital overload) while allowing you to boost overall signal level. If your recording setup includes a preamp, you could put the compressor between the preamp and the audio interface in the signal chain.

| FIGURE 12-8 | In this signal path, the mic is feeding a preamp, which boosts it's the mic's signal; the compressor is used to prevent overload as the mic's signal feeds the audio interface. |

TIP *No matter what type of effect you're using, make sure that it matches both the source and your audio interface. For example, unless the device in question has a built-in mic preamp, you can't plug a microphone directly into an effects device. A better signal path would look like this mic-mic preamp-compressor-audio interface (see Figure 12-8).*

Patchbays and Switchers

If your studio is small, you probably won't mind having to manually plug cables in and out of your interface as needed. But expand the studio to include a few preamps, outboard signal processors, or a mixer, and you'll soon find yourself wishing you had a central terminus for all those wires. A *patchbay* lets you plug all your audio connections into a central location. Instead of having to reach behind and plug into a device directly, you can route audio from one device to another by using short cables called *patch cords*. A patchbay is a huge timesaver.

Switchers are like patchbays, except, instead of patch cords, you use a switch to route signal. A switcher is handy if you have a few signals to deal with. For example, you could use one to switch your audio interface's monitor output between two sets of speakers.

Set Up Your Studio

And now, for the next 12,000 pages, we're going to discuss the proper way to set up your studio. Okay, it's not going to be that long—but it could be. What constitutes a "correct" studio setup is open to debate, and will change depending on your equipment and your own momentary needs. In professional circles, acoustical engineers earn big bucks designing recording studios, where every wire, wall, duct, and dust mite seems to be in the blueprint.

But even though the ideal studio is a custom construct, there are a few general guidelines that might be helpful as you set up your own rig, be it an iBook and a pair of headphones, or a G5 that's mated to a multichannel interface, mixer, and monitoring system.

Get Comfortable

The most important component in your studio is you. Set your computer and controllers so that you can sit at them comfortably for hours on end. The display monitor should be at eye height, with the keyboard, mouse, and MIDI controller within easy reach.

Position the Computer

Because your Mac is the heart of your studio, it deserves a featured place at the table. If you're using a laptop, the computer's position is obvious, but with a desktop, matters are a little more complicated. The computer should be close enough at hand that you can reach the CD drive and power switch. But desktop computers, especially G4s, can make a lot of ambient noise (if your own fans are as loud as the fan on your Mac, you'll be a star in no time). You can get extension cables to put the computer out of the room, but this is both expensive and complicated. Another idea is to buy or build an isolation cabinet that contains the computer and keeps it quiet.

 *If you go the "iso" route, bear in mind that you* must *keep the cabinet properly ventilated. Otherwise, you'll fry your Mac.*

List Your Connections

Putting together a studio involves a lot of connections and cables—audio, MIDI, computer, power—and it adds up very quickly. If you simply start plugging stuff in, you may end up with a big mess. So start by listing each piece of gear and its cables. Account for all power connections and decide where you want to put them. Get all the power strips you'll need *before* you start running wire.

When setting up a studio, it's best that all the audio gear be on one circuit. When you have gear on two separate electrical circuits, you may experience a "ground loop," which can cause a loud hum.

When you count audio connections, take note of the type of connector used and the output level of the device. Account for any mismatches by making or buying special cables or adapters.

I also recommend that you label your cables. You can use a numbering system, color coding, or simply name the cable after the piece of gear to which it connects. Later, if you have to troubleshoot your rig, it will be much easier if the cables are labeled.

Position the Speakers

When your computer's in place, you're ready to mark the "sweet spot" and set up the speakers. As mentioned above, position near-field monitors so that they're at ear height and equidistant from your listening position.

Place the speakers on a firm, solid footing to avoid rattling. Don't put anything between the speakers and your ears.

 *If the speakers are going to be next to a computer display monitor, you should use shielded monitor speakers, which won't interfere with the display's picture.*

Position Other Peripherals

This can be the trickiest part of the whole operation. Your MIDI controller needs to be in easy reach, but it can't interfere with your computer keyboard and mouse; your instruments should be handy, but they shouldn't be in the way when you move your chair to get to your mixer. Your mixer should be in arm's reach, but ... I could go on and on. The best thing to do is to prioritize your gear based on what you use most. If your focus is on audio recording, you may not need to have your MIDI controller on your desk (and you may not need more than a compact controller). If you play piano, you'll want a full-sized controller as the centerpiece of your studio, and should build around that. If your studio doubles as your office, you might not want audio gear and cables getting mixed up with your printer and PDA cradle, and so forth.

TIP *If you have a number of outboard signal processors, you should position them together in a rack. Most devices on the market fit a standard 19"-wide audio rack size, and racks are available from most music equipment suppliers.*

Run the Cables

When all your peripherals are in position, it's time to cable them in. Cabling can be a pain in the neck and other places, so it's best to do everything at once if you can.

12

Run the cables together as neatly as possible, and leave some slack so that moving a piece of gear in the rack (or moving the rack itself) won't unplug it. If you're using a patchbay, double-check that the cables are in the correct positions as you plug them in.

 Try to leave some space to get behind your gear so that you can get at cables after they're installed for troubleshooting or repatching purposes.

Turn It On and Test Connections

There's one more job to do before you're done—test the connections. This is a boring job, but it beats sitting there wondering why you're not getting sound in the middle of a recording sessions. To test connections, you can use a portable device known as a signal (or tone) generator. Plug it into each device's audio cable (or jack on the patchbay), and use the respective device's meters (or audio monitors) to check that it's receiving signal.

 *If you don't have a signal generator, you can use another sound source, such as an electronic tuner that generates a tone, a portable CD or tape player, or an electric instrument that you know to be working.*

Plan to Expand

Your connections are clean, your speakers are working, and you're ready to make music. Excellent! Just remember before you move on that you might expand your studio in the future. Now is a good time to account for any gear you might add. It's a good idea to run and label some extra cable and leave a few open slots in the power strip. Hey … you never know.

Moving On

The modern musician not only has to know about his or her own instrument, but must be computer savvy, have an idea about audio recording, acoustics, effects mixing, CD burning, and more. It can be overwhelming. Hopefully, once you decide what works best for you, the studio you set up will be an oasis, a place where you can forget about the technology and just make music.

In our next chapter we'll look at some ways you can expand on the capabilities of GarageBand with additional software.

Chapter 13

Extend the Power of GarageBand with Additional Software

How to...

- ■ Add Jam Pack
- ■ Expand your loop library
- ■ Use the Apple Loop Utility to tag an Apple Loop
- ■ Add third-party plug-ins
- ■ Bring sound into GarageBand with ReWire
- ■ Edit your files with audio editing software
- ■ Convert a standard MIDI file into a software instrument loop

On its own, GarageBand can keep you busy making music in lots of different ways. But your ability to compose and produce with GarageBand does not end within the confines of the program itself. You can augment its power with additional software, such as Apple's Jam Pack, which gives you more loops, instruments, and effects. Then there are new collections of Apple Loops—and "standard" audio loop files that you can convert into Apple Loop format with the free Apple Loop utility—which give you more raw audio with which to work. You'll find third-party plug-ins that let you add to your palette of effects and software instruments, while ReWire lets you synchronize another application to GarageBand's playback and "connect" it to GarageBand's audio mixer. Audio editing software lets you adjust your audio files very precisely and fix problems that GarageBand can't address on its own. Finally, a host of other useful audio and MIDI utilities make your life easier and more exciting. As GarageBand gains in popularity, there will be more compatible software to choose from.

This chapter is a survey of some of these applications, and will offer a few basic tips on how to use them.

Work with Jam Pack

Apple's Jam Pack is sort of like Hamburger Helper: It's not much without the burger (GarageBand), but just one box will help you get a lot more out of the meal.

Jam Pack is a collection of loops and effects that integrate perfectly with GarageBand's built-in library. Once installed, the connection is seamless: you won't know where standard GarageBand material ends and where Jam Pack begins.

Jam Pack includes

- Two thousand additional Apple Loops

- One hundred Software Instruments

- One hundred effect presets

- Fifteen amp simulation presets

System Requirements

Jam Pack adds functionality to GarageBand, but it doesn't significantly increase the workload on your computer—other than to add more data to your hard drive. System requirements are basically the same as those of the host program, though, obviously, you need to have GarageBand installed before you can run Jam Pack. Here's a rundown of Apple's system requirements, which we discussed in Chapter 2:

- Installed copy of iLife '04.

- Macintosh computer with G3 600 Mhz processor or higher to use Apple Loops (G4 or G5 required for software instruments).

- A minimum of 256MB of physical RAM

TIP | *As with GarageBand, the more RAM the better. A gigabyte or more of RAM would not be considered excessive.*

- A DVD optical drive (such as a Combo drive or SuperDrive). DVD is essential because of the storage space required to hold all of the loops that come with Jam Pack—they don't all fit on a standard CD-ROM.

- Mac OS X version 10.2.6 (Jaguar) or later.

CAUTION | *OS updates can be tricky. Normally, we'd advise you to use the latest version of the software available. However, if in addition to GarageBand your system includes other audio software and hardware, check with your vendors to make sure that it's all compatible with the latest OS release.*

- At least 3GB of free hard disk space.

13

Install and Use Jam Pack

To install Jam Pack, simply pop the disc into your DVD drive and follow the online instructions. After checking that your system is compatible with Jam Pack, the installer places the loops, samples, and effects in the appropriate folders for you. The GarageBand library will update itself to show the new loops, instruments, and effects.

 *You can look at the newly installed files in Library/Application Support/ GarageBand/Apple Loops.*

Once Jam Pack is installed, its contents appear alongside the original GarageBand loops, effects, and instruments. Figure 13-1 shows the Track Info Inspector before and after Jam Pack installation.

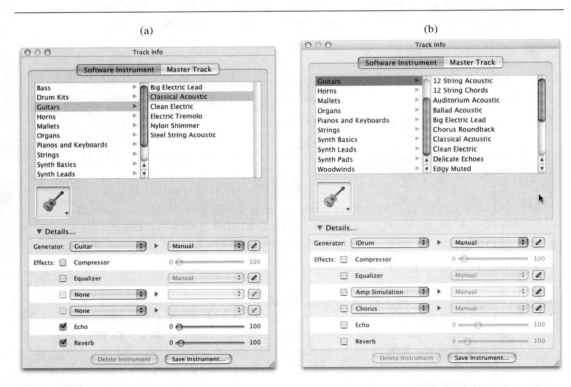

FIGURE 13-1 When you install Jam Pack, its contents are immediately available in the Track Info Inspector and loop browser. Here's a look at the inspector before (a) and after installing Jam Pack (b).

Expand Your Loop Library

GarageBand—especially if you augment it with Jam Pack—comes with thousands of loops, and they may keep you busy for quite a while. But you may also find that you want to go beyond the "official" loops and add more audio files to your collection. Fortunately, a whole industry has sprung up around the creation of third-party loops, and you can find loops in many genres and styles for sale in a range of formats. These include

- Files in Apple Loop format

- Files in other audio file formats such as WAV, AIFF, and MP3

- Files on audio CD

Add Apple Loops

The easiest way to expand your library is to add files in the Apple Loops format. Actually, Apple Loops are AIFF files that have been encoded with special metadata that tags the file with tempo and pitch information. This information is then used by GarageBand in order to synchronize the file with the song's tempo and key, and to transpose the file accurately. An Apple Loop also contains special data tags called "descriptors," which let the Loop Browser find the file in a keyword search.

Apple Loops are available from a range of sources. Vendors such as Drums on Demand (www.drumsondemand.com) and PowerFX (www.powerfx.com), AMG, and others create loops in a range of different styles, and many of these are available in Apple Loops format.

13

> TIP   *There are also sources for free loops online. Check forums like MacMusic.org to see what's available.*

Put New Apple Loops in Your Library

There are several ways to add a loop to your library. You can

- Drag a loop from the Finder into the timeline.

- Copy the loops into your Loop Library folder.

- Drag a loop or folder full of loops into the Loop Browser.

Drag a Loop into the Timeline

The easiest way to add a loop to your project is to drag it from the Finder into the timeline. The advantage of this method is that you have immediate "hands-on" contact with the loop as you place it—you won't need to search for it in the Loop Browser.

The disadvantage is that the loop you've added won't be immediately available to your other projects until you drag it into the Loop Browser.

You can drag MP3s, AIFF, or WAV files into the timeline. These files will work in your project, but GarageBand cannot automatically match their tempo and pitch to your song. Unlike Real Instrument Apple Loops, which are blue in color, the regions created from these untagged audio files are purple.

Drag Loops into the Loop Browser

With version 1.1, GarageBand has improved the way in which you can index loops. One of the best new features lets you drag an Apple Loop—or a folder full of them—into the Loop Browser; the files will be automatically indexed, and you can choose where they will be stored.

NOTE

Only Apple Loops (specially encoded AIFF files) can be indexed in the browser. Non Apple Loop-encoded AIFFs are not indexed. WAV, MP3, and other formats are cannot be imported into the browser at all.

Apple Loop AIFFs usually use a special icon. This distinguishes them from standard AIFF files and other audio files, such as WAVs and MP3s.

A_ReasonBassLoop
95Gm1.aif

Add an Audio File to the Loop Browser from the Current Volume

The simplest way to add a loop to GarageBand is to choose one on the current hard disk volume. This obviously assumes that you've created or purchased some Apple Loops and have them stored on your system's (and GarageBand's) hard disk partition.

■ Locate the loop file or files in the Finder.

■ Drag the file into the Loop Browser (see Figure 13-2).

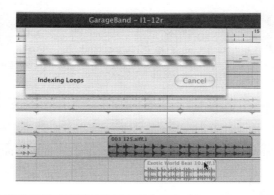

FIGURE 13-2   You can drag an audio file—or a folder full of them—into the Loop Browser. GrarageBand automatically indexes the file(s) and makes them available for all of your projects.

NOTE   *When you drag a new audio file into the Loop Browser, it will clear the current search.*

Add an Audio File to the Loop Browser from a Different Disk or Partition

Loop libraries can become extensive, and can take up quite a bit of disk space (if you need a reminder, take a look at the size of the Jam Pack disc: nearly 4GB of data are crammed onto it). Your boot volume is not always the ideal place to store such material, which is one reason why many professional studio denizens like to use separate hard drives for various types of audio files.

You may, for example, want to use an external FireWire drive to store all your loops. Not only will this reduce the performance load on the system drive when GarageBand is working; it will also make your collection of personal loops more portable if you want to work with other people in their GarageBand studios.

NEW IN 1.1   When you drag a file or files from a different volume into the Loop Browser, GarageBand automatically asks you where you want to store them (see Figure 13-3). You have the following choices:

■ **Add the Files to the Library**   The files will be copied to the main GarageBand library and will be available every time you start the program, but will take up more disk space.

13

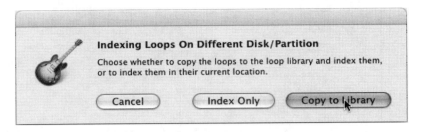

When you drag a file from a different disk or partition into the Loop Browser, GarageBand lets you choose how to handle the files.

- **Index Only**   GarageBand will reference the files, but won't copy them. This saves disk space, makes the files more portable, and may improve performance. Just be sure to have the volume containing the files open when you open the song referencing the files.

CAUTION *If GarageBand opens a song and does not find the files it needs, it will let you know with an error message (see Figure 13-4). You can have GarageBand search for the missing files.*

TIP *If you're copying Apple Loops from a data CD, GarageBand will automatically index them, copy them to the current volume, and add them to your library.*

GarageBand lets you know if any of the files needed for a particular song are AWOL.

Use the Apple Loop Utility

Thanks to the popularity of Final Cut Pro, Soundtrack, and GarageBand, Apple Loops are quickly gaining a foothold as an audio file format. But, despite this growing popularity among third-party loop programmers, the majority of audio files you'll find are not in Apple Loop format. These might include

- AIFFs that have been "ripped" from an audio CD

- AIFFs that have been created with other audio applications, such as Logic, Peak, Performer, Cubase, and others

- Standard WAV files

- ACID format WAV files

- MP3s

- Other audio file formats

Fortunately, there's a way to convert many of these formats to Apple Loops. The Apple Loop Utility (also known as the Soundtrack Loop Utility) can analyze an AIFF or WAV file; apply "tags" that indicate the file's length, pitch, and characteristics; and save it as an Apple Loop, which can be stretched and transposed in GarageBand.

The Loop Utility (see Figure 13-5) comes with Soundtrack, but is also available to GarageBand users as a free download at http://developer.apple.com/sdk/#AppleLoops.

Install the Loop Utility

The process of downloading and installing the Loop Utility follows standard OS X operating procedure. The downloader will create a disc image on your desktop; simply launch the installer, follow the directions, and you're home.

Because the Loop Utility is so useful, keep it in the Dock for easy access.

Open a File in the Loop Utility

There are three ways to open an audio file in the Loop Utility.

- Drag the file from the Finder onto the Loop Utility icon.

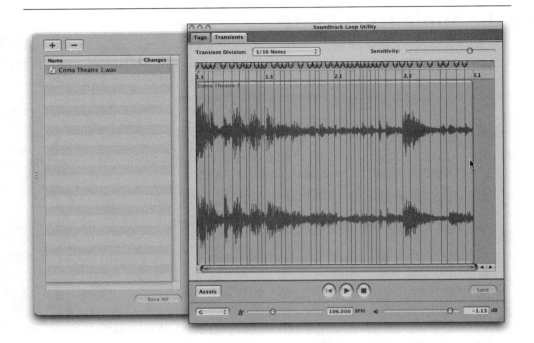

FIGURE 13-5 The Loop Utility lets you turn ordinary audio files into "elastic" Apple Loops.

- OPTION-click on the file and choose Open With Loop Utility.

- Open the Loop Utility first and load the file.

The Loop utility can open Apple Loop AIFFs, standard AIFFs, and WAV files. MP3s and other formats must be converted before you can open them in the Loop Utility.

 *You can drag a whole folder of files into the Loop Utility and "batch tag" them as a group. This is very handy if, for example, you've got a collection of drum loops that work well together.*

Navigate the Loop Utility

The Loop Utility consists of two man window panes. The Tags view (see Figure 13-6) is where you can add keyword tags to your file. These allow GarageBand to index the file and then find it in the loop browser.

The Transients view (see Figure 13-7) shows the waveform and the *transient markers,* special data that helps GarageBand identify the file's rhythmic feel so that it will play back properly at the current tempo.

From either pane, you can play the file with the transport buttons located at the bottom of the window. You can also access different files from the Assets drawer. You can load multiple files, select one or more, tag them either individually or as a batch, and save the files as an Apple Loop AIFF.

Use Tags View

The Loop Utility's Tags view lets you add different types of information to your file. User-definable categories include Properties, Search Tags, and Descriptors. The file

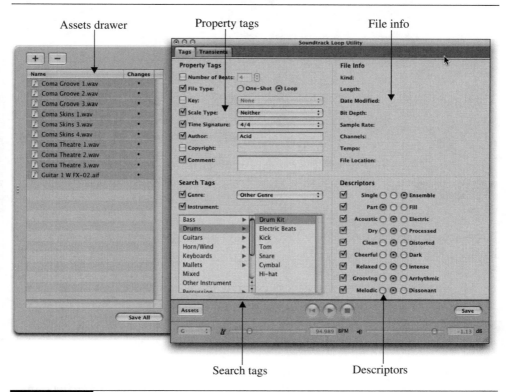

Assets drawer   Property tags   File info

Search tags   Descriptors

FIGURE 13-6   Tags view

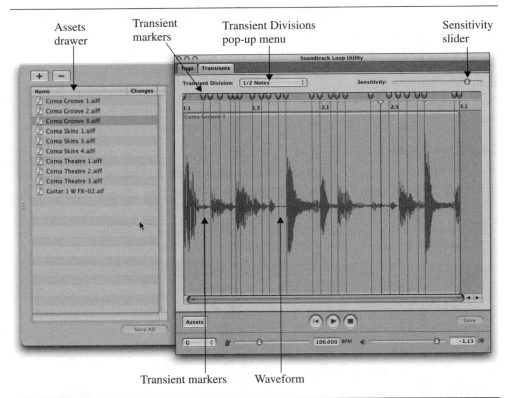

FIGURE 13-7   Transients view

info—which includes the file's format, resolution, and length—is read automatically by the Loop Utility.

- **Number of Beats**   An accurate beat count is essential if you want GarageBand to identify the loop's tempo correctly.

- **File Type**   You can determine whether the file will repeat (Loop) or play back once (One Shot). The latter is good for sound effects and cymbals.

- **Key**   For pitched material (for example, a piano or bass loop), you need to define the key. GarageBand uses this information as a reference when importing the loop into your project.

- **Scale Type**   Choices include Major, Minor, or Both. This information lets you match your loops to the mood of your music.

- **Time Signature**   This defines how many beats per measure are used in the loop.

- **Author, Copyright, and Comments**   This option lets you credit the file appropriately. These do not appear in GarageBand.

- **Genre**   Here, you define what type of music the file fits best.

- **Instrument Tags**   Here, you define what type of instrument the file contains.

- **Descriptors**   These tags let you add some more subjective description to your file, such as its mood, sound, instrumentation, and so on. You can tag a file with as many as nine different descriptors.

Use Transients View

Transients view may seem a little intimidating at first, but this powerful tool is relatively easy to use. Basically, your mission in Transients view is to place transient markers at the appropriate positions, thereby enabling GarageBand to read the file's rhythm correctly on playback. The good news is that, most of the time, the Loop Utility does the work for you. It analyzes a file's transients (places where the waveform peaks) and sets markers there. You can, however, add or remove markers and change their position in time.

- **Transient Division**   Defines the time unit of the transient markers— similar to the grid settings used in GarageBand. For example, you can set transient division to eighth notes, sixteenths, quarter notes, and so on.

- **Sensitivity Slider**   Increases or decreases the number of markers in the file.

- **Transient Handles**   Lets you drag a transient marker to a new location.

Play a File in the Loop Utility

The Loop Utility lets you play the file and hear your work. The playback controls (shown here) is available at the bottom of the window at all times and includes buttons for play, stop, and return to start. Here, you can also hear the file at different tempos and keys using the appropriate fields.

13

Save a File in the Loop Utility

Once you're done tagging your file, you'll need to save it so that GarageBand will know it's an Apple Loop. You can do this via the Assets drawer or the File menu. The Assets drawer is handy because it allows you to save multiple files with the Save All button. The Assets drawer's Changes column also indicates which files have been edited and which have not.

 *When you're saving files that you've tagged in the Loop Utility, it's probably a good idea to save them all in a central location—for example, a My Apple Loops folder. Within that folder, you can create subfolders for specific instruments, collections, projects, etc.*

Add Third-Party Plug-ins

Like most music software, GarageBand lets you add effects and software instruments that have been developed by third-party developers. These "plug-ins" work within GarageBand and can be accessed in the same way you access the program's built-in effects and instruments.

There are two reasons you might want to add a third-party plug-in. First, to get a feature that's simply not available in GarageBand. For example, Antares's specialized pitch-correction program Auto-Tune (shown next) is very useful for fixing pitch

Voices from the Community

Do the Demo

If you're interested in expanding on the capabilities of GarageBand, good news: There are loads of plug-ins on the market that work in Apple's AU format, and the list is growing every day. You'll find effects that do common jobs (compression, RQ, reverb) and processors that walk the audio wild side, twisting your music beyond recognition. It's similar with software instruments (I use the term generically here). You'll find both the traditional and the whacky, from samplers, to synths, to drum machines. When it comes to software, pretty much anything goes.

The challenge is often in finding what's out there—and then choosing which of the myriad of tools you want to add to your "Garage." Publications like *Keyboard* and *Electronic Musician* are a good starting point. They offer info and reviews of many of the latest commercial plug-ins (as well as third-party loops, which can be another resource for expanding your music-making capabilities), and they're loaded with ads from the manufacturers. Online, sites like Harmony Central (www.harmony-central.com) and Hit Squad (www.hitsquad.com) are extremely valuable. Harmony Central offers new product information (not just software, but just about everything in music and audio), user reviews, forums, links, and other information. Hitsquad is a gateway to music software for all the major platforms. Here, you can find links to shareware, freeware, and demos from commercial developers. (See Appendix A for a list of valuable web sites.)

And that brings me to my last point. There's nothing like firsthand experience when testing software. If you want to see how well a plug-in works in your system, download a demo version of the software. Most vendors offer them online. Generally, you'll find two kinds of free demos online: "Trial" versions are fully-functional but work only for a set number of days. If you like the plug-in, you can often purchase an authorization for permanent use of these demos without having to re-install. Other demos are unlimited time, limited function. They may have some features disabled, but still give a general idea of how the plug-in works and sounds. Either way, testing demo software can be both fun and informative. It'll give you a tangible idea of the features you can add to your virtual studio.

—*Guitarist, producer, and journalist Danny Miles spends so much time in the virtual studio that he sometimes feels like the figment of someone else's imagination.*

13

problems on vocal tracks—not something you can do with GarageBand's standard assortment of tools. Second, you may want a plug-in that performs the same function as one in your GarageBand toolkit, but does it with a different sound. Waves and TC Electronic plug-ins, for example, include EQs, compressors, reverbs, delays, and the like—very common effects. But they're valued for their distinctive sounds. The same holds true for software-based synthesizers, samplers, and drum machines. Companies like Native Instruments make a living by creating very detailed and powerful emulations of vintage gear, as well as some sounds you can't find in the hardware world. For many producers, their collection of plug-ins is similar to a collection of traditional instruments.

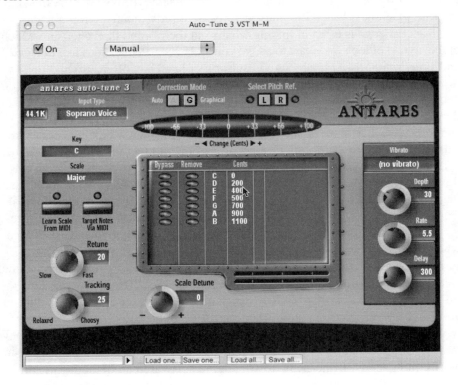

Audio Units

Plug-ins come in a number of formats: Steinberg's VST (Virtual Studio Technology), Mark of the Unicorns' MAS (MOTU Audio System), Digidesign's RTAS (Real Time Audio Suite), and others.

With the development of OS X, Apple created a plug-in format of its own: Audio Units, or AU. AU plug-ins are compatible with GarageBand, Soundtrack, Final Cut Pro and Express, and the Logic series, and are available from a variety of manufacturers.

 CAUTION   *These various formats are not interchangeable and your plug-in's format* must *match that of your host software in order to work.*

Install AU Plug-ins

The nice thing about the AU format is that any plug-ins you install are immediately available to *all* of your AU-compatible programs. When you install a plug-in, it will be copied into the Library/Audio/Plug-ins (Figure 13-8 shows the subfolder Components, which contains AU plug-ins.)

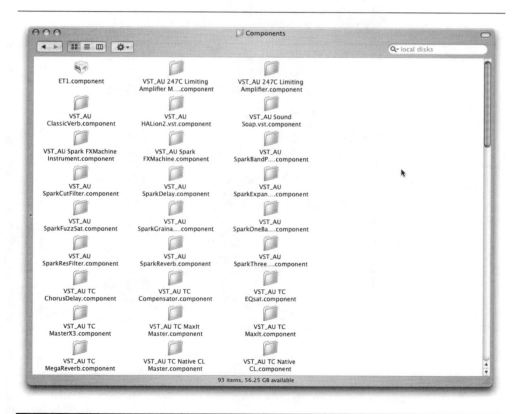

FIGURE 13-8   When you install an AU plug-in, the system puts it into the Library folder, so that it's available to all of your AU-compatible applications.

The installation process is similar to that of any other OS X software. However, as with other audio applications, check that the version of the plug-in that you're installing is compatible with the current version of your operating system.

Access AU Effects Plug-ins

Once you've installed a plug-in—or set of plug-ins—you'll be able to access it from the Additional Effect insert pop-up menus in GarageBand's Track Info and Master Track Inspectors. Figure 13-9 shows a menu full of third-party plug-ins.

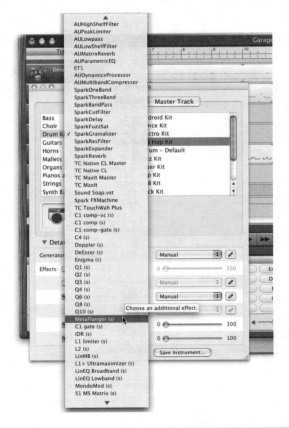

FIGURE 13-9   Flip up the Additional Effect insert pop-up menus to see the AU plug-ins installed on your system.

Select the AU plug-in to add it to your signal chain. In most cases, the plug-in will work just like a standard GarageBand plug-in. You can edit the AU plug-in in the same way in which you edit a standard plug-in—by clicking the Editor button. The plug-in's editor will open, showing its native interface. Figure 13-10 shows a reverb effect by the developer Waves.

NOTE   *See Appendix A for a list of plug-in vendors.*

Access AU Instrument Plug-ins

The AU format can also be used to add to your collection of software instruments. The variety of AU software instruments available is mind boggling—from simple synthesizers, to samplers, to drum machines such as the iDrum (see Figure 13-11), which lets you program a drum pattern with a custom set of samples and play it in sync with GarageBand.

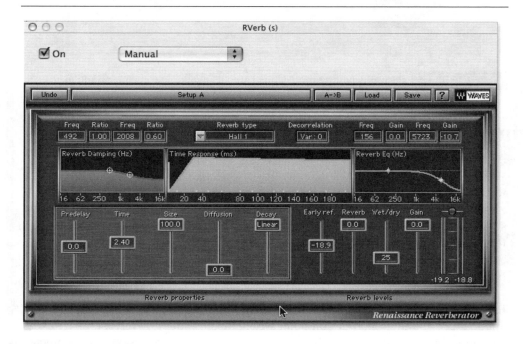

FIGURE 13-10   Waves' famous Renaissance Reverb is available to GarageBand users as a third-party plug-in.

13

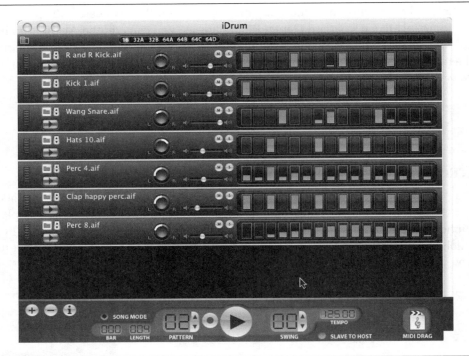

FIGURE 13-11   iDrum is among the AU instruments available to GarageBand users.

Bring Sound into GarageBand via ReWire

NEW IN 1.1   After its initial release, GarageBand became compatible with ReWire, an audio-streaming protocol that lets two applications work together. GarageBand's ReWire implementation has improved greatly with version 1.1

In a "real" recording studio, it's not uncommon to have a wide range of different sound sources operating at the same time. Tape machines, MIDI-controlled sound modules, and effects are all separate units, but all can be blended together with a mixing console and synchronized by special time code so that they run as one big system.

The mixer concept is a little different in a computer environment. In standard form, a piece of software uses its mixer to mix its own tracks, and that's it. Other applications running on your computer would also use their own respective mixers. Not only is this a little unfriendly, but in some cases the application may compete for the use of the audio interface.

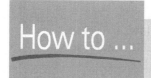

Use VST Plug-ins with an Audio Units Program

VST, the plug-in format developed by Steinberg for its Cubase and Nuendo applications, is the most common plug-in format in current use. It's supported by a wide variety of applications, but not by GarageBand or Apple's other Audio Units apps. Fortunately, thanks to the developer FXpansion, AU users don't have to be left out in the cold.

FXpansion's VST-to-AU adapter (shown next) searches your system for VST effects and creates a link, called a "wrapper," that allows them to appear alongside the AU plug-ins in GarageBand. You can learn more about this handy software at www.fxpansion.com.

VST–AU Adapter Configuration Utility

v1.30.02 – do not distribute – (C) 2002–2004 FXpansion Audio UK Ltd

Detect and convert VST plug-ins

Remove converted VST plug-ins

Options

Create AudioUnits in which library?   ● Global   ○ User

Print extra diagnostics and log to console: ● Off   ○ On

Try to reduce host app load times: ○ Off   ● On

Convert newly installed plugins only: ○ Off   ● On

Scan only local Vstplugins folder: ● Off   ○ On

Status messages:

Beginning scan of Carbon VST plug-ins...
Couldn't find folder (local VSTplugins folder, #1)

Quit

13

Once installed, the VST plug-ins work just like their AU counterparts. You can add them to your project and edit them freely. Both effects and software instruments are supported.

ReWire, which was initially developed by Propellerhead, allows two pieces of software to sync to the same clock and work together in one audio stream, solving this problem. With ReWire, one application acts as the host. The host accepts signal from another piece of software, known as the "slave."

GarageBand works as a ReWire host, which makes it compatible with software such as Propellerhead Reason and Ableton Live. These applications, which are very cool in their own right, can be a powerful addition to your GarageBand setup.

You can learn more about Reason and Live by visiting the companies' respective web sites: www.propellerhead.se and www.ableton.com.

Launch a ReWire Application

GarageBand's ReWire interface is what you might call minimalist—as in invisible. Unlike other ReWire hosts, such as Logic or Steinberg's Cubase, there are no special inputs or tracks for ReWire streaming. To activate a ReWire application, launch GarageBand, then open the ReWire application.

NOTE *You must have GarageBand open before launching the ReWire application. Otherwise, the ReWire application will take possession of the audio interface and run independently.*

Once the ReWire application is open, you can load up the appropriate file (or start a new one). When you play a sound in the ReWire Application, it will be heard through GarageBand's audio outputs.

Synchronize the ReWire Application to GarageBand

GarageBand automatically syncs the ReWire application to match its tempo. When you change tempo in GarageBand, the other application will follow along, and vice versa, although GarageBand does not support multiple tempos in a single song. Playback and other transport functions can be controlled by either program.

Add the ReWire Application to Your GarageBand Mix

GarageBand automatically streams the audio output of the ReWire application to mix with its own sounds. As mentioned above, GarageBand doesn't let you control the ReWire stream with a dedicated channel, as you can on some other applications. To adjust the mix of the ReWire applications relative to your GarageBand tracks, you must use the ReWire app's own volume control.

NOTE *As of version 1.1, GarageBand only supports ReWire's main outputs. You can't stream individual ReWire tracks in GarageBand.*

The Hardware Difference

AU and VST plug-ins are designed to operate in a "native" environment, which means that your computer's own processor is used to run them. Some other plug-in formats, such as Digidesign's TDM format, use separate hardware digital signal processors (or DSPs), which are dedicated to audio processing. The advantage of a system like this is that the effects processing doesn't increase the strain on your computer. Unfortunately, these high-end-systems are pricey and are not available to users of "native" programs like GarageBand.

However, for native plug-in users, there are some hardware solutions available. TC Electronics' PowerCore (shown next) is a VST-compatible DSP plug-in system that offers high-quality signal processors that operate just like other VST plug-ins, except that they run on a special hardware unit instead of your computer's built-in processor. Models are available in PCI or FireWire configurations. You can use PowerCore plug-ins in GarageBand via a VST wrapper, though these plug-ins do sometimes exhibit greater latency than conventional AU effects. Universal Audio's UAD-1 offers similar power in PCI card.

13

Include the ReWire Stream When You Export to iTunes

When you add a ReWire stream to your mix, GarageBand treats it like any other part of the signal path. If you export your mix to iTunes, the ReWire stream will be included. This lets you create some very complex mixes that go way beyond the standard capabilities of GarageBand.

ReWired: Reason and Live at a Glance

Propellerhead Reason and Ableton Live have gained a huge following in the music community in recent years, thanks to the flexibility and speed with which they let you compose and produce music. It's probably not much of a reach to say that these two applications have exerted great influence on music software developers—including the folks who brought you GarageBand. Although both are ReWire applications, each is quite different. Reason and Live are both complex enough to merit books of their own, but here is a quick overview of each.

Reason

Propellerhead Reason (see Figure 13-12) offers a virtual rack full of synthesizers, samplers, drum machines, and effects. Among its modules are analog synthesizers, old-style step sequencers, strange digital synths, and a loop player called Dr. Rex that can play specially encoded audio loops at various tempos. Reason does not offer any audio tracks of its own, but focuses instead on software instruments. You play these with a MIDI controller and record your performance into Reason's internal sequencer (similar to GarageBand's own software instrument tracks), or you can use some of Reason's pattern-based "hardware" drum and sequencer modules to program parts manually. One of the most fun aspects of the program is its virtual patchbay, with which you can cable different modules together in all kinds of creative ways.

Live

Ableton Live (see Figure 13-13) is a bit like GarageBand in that it can work with encoded audio loops and match them to a song's tempo. However, Live has some other very unique features, the most important being its ability to trigger audio loops—either individually or in groups—with a command from your QWERTY keyboard or MIDI controller. This ability to "play" audio makes Live a very powerful tool for remixing, DJing, and other electronic music pursuits.

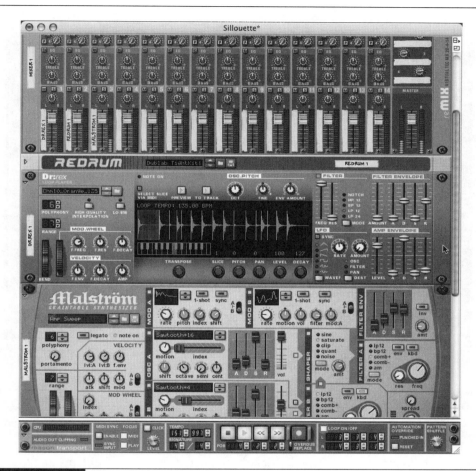

| FIGURE 13-12 | Propellerhead Reason |

Work with Audio Editing Software

GarageBand lets you edit an audio file's regions in its timeline and editor windows, but it's not designed to do anything to the audio file itself. Most of the time, that's not a problem. But there are times when you may need to get down "inside" the audio file and perform edits that are beyond GarageBand's reach.

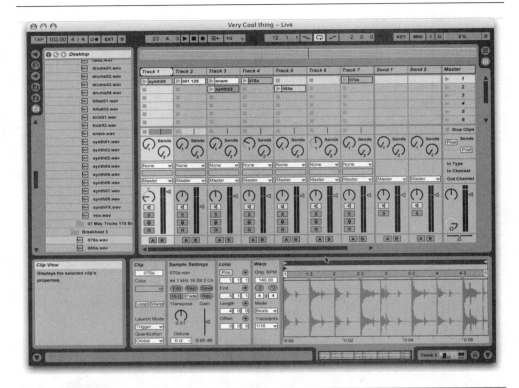

FIGURE 13-13 Ableton Live

A dedicated audio editor program like BIAS Peak (see Figure 13-14) lets you work with your file in very precise detail. You can use it to fix problems and to enhance the sound.

Open a File in the Two-Track Editor

When you record an audio file into GarageBand, the program puts it into a special package file, which means that the audio files are not immediately visible on your desktop. To access the individual files, first navigate to the project package file. CONTROL-click on the package and choose Reveal Package Contents (see Figure 13-15).

When you locate the audio file you want to work with, CONTROL-click it and choose your audio editor from the Open With menu. You can also open the file by dragging onto the audio editor's icon.

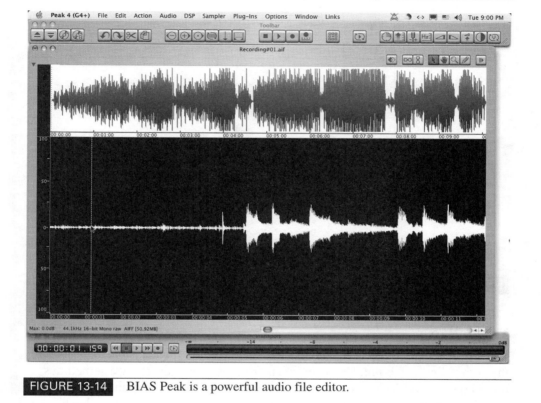

FIGURE 13-14 BIAS Peak is a powerful audio file editor.

CAUTION *Don't double-click the file: doing so will open it in GarageBand.*

Work with the File in the Audio Editor

An audio editor such as Peak gives you a wide range of tools with which to work. You can edit an entire audio file, or only a small part of the file. As you can see in Figure 13-17, the display is similar to that of the editor window in GarageBand. The file is depicted as a waveform. To select a portion of the file, drag the mouse over the waveform, as shown in Figure 13-16.

Peak is a powerful program, and it can do a lot of different things to your audio file. We won't even attempt to cover them here, but we should take a look at some of the most common ways to use Peak to enhance your GarageBand audio files.

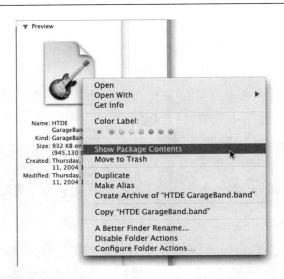

FIGURE 13-15 Use CONTROL-click to reveal the contents of a GarageBand song's package file.

Normalize

In a well-recorded digital audio file, the loudest parts of the signal come to just below the zero "clipping" point. However, in an effort to avoid "overs," we sometimes record our audio files at too low a level. Peak's Normalize command analyzes the selected part of an audio file (or the entire file if you "select all") and adjusts it so that its peak reaches a preset level. All the rest of the audio selected area gets raised along with it, but the relative difference between loud and soft remains. Normalize is great because it lets you make your file louder without having to worry about making it clip.

Silence

When you record a file with lots of spaces between musical passages, the ambient noise that fills those spaces can sometimes be distracting. The classic example is the vocal track, in which "spill" from the headphones can be heard every time the singer rests. GarageBand lets you edit these spaces out, but its grid settings may not always allow you the utmost flexibility in dealing with noise. You can select the offending areas in Peak and silence them completely.

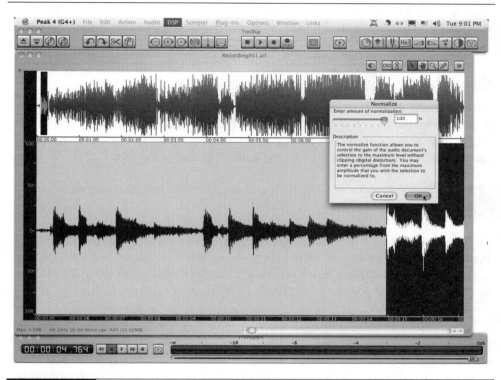

FIGURE 13-16   Drag the mouse to select part of the waveform.

Fade In and Fade Out

In Chapter 10, we discussed the way to create fades with GarageBand's envelope curves. But sometimes, you may need to use a fade on the file itself to eliminate a noise (such as a click or a pop), or simply to create an audio effect. Peak lets you select a portion of the file and apply a fade to it. This fade will then become a permanent part of the file's sound.

Add Effects

GarageBand lets you add effects in "real time" as your tracks play back. But there are also situations when you might want an effect to be built into an audio file. For example, if you have a bass loop, you might want to add compression permanently, thereby freeing up GarageBand's system resources for other effects. Peak lets you process a file—or portion of a file—through effects processors and will "write" the effect so that it becomes a permanent part of the file.

13

 *Here's a cool trick. Take a drum loop and select the parts of the loop where the snare plays. Add reverb to the snare hits and save the file. The snare hits will now stand out from the rest of the loop.*

Save the File and Use It in GarageBand

After you edit a file in Peak (or other audio editor), you can save it and reintroduce it into GarageBand. The simplest way is to save the file to its original location. This will overwrite the old file. When you next launch the song in GarageBand, the program will automatically load up the edited version of the file.

 *If you overwrite the original version of the file, any edits you make are permanent and can't be undone.*

The other option is to save a copy of the file to a new location, and then replace the original in the timeline with the copy. While this involves an extra step, it does allow you to give the file a descriptive name, and also gives you the ability to fall back on the original version of the file if the edits aren't to your liking.

CAUTION *Audio editors can do more than simply process an existing audio file. They can completely alter the file's structure. While this is a useful feature, you need to be careful when working with GarageBand files, and especially with Apple Loops. You can, for example, trim the file to remove a portion of the audio—a common way to reduce noise. However, if you do this to an Apple Loop, you can cause the file to play out of sync: its length will have changed, and GarageBand won't know how to handle that. If you do anything that affects the file's length, save the edited version as a separate copy. You may also want to retag the file in the Loop Utility.*

Add Standard MIDI Files to Your GarageBand Project

The audio applications we've mentioned are just a fraction of the music software you'll find, both from commercial sources and from shareware and freeware developers. One of the most useful is a piece of freeware called Dent du Midi by Bery Rinaldo (see Figure 13-17) (http://homepage.mac.com/beryrinaldo/ddm/).

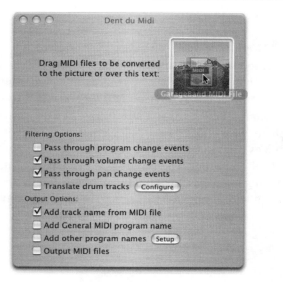

GarageBand MIDI File

FIGURE 13-17   Dent du Midi lets you convert a standard MIDI file into a software instrument loop.

Dent du Midi can convert a standard MIDI file into a GarageBand-compatible AIFF that contains MIDI data. This file can be dragged into the timeline like any other software instrument loop (see Figure 13-18).

The new loop can be assigned to any instrument and edited just as you would a standard GarageBand Software Instrument loop.

13

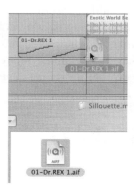

FIGURE 13-18   The standard MIDI file works much like any other software instrument loop.

Play GarageBand Without an External Controller

You've got GarageBand installed on your PowerBook, and you're sitting in a train, plane, automobile, or cafe when inspiration strikes. You rev up GarageBand and then you realize that there's a problem: You have no MIDI controller. You could use the mouse and GarageBand's keyboard to enter notes, but this can get awkward and is not very effective for chords. Fortunately, there's a piece of freeware by Chris Reed called Midi Keys (shown next) that lets you use your computer's QWERTY keyboard as a MIDI controller. The program is available online in Beta form, and though it's not as elegant as having a hardware controller, it does work pretty well in a pinch. You can learn more about it at www.manyetas.com/creed/ midikeys_beta.html.

Once you download the program, all you need to do is launch it and route it to GarageBand by selecting Virtual source in the Destination pop-up. In GarageBand, open and select a software instrument track, then switch over to Midi Keys, and play your computer's keyboard. You should hear some sound coming through GarageBand, If you plan to record, I recommend doing so with count-in, or better, the cycle activated. This will give you time to switch over to Midi Keys and start jamming. It can be a bit awkward, compared to a standard hardware controller, but it works well enough to get that idea down before it fades away.

 *Be sure you're in Midi Keys before you start playing the keyboard: many of the letter keys activate commands in GarageBand; you may, for example, inadvertently toggle the mute, solo, or cycle status or put your song into record prematurely.*

Moving On

The programs we discussed are just of the few of the applications you can use alongside GarageBand. For example, you can export your mixes and load them into iMovie to use as a soundtrack to your digital video. You can share your GarageBand loops with Soundtrack users and vice versa. You can create complex sequences in Logic and export them as standard MIDI files, which you can convert and load into GarageBand. The Internet is a great source of information on the ever-changing world of audio software. See Appendix A for some useful online resources.

13

Chapter 14

Tech Tips and Troubleshooting

How to…

- Troubleshoot audio connection problems
- Troubleshoot MIDI connection problems
- Troubleshoot playback and recording problems
- Prevent problems from happening

A computer-based recording studio is a powerful tool, and it can sometimes feel like magic when you boot up a machine that is more closely associated with spreadsheets and word processors and use it to kick out the jams. But the magic can wear off pretty quickly when something goes wrong.

A recording studio—even one dressed up in a cute and friendly package like GarageBand—is a complex ecosystem. Every part has a role to play. You might have a great computer, interface, and collection of plug-ins, but a simple audio cable can derail your best laid plans.

This chapter shows you how to troubleshoot the problems you're most likely to run into with GarageBand: audio connection problems, MIDI connection problems, and playback and recording problems. The chapter also gives you tips on getting your Mac into the best possible shape for running GarageBand as well as it can.

Troubleshoot Audio Connection Problems

A recording studio, like any chain involving different parts, is only as good as its weakest link. A bad audio cable—or a bad connector between audio cable and your computer—can cause signal loss that results in distortion, weak tone, or even silence.

Both analog and digital audio connections can give you plenty of grief if you don't set them up correctly. This section offers you suggestions for dealing with common problems.

> **TIP** *If you have the choice, choose balanced connections over unbalanced connections, because they'll usually give you better results. See the section "It's All About Connections" in Chapter 7 for details on balanced and unbalanced connections.*

Before You Panic: Audio

■ Make sure the audio source (the signal you're recording into GarageBand) is powered on and connected to your audio interface.

■ Make sure that the audio interface is powered on and connected to the computer.

■ If you're using a hub between the interface and computer, make sure it's on and properly connected.

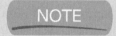 *The use of a USB hub between interface and computer is generally not recommended.*

No Sound from Input

Check that the cables are firmly connected in the right places. Unplugging and replugging a cable can often solve a problem.

 *If your setup includes more than a few cables, label all your cables at both ends (I like color coding myself, but text is just as effective). Few things are more irritating than troubleshooting your whole setup only to find you'd pulled the wrong cable in the first place.*

Still no sound? Check that you're using the right kinds of cable. After that, check that the cable isn't defective. The easiest way to check is to swap in a cable that you know to be working.

Still no sound? Check that you haven't connected an analog source to a digital input, or vice versa. Either is a good recipe for continued silence.

 *As discussed in Chapter 7, digital inputs are designed to receive a digital signal. To connect an analog source to a digital input, you must use an analog-to-digital (A/D) converter.*

Still no sound? Check your input settings in Sound preferences (go to the Apple menu and click System Preferences, click Sound, and click the Input tab) or the Default Input on the Audio Devices tab in Audio MIDI Setup (in Applications/Utilities).

14

Then switch to GarageBand, display Audio/MIDI preferences, and check the Audio Input pop-up to make sure GarageBand is using the right device.

 *Problems can also occur if another application has taken over control of your audio interface. Some audio drivers can only deal with one application at a time. If you're not hearing GarageBand, but are hearing the other applications, quit all audio applications and restart GarageBand. In some cases, you may need to log out, or restart your computer, to regain control of the interface.*

Interrupted or Partial Sound

If the sound is interrupted (it comes through only some of the time) or partial (only some frequencies come through), you've probably got a loose connection, a damaged or dirty connector, or a damaged cable. First, check that each connection is tight; plug and unplug the cable to clean the connection; failing that, swap in another cable and see if that fixes the problem.

Distorted Sound

Unless you're talking about the intentional fuzz and overdrive sounds that you might use to give your music an edge, distortion is generally not a good thing. Digital distortion, or clipping, is usually the result of too hot a level on input. This can be caused by the following.

Output Too Hot for Input

All audio devices are designed to have a nominal output level. Most of the gear you'd find in a professional studio are designed to operate at +4dB—which is considered "hot" (or loud). Consumer devices tend to run at a lower level: –10dB. If you feed a +4dB device to a –10dB input, you may end up overloading the input. You can compensate by lowering the output volume of the +4dB device and/or lowering the input level if the –10dB device

Levels Set Too High

Even if the devices match in level, it's possible to get distortion if your levels are set too high. For example, if you're using a mic in front of a loud guitar amp, the signal coming back might be too hot for your audio interface, and, therefore, GarageBand. Lower the input level of the interface first; if the signal is still too hot, lower the level of the source (in this case, turn down the amp), or move the mic back a bit (doing so may affect the tone). If the microphone has a built-in pad—a switch used to reduce the mic's level—you could engage that as well.

Distortion can occur before the signal gets to GarageBand. If you're using outboard gear such as mixers, preamps, or effects, make sure that their levels are set correctly so that they're not overloaded.

Sound Too Quiet

If the sound is too quiet, your signal is too low for the input you're using. Again, check that it's the right kind of signal for the input: Check that you haven't plugged a microphone into an instrument-level or line-level input rather than a mic input. Likewise, check that any instrument that needs amplification to bring it up to line level is routed through a preamp.

If all's well on that front, increase the output level on the instrument to boost the signal.

No Sound from Output

If you appear to be getting no output from GarageBand, display the Audio/MIDI preferences (open the GarageBand menu and choose Preferences, and click Audio/MIDI) and check the setting in the Audio Output pop-up. If it's right, check that you haven't muted the output volume on your Mac or on the external audio interface. Also check that you haven't confused your analog and digital outputs.

Latency When Recording Real Instruments

To minimize the latency when recording real instruments, display the Audio/MIDI preferences and select the Minimum Delay When Playing Instruments Live option button rather than the Maximum Number of Simultaneous Tracks option button in the Optimize For area.

In GarageBand 1.0, the Optimize For option buttons had different names. The Maximum Number of Simultaneous Tracks option button was named Better Performance, and the Minimum Delay When Playing Instruments Live option button was named Faster Response. If you're still seeing the old names, you should update to the latest version of GarageBand.

Troubleshoot MIDI Connection Problems

MIDI is pretty cool: it lets you operate a range of devices with a controller, and lets you record and edit your music in precise detail. But when MIDI goes wrong, it can be pretty vexing to troubleshoot. Problem areas can include connections, interfaces, and drivers.

Before You Panic

- Make sure your MIDI controller is powered up and connected to the interface.

- Make sure that the interface is powered up and connected to the computer.

- If you're using a hub between the interface and computer, make sure it's on and properly connected.

- If possible, test MIDI setup with another device or software.

- Log out or restart your computer.

GarageBand Doesn't Recognize a MIDI Device

GarageBand recognizes some USB MIDI keyboards straight out of the box without your needing to install a driver. For example, you can plug in the Apple-recommended M-Audio KeyStation 49e and start playing without further ado. For other MIDI keyboards, and for most MIDI interfaces, you'll need to install a driver. If in doubt, consult the manufacturer's documentation or web site to find out if your MIDI device needs a driver.

The easiest way to check that GarageBand recognizes a MIDI keyboard is to play a few notes on it. Select a software instrument track in GarageBand and strike a few keys. You should hear the associated notes or sounds, and the MIDI status light to the left of the tempo readout should flash at each key struck.

If the MIDI status light doesn't flash, check that the keyboard is connected to your Mac and is powered on. Then open Audio/MIDI preferences (open the GarageBand menu and choose Preferences, and click Audio/MIDI) and check that the MIDI Status readout shows a MIDI input.

If the MIDI Status readout shows "0 MIDI Input(s) Detected," try unplugging the keyboard and then plugging it back in.

TIP *If you're using a stand-alone controller that's connected to your interface via MIDI cables, make sure the problem is not there by playing the controller and watching the interface's status lights.*

MIDI Device Stops Working

If the MIDI device was working before but has now stopped working, follow as many of these steps as necessary:

1. Unplug the MIDI device, and then plug it back in.

2. Restart GarageBand.

3. Restart Mac OS X.

4. Reinstall the driver for the audio device.

If you plug in a MIDI device when GarageBand is running, GarageBand may get confused about which device you want to use. If this happens, GarageBand displays the Audio Device Added dialog box (shown here), suggesting that you quit GarageBand and select the device you want to use. Click Quit, and GarageBand will prompt you to save any unsaved changes to the song you're working on. Then restart GarageBand.

MIDI Keyboard Plays the Wrong Software Instrument

On a Mac that has Fast User Switching enabled, you may find your MIDI keyboard plays a software instrument other than the one you've selected. This can happen when another user has GarageBand open in their user session on your Mac. You may get the software instrument that they've selected rather than the one you've selected.

To fix this problem, have the other user log in and quit GarageBand, then log back in to your account. To prevent this problem from happening in the future, turn off Fast User Switching (see "Turn Off Fast User Switching," later in this chapter). GarageBand is such a demanding application that running two or more sessions of it at the same time is a recipe for poor performance.

"Error While Trying to Synchronize Audio and MIDI" Message

You may see this error message if you plug an audio device into, or unplug it from, your Mac's audio input port while GarageBand is playing back audio. Dismiss the message box, click the Play button or press SPACEBAR to stop playback, and then click or press again to start it once more.

This is essentially a "don't *do* that, then" error message: to avoid producing the error, don't plug or unplug audio devices during playback.

"Phased" Signal on a Real Instrument Track

If you hear a strange sound on a real instrument track—sort of a thinner, swishier version of the sound you were expecting—chances are that you've turned on Play Through in Audio MIDI Setup *and* turned on monitoring in GarageBand. This produces a "phased" signal: You're asking your Mac or audio interface to play the same signal twice, but with different latency, and the delay between the two causes some of the sound waves to cancel each other out. (Actually, this short delay is the basis of the flanger effect).

To stop this from happening, open Audio MIDI Setup (in the Applications/Utilities folder), select the device on the Audio Device tab, and clear the appropriate check boxes in the Thru column.

GarageBand Starts Using a Different MIDI Device

If GarageBand starts using a different MIDI device for input or output than the device you specified, it usually means that your device has become disconnected or turned off. Reconnect the device (or switch it on again), make sure Audio MIDI Setup recognizes it, and restart GarageBand if necessary.

Audio MIDI Setup Doesn't Show Your MIDI Interface

If Audio MIDI Setup doesn't show your MIDI interface, click the Rescan MIDI button (or choose MIDI Devices | Rescan MIDI System) to force it to rescan the system. Failing that, check that the MIDI interface is connected properly to your Mac and turned on, and that you've installed any drivers it needs.

Troubleshoot Playback and Recording Problems

With your audio connections and MIDI all working, you're ready to deal with playback and recording problems.

Troubleshoot Noise or Distortion During Playback

Noise or distortion during playback usually means that *clipping* is occurring. In lay terms, clipping is what happens when you try to put too loud a signal through a playback device. You can deal with this clipping in the following ways:

■ If clipping is occurring throughout the song, turn down the output volume on the song as a whole.

- If one track is causing the problem, turn its volume down. If just parts of the track are guilty, create a custom volume curve (see Chapters 9 and 10) to lower the volume of those parts below the clipping threshold.

- Reduce the number of effects on the track.

- Re-record parts of the track at a lower volume.

Clipping can also occur when you're recording a Real Instrument and you've turned up the track volume level too high for the output level of the instrument. You'll be able to guess the ways of avoiding this type of clipping: Check the output level of the instrument before recording. Play the loudest passage (or scream into your microphone) and set the output level of the instrument or audio interface accordingly.

Once you've recorded a Real Instrument at a high enough volume to cause clipping, there's not much you can do about the results beyond deleting the offending passages and re-recording them.

Noisy "Silences"

If your tracks suffer from noise on their quieter or silent passages, use the Gate effect to remove it. Solo the track, open the Track Info Inspector, apply the gate, play the track, and drag the Gate slider to a level that removes the noise from the quieter passages but doesn't affect the remaining passages.

TIP *You can also cut out "silent" passages manually by editing them in the timeline or editor. Refer to Chapter 8.*

GarageBand Hangs

If you ask GarageBand to bite off more than it can chew, it's apt to hang. If it senses doom in the air, GarageBand may cough up a complaining message, such as those discussed in the next section, but often you'll just see the Spinning Beachball Of Death (SBOD) and hear either short or sustained interruptions to the audio as GarageBand struggles to cope.

The best thing to do when GarageBand hangs like this is to give it time and see if it can recover. Watching GarageBand struggle through the rest of your song, punctuating what little music it manages to play back with bursts of static, is not much fun. So get up and walk away from your Mac for a few minutes. Play an ancestral lament on your guitar, pound out an intricate tattoo on your drums, or just go and get some liquid refreshment. When you return, you should feel happier, even if GarageBand doesn't.

14

If GarageBand is still stuck, but the SBOD has disappeared, it's time to force quit. (Unfortunately, you'll lose any unsaved changes.) OPTION-click the GarageBand icon on the Dock and choose Force Quit from the menu. Alternatively, go to the Apple Menu and click Force Quit to display the Force Quit Applications dialog box, select GarageBand, and click Force Quit.

You can also press COMMAND-OPTION-ESCAPE to open the Force Quit dialog box.

"System Overload" or "Disk Too Slow"

If GarageBand detects that it can't keep pace with your song before it's overwhelmed, it displays a message such as the following:

- "System overload"

- "Disk is too slow"

- "The hard disk is not fast enough to deliver all audio data in time. Try muting some tracks."

- "Part of the song was not played. This song has too many tracks, effects, or notes to be played in real-time." (There are several versions of this message that mention different specific offenders—for example, "too many real instrument tracks.")

Apple has changed the wording of some of these errors in the different versions of GarageBand so far, but the message remains clear: You're overdoing things. Reduce the number of tracks or voices (as discussed earlier in this chapter), or free up resources on your Mac, as discussed later in this chapter.

 *If GarageBand starts balking at a song that it used to be able to play, quit GarageBand and restart it. If that doesn't improve matters, quit as many other applications you're running as possible. Restart your Mac if necessary.*

Pops, Clicks, and Dropouts on Playback

Pops and clicks when GarageBand is playing music typically indicate that your Mac's processor is overloaded. You might miss the occasional pop or click, but the next stage of overload is marked by large sections of the audio dropping out, which is hard to miss. GarageBand may also beep in embarrassment and stop playing the song.

Again, reduce the demands of your song (as discussed earlier in this chapter), or free up resources on your Mac, as discussed in the upcoming section "Reduce GarageBand's Demands on Your Mac."

Reduce GarageBand's Demands on Your Mac

If GarageBand is overloading your Mac, you can improve performance by reducing GarageBand's demands as far as possible (as discussed in this section) and improving your Mac's performance (as discussed in "Computer Issues," later in this chapter).

Optimize GarageBand for Playback

As you saw in "Latency when Recording Real Instruments," earlier in this chapter, you'll typically want to minimize latency when you're recording Real Instruments. To do so, select the Minimum Delay When Playing Instruments Live option button in GarageBand's Audio/MIDI Preferences. But when you want GarageBand to play back as many tracks as possible without choking, you need to select the Maximum Number of Simultaneous Tracks option button in Audio/MIDI preferences to increase the buffer size and improve playback.

Reduce the Number of Tracks and Voices

Next, reduce the number of tracks and voices GarageBand is using. Open Advanced preferences and open the Real Instrument Tracks pop-up, the Software Instrument Tracks pop-up, and the Voices per Instrument pop-up. (See "Advanced Preferences" in Chapter 3 for more details on these settings.) Remember, every note you play in a Software Instrument at one time is one voice. If you're mostly playing single-line parts and sparse chords, you can get away with a lower setting without having to make musical compromises.

14

Reduce the Number of Effects

As you've read earlier in this book, effects can demand a large amount of processing power. If GarageBand is struggling to play a song, see if removing some of your less essential effects makes a difference.

Delete Silent Sections from Real Instrument Tracks

Delete any silent sections from your real instrument tracks to reduce the amount of data that GarageBand has to process. Double-click the real instrument track you want to affect so that GarageBand displays it in the editor, and then select each section you want to remove, and choose Edit | Delete or press DELETE.

 *You can also do this in the timeline by using the Edit | Split command (COMMAND-T). Split the region on either side of the area you want to remove.*

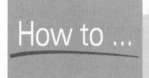 **Monitor GarageBand's Demands on Your Mac**

The easiest way to get a rough idea of how heavily GarageBand is using your Mac's processor is to watch the color of the Playhead. When GarageBand is resting, or when it's playing music comfortably within the capability of the processor, the Playhead is white. When the processor starts working hard, GarageBand turns the Playhead yellow and then orange; and when the processor starts to overload, GarageBand turns the Playhead red. By checking the Playhead's color periodically, you can see whether your Mac is within its comfort zone or whether it's struggling.

For more detail on how your Mac is coping with GarageBand, the other applications you're running, and Mac OS X and its services, run your Mac's Activity Monitor application. This utility can give you a continuous update on your Mac's resources, and it can display them in the Dock. To activate it, click the Finder button on the Dock, choose Go | Utilities, and double-click the Activity Monitor icon.

 *You can open the Utilities Folder from the Finder by pressing COMMAND-SHIFT-U.*

In the Activity Monitor, select the My Processes item in the Show pop-up to restrict the display to the processes started by your user session, thus excluding processes used by the system and by other users. Click the %CPU column heading once or twice (as necessary) to sort processes by CPU usage in descending order.

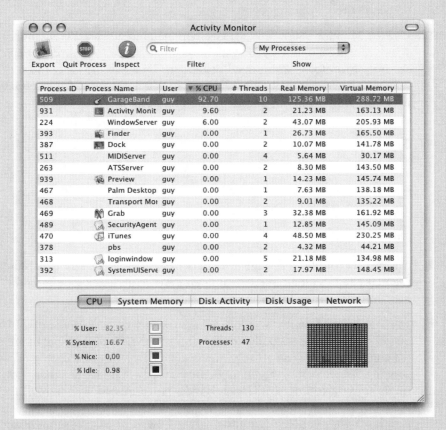

The key commands for Activity Monitor are on the Monitor menu:

■ Use the Monitor | Dock Icon submenu to specify what to display for the Activity Monitor's Dock icon: the application icon, the CPU usage, the CPU history, the network usage, the disk activity, or memory usage. The CPU history is perhaps the most useful for GarageBand, because you can see several seconds' worth of processor usage easily.

■ Use the Monitor | Update Frequency submenu to specify the frequency of updates: 0.5 second, 1 second, 2 seconds, or 5 seconds. More frequent updates give you a more precise picture of what's happening, but they consume more system resources.

■ Use the Monitor | Show CPU Usage command to display a CPU monitor window, which enables you to monitor processor activity even when Activity Monitor is minimized or hidden. To make the CPU monitor window appear on top of other windows so that it's always visible, choose Monitor | Show CPU monitors on top of other windows.

■ You can also display a floating readout of the CPU activity. From the Monitor menu, open the Floating CPU submenu. You can display the monitor horizontally, vertically, or not at all.

■ In the Activity Monitor window, you can see what percentage of CPU power GarageBand is taking and how much memory and virtual memory it's consuming. You can also see how much of each resource each process is using, which can help you to identify greedy applications that you might turn off to improve GarageBand's performance. Inevitably, Activity Monitor takes some processing power and memory to run, so turn it off after you've used it to analyze how your Mac is running and what improvements you might make.

Simplify the GarageBand Window

If all you want to do is hear your full set of tracks without any of them dropping out, you can give GarageBand a better chance of playing them by reducing the complexity of its window:

■ If the editor is displayed, hide it by pressing COMMAND-E or choosing Control | Hide Editor.

- If the track mixer is displayed, hide it by pressing COMMAND-Y or choosing Track | Hide Track Mixer.

- Minimize the GarageBand window so that Mac OS X doesn't have to update it at all.

- Simplify the way the timeline scrolls on playback by clicking the Timeline Lock button, located at the bottom right-hand corner of the timeline.

Bounce Several Tracks Down to a Single Track

The more tracks you add to a song, the more the performance demands on your processor stack up. One way to reduce the number of tracks in a song is by "bouncing" several tracks down to a single track.

 *We discussed bouncing as a creative tool in Chapters 9 and 10.*

Computer Issues

Even if you pass through life largely untainted by cynicism, you might be forgiven for concluding that iLife '04 is designed to force you to buy a G5 Mac. As in earlier versions of iLife, iTunes and iPhoto deftly encourage you to stuff your hard disk with the music you own and the pictures you take—after which, consuming your last remaining gigabytes is the work of a few minutes' importing video from your DV camcorder with iMovie. iDVD has removed your last excuse for not buying a SuperDrive (but at least you can use that SuperDrive to archive large chunks of older data and reclaim hard disk space). And now along comes GarageBand to consume every last processor cycle your Mac can offer!

If you have that G5 already, you're sitting pretty for using GarageBand (but you're probably chafing to buy one of the faster dual-G5s that Apple is rolling out). If you're still with the G4 or G3 generation, this chapter shows you how to make the most of what you've got.

Processor Issues

GarageBand demands a huge amount of processing power, especially for producing Software Instruments and applying effects. If your Mac can't offer enough processor cycles for what you're trying to do in GarageBand, performance will suffer, as described earlier in this chapter.

14

You can deal with this problem in four ways: by reducing GarageBand's gluttony (as discussed earlier in this chapter), by making sure as many processor cycles as possible are available to GarageBand, by upgrading your Mac's processor (on some Macs only), or by buying a new Mac.

Make Processor Cycles Available

There's not much to say here beyond the obvious:

- To make as many processor cycles as possible available to GarageBand, run as few other applications and services as possible when you're using GarageBand.

- If you're using GarageBand on a PowerBook or iBook, make sure you've selected the Highest setting in the Processor Performance pop-up on the Options tab of the Energy Saver sheet in System Preferences. Using the Reduced setting gives GarageBand exactly the kind of hit you don't need.

Upgrade Your Processor

If you feel that your Mac is underpowered in the processor department, you may be able to upgrade to a faster and more modern CPU. At this writing, you can upgrade various desktop Macs (for example, G3 and G4 PowerMacs) and some G3 PowerBooks (such as the Lombard and Pismo PowerBooks). You'll find good advice on processor upgrades at Mac sites such as MacSpeedZone (www.macspeedzone.com) and MacWorld (www.macworld.com) and at manufacturers' sites such as Daystar Technology (www.xlr8.com), Sonnet Technologies (www.sonnettech.com), and PowerLogix (www.powerlogix.com).

The main problem with processor upgrades is that they're too expensive to make financial sense unless you've already performed other upgrades on your Mac. For example, say you have a G3 PowerBook. You can give it a G4-level processor for $250 to $300, but you'll probably need a bigger hard drive ($150 to $250) and more RAM ($80 to $200) as well, which starts to bring you into the zone of a discounted new iBook. So with hardware prices continuing to fall, the processor upgrade typically makes sense only if you've already given your Mac the other upgrades, leaving only the processor lagging.

RAM Issues

As you learned in Chapter 2, GarageBand requires 256MB of RAM, but it's a better idea to have much more memory—at least 512MB for casual use of GarageBand, and 1GB for serious use. Having more RAM than that—recent PowerBooks can hold 2GB, and G5 PowerMacs can hold up to 8GB—will do you no harm except for putting a dent in your bank balance.

Add RAM

Memory is one of the easiest upgrades to most Macs, provided that your Mac has one or more memory slots free and that you get exactly the right type of RAM that your specific model requires. Check your Mac's manual or the Apple Support site (www.apple.com/support) for details of the memory needed and how to install it.

When buying a new Mac, either load it up with RAM straight off the bat or leave one or more memory slots free so that you can add memory easily later. For example, say you're buying a G4 PowerBook, which has two memory slots, and you decide to get 512MB RAM. It's much better to get a 512MB chip in one memory slot and keep the other slot free for expansion than to get two 256MB chips and have no room for expansion without discarding a chip. This approach is also more expensive in the short term (because high-capacity chips are proportionally more expensive than lower-capacity chips), but it will save you money in the long term.

Give GarageBand as Much RAM as Possible

Having plenty of RAM is great, but if you use your Mac extensively, the applications and system processes will be queuing up to consume the RAM like children around a freshly split piñata. To get the best performance from GarageBand, give it as much RAM as possible, as discussed in the following subsections.

Quit Any Applications You're Not Using   Other applications can compete for RAM with GarageBand. If GarageBand bogs down, quit all unnecessary programs.

Turn Off Services You Don't Need   Next, turn off any services that you don't need. Common candidates for the ax are network services that your Mac is providing to other computers on your network (go to the [Apple] menu, click System Preferences, click Sharing, and then work on the Services tab).

Turn Off Fast User Switching   GarageBand is greedy for memory, but other users' sessions can be even greedier. To get the best performance with GarageBand, ensure that no other user session is running in the background when you're using GarageBand. You can take care of this for sure by switching off Fast User Switching:

1.   Go to the Apple menu and click System Preferences.

2.   Click Accounts.

14

3. Click Login Options.

4. Clear the Enable Fast User Switching check box.

5. Choose System Preferences | Quit System Preferences to close System Preferences.

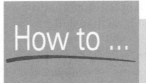 **Check How Much RAM You Have**

If you're not sure how much RAM your Mac has, check by choosing [Apple] | About This Mac. The Memory readout in the About This Mac dialog box shows the total amount of RAM installed.

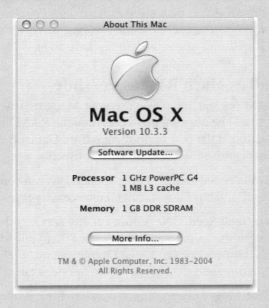

To learn the configuration of the memory, click the More Info button to launch System Profiler. In the Contents pane, expand the Hardware section by clicking its gray triangle if it's collapsed, and then click the Memory item. The resulting readout shows the size, type, and speed of memory chip installed in each memory slot.

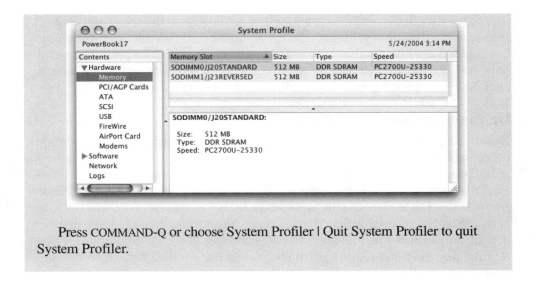

Press COMMAND-Q or choose System Profiler | Quit System Profiler to quit System Profiler.

Disconnect from the Network   These days, more and more applications assume you'll have an Internet connection whenever they want it. But with GarageBand, you can usually work more effectively when disconnected from the network. You'll probably benefit from the lack of distractions, and your Mac won't have to expend the resources of maintaining and monitoring your network connection.

Disconnect Unnecessary Hardware   You can further reduce demands on your Mac by temporarily disconnecting from your Mac any hardware you don't need for working in GarageBand: your Palm, your iPod, your scanner, your printer, and so on.

Maintain Your Hard Drive

After your processor and RAM, the next most important component of your Mac for GarageBand is its hard drive. You'll need several gigabytes of free space for installing GarageBand itself, the loops that come with it, and the Jam Pack or such other loops as you add. You'll also need space to store the songs you create. In particular, the real instrument tracks you record by playing a physical instrument take up a considerable amount of space.

Keep Your Songs Out of FileVault

Mac OS X's FileVault feature encrypts your home folder and all its contents so that they're protected from snooping at any time you're not logged in. (When you're

14

logged in, your folders are decrypted.) FileVault decreases the speed at which your Mac can read data from your home folder. So if you use FileVault, store your songs in a folder outside your home folder so that you don't suffer this performance hit. (Alternatively, turn off FileVault: go to the Apple menu and click System Preferences, click Security, click Turn Off FileVault, and follow the instructions.)

Defragment Your Hard Drive

Historically, computer users have needed to defragment their hard drives to improve performance (or, more accurately, to prevent performance from deteriorating further). A hard drive is divided up into physical *sectors* that are mapped into logical *clusters*. Each file larger than the cluster size is saved in multiple clusters. If contiguous clusters are free, Mac OS X saves the file in them; otherwise, it must use clusters in different parts of the disk. Files distributed in far-flung clusters take longer for the disk head to read, thus reducing performance. Files that are spread out like this are *fragmented*. Rearranging the files so that they're less spread out is called *defragmenting* or (sometimes) *optimizing*.

Apple says that "You probably won't need to optimize at all if you use Mac OS X" because present-day hard drives have higher capacities; Mac OS X's delayed-allocation capability helps keep files together, as does its Hot File Adaptive Clustering (don't laugh); many applications rewrite files each time they save them rather than appending data to the existing file; and hard drives use read-ahead and write-behind caching to reduce the impact of fragmentation on performance.

Apple doesn't include a defragmentation utility with Mac OS X, so you need to buy a third-party utility (such as Plus Optimizer or Norton Utilities Speed Disk) if you want to defragment your hard disk.

Reduce Startup Items

To lighten the load on your Mac, consider reducing the number of items Mac OS X opens each time you log in. Open the [Apple] menu and click System Preferences, click Accounts, select your account, and then click the Startup Items tab to see what's running. Remove any items that you can do without in your pursuit of performance.

Eliminate Avoidable Noise

By this point, things should be looking pretty good. You've figured out how to reduce GarageBand's demands to a level that your Mac can handle, and you've streamlined your Mac OS X setup to give GarageBand the most processor cycles and RAM possible. You may also have enhanced your Mac with extra RAM or an additional high-speed hard disk.

So far, so good. But you can still wreck your recordings by picking up noise on your real instrument recordings. Here are brief tips for eliminating avoidable noise:

- When recording stringed instruments or anything miked, keep them away from your Mac and your monitor so that they don't pick up hum from them. CRT monitors generate more hum than LCD monitors, but even LCDs can affect some guitars, especially those with single-coil pickups.

- Use balanced cables instead of unbalanced cables wherever possible, especially for long cable runs. (Instrument cables—such as those between a guitar or bass and your preamp—are always unbalanced.)

- If the pickup on your guitar or bass has a setting for canceling hum, use that setting. However, for many styles of music, you may opt to stay with a single-coil sound and live with the resulting noise). If so, you can temporarily turning off the display monitor, or step away from the computer until the guitar is out of hum range.

If your microphones are picking up ambient noise from the computer, reduce the amount of noise your Mac (or any external drives, which can be even noisier) is making. G5 PowerMacs are much quieter than G4 PowerMacs, so this tends to be more of an issue with G4s. Solutions range from using extension cables to move the Mac to a distance where the noise is negligible, muffling it while recording with a blanket or box (make sure it doesn't overheat), and building a ventilated cabinet with holes to run cables through (commercial audio-spec computer isolation cabinets are available, though these can cost as much as a computer).

TIP *Assuming you're using a directional mic, be sure to position your sound source so that you can face the mic away from the computer or other noisy gear. This will help reduce pickup of noise because the mic's "null point" will be pointed at the noise, while its major pickup area will be pointed away from it.*

14

Protect Your Data

Finally, a word to the wise: although audio, MIDI, and computer problems can be a hassle, all of these things can be replaced. Expensive, yes; painful, I know, but possible.

But your songs are irreplaceable, especially if you've captured some magical moments with an inspired recording or an improvised performance. It's pretty hard to re-create those later.

Back up your work—not regularly, but constantly. There are plenty of good backup applications available, including Retrospect Desktop 6.0 by Dantz and others. These applications can back up your work automatically and synchronize your backup storage with your main hard drives, so that the backup matches the most recent version of your work.

But you don't even need backup software: You can buy an inexpensive external drive and devote it to data backup; at the end of each session, copy the latest version of the file to the drive. Save the song as an "archive" so that all the loops and audio files used in the song are stored in one package file. If your system includes a CD burner, save your song to CD-ROM. A SuperDrive (or other DVD burner) is even better because it can hold projects that are larger than 700MB.

Use GarageBand's Save as Archive option (found in the File menu) to create a page file that contains all the loops used in your song, then save this file to your backup medium.

Wrapping Up

The most important thing to do when things go wrong is to stay calm and not rush to find the answer. I once reformatted a hard drive that I thought was corrupted, only to find out later (when a similar problem occurred on a drive I knew to be good) that the problem was caused by a "sharing" setting I'd made. I was anxious and annoyed, so I'd clicked the OK button and trashed about a gigabyte worth of music for nothing.

When you can't solve a problem on your own, and tech support is no help, use resources like the communities highlighted in Appendix A, magazines, and nonmusical computer books. Even if you're only using your Mac for music, remember that it's a computer, and is prone to the same computer issues as any other.

Final Word

And that's it! Hopefully, by now, you've been making music in GarageBand, sharing it with friends and fellow musicians, and have had some fun in the process. The following appendixes offer resources and a glossary. Like the rest of the material in this book, they're meant to be a starting point for your own creative exploration. Have fun!

Part V

Appendixes

Appendix A Resources

A computer-based music setup can be incredibly fun or incredibly frustrating— or, incredibly, both at once on occasion. There's so much to do and so many opportunities to learn that it can be overwhelming. Plus, your work with GarageBand can be solitary compared to other musical pursuits. When you're stuck, it's not like you can turn around and ask someone.

Now for the good news. The Internet is full of information about music, software, hardware, sounds, and production. The following list represents a few of the better sites at the time of writing.

Support

When things go wrong, the first place to turn is Apple's online support, www.apple.com/support/garageband/. There, you'll find tutorials, information about updates, information about compatible devices, downloads, and links to information about other iLife products. You can search support for specific information, or look through a list of FAQs.

Newsgroups, Forums, and Message Boards

Newsgroups and message boards are great resources because they give you the opportunity to interact with other people who are going through the same experiences as you. You can post a question and have it answered by a number of different people: You may get several different answers, but in the end, you may get a "real world" perspective from someone with the same setup as yours, who may have solved the same exact problem. That kind of info is simply not available in any manual or book. After a while, you may find yourself posting the answers.

Newsgroups are also a good place to find collaborators, gear, and information about updates, rumors, and hardware.

GarageBand-Specific Web Links

GarageBand has developed a cult following in a very short time. So, in addition to the more general music sites you'll find on the web, there are some sites that focus on GarageBand and its user community.

Apple's Official GarageBand Discussion Site

Apple runs a very lively discussion on GarageBand, which you can access online. From what I've seen of the group, a wide variety of topics are covered with candor. The advantage of the official Apple discussion is that you may just get an answer from an Apple employee. Access it at http://discussions.info.apple.com/garageband/.

Independent GarageBand-Related Sites

If the list below is any indication, GarageBand is becoming a hot topic on the Internet. The sites below (all of which were active at press time) offer tips, discussions, tutorials, links, discussions, reviews, sounds, and more.

- **Mac Jams**   www.macjams.com

- **iCompositions**   www.icompositions.com

- **MacJukeBox**   www.macjukebox.net

- **Mac Idol**   www.macidol.com

- **MacMusic**   www.macmusic.org

- **Music on the Mac**   www.musiconthemac.com

- **OSX Audio**   www.osxaudio.com

- **The Garage Door**   www.thegaragedoor.com

- **Soundtrack Lounge**   www.soundtracklounge.com

General Music and Computer Music Sites

GarageBand is just one of the many music applications available. The wider music community has a huge presence on the Net. You'll find sites that focus on computer music, sites devoted to a style or genre of music, sites that cover a specific instrument, and sites that cover all of the above.

General music sites give you information about all kinds of music and all kinds of instruments. Of these, Harmony-Central (www.harmony-central.com) is probably the most comprehensive. It features user reviews, press releases from all over the industry, discussion, and more.

There are also more specific music sites on the Net. Some of these include

A

- **Guitar.com**   www.guitar.com

- **The Synth Zone**   www.synthzone.com

- **Synthtopia**   www.synthtopia.com

- **Drum Web**   www.drumweb.com

- **Musicians.net**   www.musicians.net

- **GetSigned.com**   www.getsigned.com
- **Songwriter101**   www.songwriter101.com
- **CD Baby**   www.cdbaby.com

Mac User Sites

Mac users are a close community, and there are several sites online where you can find information on a variety of Mac topics.

- **XLR8 Your Mac**   www.xlr8yourmac.com
- **Low End Mac**   www.lowendmac.com
- **Version Tracker**   www.versiontracker.com

Music and Computer Media

Magazines—and their web sites—are a great way to stay current on GarageBand, Macs, and other computer-music topics.

- **Electronic Musician**   www.emusician.com
- **EQ**   www.eqmag.com
- **Guitar Player**   www.guitarplayer.com
- **Guitar World**   www.guitarworld.com
- **Keyboard**   www.keyboardmag.com
- **Mac Central**   www.maccentral.com
- **Mac World**   www.macworld.com
- **Mac Addict**   www.macaddict.com
- **Mix**   www.mixmagazine.com

Music Sharing Sites

One of the coolest things about making music with GarageBand is the ease with which you can share it with the world at large. There are lots of music-sharing communities and resources for musicians on the Internet. Ironically, one is called

GarageBand.com, though it's not affiliated with Apple or GarageBand software. Here are a few other music sharing sites:

- **Amazon Free Music** www.amazon.com (click Music, then Free Downloads)
- **Audio Lunchbox** www.audiolunchbox.com
- **MP3.com** www.mp3.com
- **Share Your Music** www.shareyourmusic.com

Musical Equipment

Software, hardware, mics, mixers, monitors, effects, controllers—these are tools of the modern musician's trade. The nice thing about going on a gear vendor's web site is that you may learn something that goes way beyond the price and specs of a specific piece of equipment. Many of these sites offer links, tutorials, and more. This list is far from comprehensive, but this should provide a good starting point as you look for and learn about gear.

Software

Here are some sites for sequencers and audio programs (many of these vendors also offer sounds and software instruments):

- **Ableton** www.ableton.com
- **BIAS** www.bias-inc.com
- **Digidesign** www.digidesign.com*
- **Emagic** www.Emagic.de*
- **Mark of the Unicorn** www.motu.com*
- **Propellerhead** www.Propellerhead.se
- **Steinberg** www.steinberg.net*

NOTE *Starred entries also offer audio hardware.*

A

Plug-in Effects and Software Instruments

You can find tons of plug-in effects and instruments online. Many of these sites offer downloadable demos that you can try out in GarageBand.

- **Antares**   www.antarestech.com
- **Arturia**   www.arturia.com
- **Audio Ease**   www.audioease.com
- **Cycling '74**   www.cycling74.com
- **FXpansion**   www.fxpansion.com
- **Glaresoft**   www.bitshiftaudio.com
- **GRM Tools**   www.grmtools.org
- **IK Multimedia**   www.sampletank.com
- **LinPlug**   www.linplug.com
- **Native Instruments**   www.nativeinstruments.com
- **Propellerhead**   www.propellerhead.se
- **Steinberg**   www.steinberg.com
- **TC Electronic**   www.tcelectronic.com
- **Universal Audio**   www.uaudio.com
- **Wave Arts**   www.wavearts.com
- **Waves**   www.waves.com

Audio and MIDI Interfaces

Computer music hardware can enhance your GarageBand experience and open the door to using more advanced music applications. These web sites not only give you information about some cool hardware, they're also a source for up-to-date drivers, tips for solving compatibility issues, and more.

- **Aardvark**   www.aardvarkaudio.com
- **Digidesign**   www.digidesign.com
- **Edirol**   www.edirol.com

■ **Emagic** www.emagic.de

■ **Frontier Design Group** www.frontierdesign.com

■ **Mark of the Unicorn** www.motu.com

■ **M-Audio** www.m-audio.com

■ **RME** www.rme-audio.com

■ **Steinberg** www.steinberg.net

■ **TASCAM** www.tascam.com

■ **TerraTec** www.terratec.com

Mixers, Monitors, Effects, and Mics

Your computer and its associated peripherals may be the center-point of your studio, but they're only a part of the potential music-making experience. The companies below make all the other stuff we discussed in Chapter 12, the tools and toys that can enhance your computer-studio and take you beyond it.

■ **Akai** www.akaipro.com

■ **AKG** www.akg.com

■ **Audio-Technica** www.audiotechnica.com

■ **Behringer** www.behringer.com

■ **Electro-Voice** www.electrovoice.com

■ **Event Electronics** www.event1.com

■ **JBL** www.jbl.com

■ **Korg** www.korgusa.com

■ **Lexicon** www.lexicon.com

■ **Line 6** www.line6.com

■ **Mackie** www.mackie.com

■ **Neumann** www.neumann.com

■ **Peavey** www.peavey.com

A

- **Roland**   www.rolandus.com
- **Samson**   www.samson.com
- **Sennheiser**   www.sennheiser.com
- **Shure**   www.shure.com
- **Sony**   www.sony.com
- **Soundcraft**   www.soundcraft.com
- **Tannoy**   www.tannoy.com
- **TASCAM**   www.tascam.com
- **TC Electronic**   www.tcelectronic.com
- **Yamaha**   www.yamaha.com

Sounds and Samples

You can augment your GarageBand library with sounds from third-party vendors. Files in Apple Loop format are easiest to use with GarageBand, but you'll also find collections in file formats such as Acid WAV, standard AIFF, and audio CD, and these can be converted to Apple Loops with the free Soundtrack Loop Utility.

- **Big Fish Audio**   www.bigfishaudio.com
- **Discrete Drums**   www.discretedrums.com
- **Drums on Demand**   www.drumsondemand.com
- **Power FX**   www.powerfx.com
- **Samples 4**   www.samples4.com
- **Sony Media Software**   http://mediasoftware.sonypictures.com/loop_libraries/default.asp
- **Sounds Online**   www.soundsonline.com
- **Time + Space**   www.timespace.com

Music Gear Retailers

Musical gear retailers offer instruments, amps, sounds, effects, plug-ins, controllers, and more.

- **American Music Supply**   www.americanmusical.com
- **Audio MIDI**   www.audiomidi.com
- **Guitar Center**   www.guitarcenter.com
- **Musician's Friend**   www.musiciansfriend.com
- **Sam Ash**   www.samash.com
- **Sweetwater**   www.sweetwater.com
- **zZounds**   www.zzounds.com

Computer and Computer Equipment Retailers

Talk to a computer musician who's been at it for a while, and he or she is as likely to want to talk about throughput, disc speed, and RAM as about guitar amps or vintage pianos. A program like GarageBand benefits greatly from additional RAM, a fast hard drive, fast processors, and high-speed peripherals.

- **ABT Electronics**   www.abtelectronics.com
- **Amazon**   www.amazon.com
- **The Apple Store**   http://buy.apple.com
- **Buy.com**   www.buy.com
- **CDW Computer Centers**   www.cdw.com
- **Club Mac**   www.clubmac.com
- **Comp USA**   www.compusa.com
- **Glyph Technologies**   www.glyphtech.com
- **J and R Computer World**   www.jandr.com
- **Mac Connection**   www.macconnection.com
- **Mac Mall**   www.macmall.com
- **Mac Warehouse**   www.macwarehouse.com

A

- **Mac Zone**   www.maczone.com
- **Mega Haus**   www.megahaus.com
- **Micro Center**   www.microcenter.com
- **Other World Computing**   www.macsales.com
- **Outpost**   www.outpost.com
- **Small Dog Electronics**   www.smalldog.com

Appendix B Glossary

It seems like every occupation has its own set of jargon. Audio production is no different. Here are a few key terms you'll encounter in your work with GarageBand and with audio production at large.

- ■ **A/D conversion**   Analog to digital conversion is the process by which analog audio signals are converted to digital audio data.

- ■ **Acid**   A PC audio application that allows for elastic audio. The Soundtrack Loop Utility can convert Acid files into Apple Loops.

- ■ **AIFF**   An audio file format that's compatible with GarageBand.

- ■ **Amp Simulator**   A GarageBand effect that emulates the sound of a guitar amp.

- ■ **Amplitude**   The loudness of an audio signal, illustrated by the height of the waveform.

- ■ **Analog input**   A connection for analog audio signals.

- ■ **Apple Loop**   A type of AIFF audio file that contains tempo, pitch, and performance data. GarageBand can automatically match an Apple Loop to any tempo.

- ■ **Archive**   Stores all of the elements of a GarageBand project in one package file.

- ■ **Attenuate**   Makes noises quieter by decreasing the audio level.

- ■ **Audio format**   Type of data file. Popular formats include AIFF, WAV, and MP3.

- ■ **Audio interface**   A hardware device that lets you route audio signals to and from a computer.

- ■ **Automation**   The automatic control of a mixer's functions, such as volume, pan, and others. GarageBand's automation includes the volume curves.

- ■ **Bit depth**   The number of bits used to represent a single sample in an audio file. GarageBand can work with 16- and 24-bit audio files.

- ■ **Boot drive**   A hard disk that contains the system software.

- ■ **Bounce**   To output all or part of a mix to a new audio file.

- ■ **CD burner**   A unit that can write data to CD-R and CD-RW.

■ **Click**   See Metronome.

■ **Clip**   (1) (v) To record digital audio at too high a level, causing distortion, or clipping. (2) (n) A short piece of audio.

■ **Clipping**   When the amplitude of a digital audio signal exceeds the maximum allowed recording level, it is chopped off (or clipped). Also called digital distortion.

■ **Compression**   (1) (Data) compression reduces the size of an audio file by compressing the data on recording and decompressing it on playback. The most popular compressed audio format is MP3s. (2) Audio processing that reduces a signal's dynamic range.

■ **Controller**   (1) A device used to transmit MIDI messages—for example, MIDI keyboard, guitar controller, or drum pad. (2) A message used to control the sound of a software instrument in real time. GarageBand can record and play back pitch bend, modulation, and sustain.

■ **Count-in**   See Pre-roll.

■ **CPU**   Central processing unit, the processor that runs the computer.

■ **Crop**   To eliminate a part of an audio file. Also known as *trim*.

■ **Crossfade**   An audio editing technique in which small amounts of data taken from before and after the edit point are mixed together to make the edit seem more natural.

■ **Curve**   A control that allows you to edit a continuous parameter, such as volume.

■ **Cycle**   (1) To repeat a section of a song over and over. (2) The control that activates GarageBand's cycle region.

■ **Cycle region**   A section of music in the timeline that repeats when GarageBand is in cycle mode. The Cycle region can also be used to define punch-in and -out points, and to select an area of the song for export to iTunes.

■ **DAW (Digital Audio Workstation)**   A software application that features multitrack audio recording and mixing. The term is often used to describe a digital audio sequencer.

■ **Decibel (dB)**   A unit of measure for audio level.

B

■ **Delay** See Echo.

■ **Destructive edits** Edits that change an audio file permanently.

■ **Digital audio sequencer** Software that combines multitrack digital recording, multitrack MIDI recording, mixing, and editing—for example, GarageBand.

■ **Digital input** A connection for digital audio signals.

■ **Distortion** (1) An audio effect that imparts a hard-edged "fuzz" to the sound. (2) An unpleasant sound caused by digital overload, or clipping.

■ **Driver** An application that allows software and hardware to communicate. To work with GarageBand, an audio interface must have a Core Audio driver.

■ **DSP (Digital Signal Processor)** Any device or software application that can process digital audio.

■ **Dual processor** A computer with two CPUs.

■ **Dynamics** A characteristic that pertains to the loudness of a sound.

■ **Echo** An effect that repeats a sound.

■ **Effect** See Signal processor.

■ **EQ (equalization)** A device that controls the tone of an audio signal by boosting and cutting specific frequencies.

■ **Expansion slot** The section of a computer motherboard that lets you add peripherals, such as sound cards, DSP cards, and others.

■ **Export** Output data from one application for use in another—for example, exporting a mix from GarageBand into iTunes.

■ **Fade** A gradual change in audio level.

■ **FireWire (IEEE1394)** A high-speed interface that's used for transferring data between peripherals such as disk drives, CD burners, and audio interfaces.

■ **Grid** Method for subdividing a song into time increments. GarageBand's grid follows musical time divisions, or "bars and beats."

■ **Groove Quantize** A type of quantization that uses a modified grid in which the space between notes is unequal.

■ **Hard disk recording**   Recording audio to a computer's hard drive.

■ **Host**   An application from which plug-ins can be launched.

■ **Import**   To bring an existing file into an application—for example, importing an Apple Loop into your GarageBand library.

■ **Index**   To catalog Apple Loops by keyword. Indexed files can be searched for with the Loop Browser.

■ **Input**   Any connection that allows a signal to enter an audio device.

■ **Insert**   An audio connection that lets you add a signal processor to a single channel.

■ **Inspector**   A GarageBand window that, when open, remains on top of others.

■ **Interface**   A device that routes a signal to and from the computer—audio interface; MIDI interface, for example.

■ **Latency**   The delay between input and output of a signal as it passes through the audio system.

■ **Library**   An organized collection of sounds, or patches. The GarageBand library is searchable.

■ **Limiting**   A type of dynamics processing that stops any signal from going over a user-specified threshold.

■ **Loop**   (1) (v) To repeat over and over. (2) (n) An audio file that's used as a repeating section of music (see Apple Loop).

■ **Loop Browser**   A GarageBand window that lets you search for indexed Apple Loops.

■ **Loop Utility**   Apple software that lets you tag audio files for use with GarageBand.

■ **Master track**   The track that controls the main output of GarageBand.

■ **Metronome**   A device used to provide a steady beat (sometimes called a "click") as a timing reference when playing music.

■ **MIDI**   The Musical Instrument Digital Interface is a data protocol that allows compatible devices to communicate. GarageBand uses MIDI messages to control its Software Instruments.

B

■ **MIDI Port**   A physical MIDI connection, as found on an interface, keyboard, controller, or other hardware device.

■ **Mix**   (1) (v) To combine multiple signals for final output—for example, mixing a multitrack song to a stereo master file. (2) (n) An audio file (usually stereo) that contains the combined tracks and effects from a multitrack recorder.

■ **Modeling**   Digital audio technology that uses software to imitate the behavior of a piece of physical audio hardware, such as a synthesizer or a guitar amplifier.

■ **Modulation**   (1) A type of audio effect in which the sound changes over time. (2) To change key in a section of a song. (3) MIDI control message used to change the sound of a Software Instrument.

■ **Monitor**   To listen to audio playback.

■ **Monitors**   Speakers (or headphones) used to listen to audio in a recording situation.

■ **Multitrack**   An audio device that's capable of recording and playing back more than two tracks at a time. GarageBand offers multitrack recording.

■ **Mute**   To silence an audio signal.

■ **Native**   An audio system that uses a computer's internal CPU to process audio signals.

■ **Normalization**   A digital process that increases the loudest part of an audio file to a predetermined maximum level, which results in the rest of the levels increasing proportionately.

■ **Note**   A MIDI event that triggers a sound in a Software Instrument.

■ **Output**   Path by which signal leaves one device so that it can go into another.

■ **Overdrive**   An audio effect that imitates the lightly distorted sound of a tube amplifier.

■ **Pan**   The control used to set the left-to-right positioning in the stereo field.

■ **Parallel**   A connection that takes sound from an audio channel so that it can be routed to an effects processor, and then returns it without interrupting the signal flow.

■ **Parameter**   Any element in an effect or Software Instrument that can be controlled.

■ **Partition**   A section of a hard drive.

■ **PCI slot**   The high-speed expansion slot on a computer motherboard. Often used for connecting audio interfaces.

■ **PCMCIA slot**   An expansion slot found on laptop computers that's sometimes used for adding high-speed audio peripherals.

■ **Piano Roll**   Type of MIDI editor that shows notes relative to a piano keyboard. GarageBand's Software Instrument regions are edited on a piano roll.

■ **Playhead**   A line that runs through the timeline to show current song position. It's also used to select the locations for pasting loops and splitting regions.

■ **Plug-in**   An add-on software application that enhances the capabilities of a host application. Examples include third-party effects and instruments for GarageBand.

■ **Pre-roll**   A feature that lets the music play back before a predefined point. For example, you can use a pre-roll to play back one measure before you begin recording.

■ **Preset**   A file in which an instrument or effects settings are stored.

■ **Punch in**   To record new material in a specific location on an existing track.

■ **Quantize**   To restrict MIDI notes so that they conform to a user-specified grid.

■ **QuickTime**   Apple multimedia file format.

■ **RAM**   Random Access Memory.

■ **Real Instrument track**   A GarageBand term for a track containing audio data or loops (generically, this would be referred to as an audio track).

■ **Real Media G2 (*.rm)**   Streaming video format from RealNetworks, Inc.

B

- **Realtime processing**   Signal processing that happens as the sound is playing.

- **Region**   A section of a Real or Software Instrument track that can be edited in the Timeline.

- **Render**   To write an audio file to disk.

- **Resolution**   The sample rate and bit depth of an audio file.

- **Return**   An input that brings a signal from an effect into the main mix.

- **Reverb**   A processor that creates ambience that imitates acoustical spaces.

- **ReWire**   An internal computer signal protocol that lets one audio application route its output to the other, and allows both applications to play in sync.

- **Rip**   To extract an audio file or files from an audio CD.

- **Sample**   (1) The smallest part of a digital audio recording. At a sample rate of 44.1kHz, there are 44,100 samples in one second of audio. (2) An audio recording that can be triggered by a sampler.

- **Sample rate**   The number of samples per second, expressed in Hertz.

- **Sample rate conversion**   A method for changing the sample rate of an audio file.

- **Sampler**   An electronic instrument that can "play" audio files, called samples. Typically, a sampler will use short samples of a recorded instrument and pitch them to correspond to the notes on a keyboard. Several of GarageBand's Software Instruments are sample-based.

- **Send**   A mixer control that routes signal to an output without interrupting a track's original signal. GarageBand's Echo and Reverb controls are examples of sends.

- **Sequencer**   A device that records and plays back MIDI and audio data— GarageBand, for example.

- **Signal processor**   Any device that changes the sound of an audio signal. Examples include Reverb, Delay, Compression, EQ, Modulation Effects, and others.

- **Silence**   Audio editing command that makes a selected part of an audio file completely silent.

■ **Snap**   Automatically places a region to a specific grid position.

■ **Soft synth**   See Software Instrument.

■ **Software Instrument**   A software-based synthesizer, sampler, or drum-machine.

■ **Solo**   A button that allows an audio track to play while muting all others.

■ **Split**   To separate a region into two or more pieces.

■ **Sync**   See Synchronize.

■ **Synchronize**   To configure two separate applications so that they play back together at the same tempo—for example, GarageBand and Reason play in sync via ReWire.

■ **Tag**   Metadata contained in an Apple Loop that offers information about the file's tempo, pitch, and keywords.

■ **Time stamp**   A tag that determines the absolute tempo and pitch of an audio file. GarageBand uses this information as a reference when changing these parameters.

■ **Timeline**   Part of the GarageBand window in which regions are arranged.

■ **Transpose**   To change pitch or key.

■ **Trim**   To adjust the boundaries of a region.

■ **Ultra ATA**   High-performance interface for internal hard disks.

■ **USB**   Universal Serial Bus. USB can be used to connect your computer to disk drives, CD burners, audio interfaces, MIDI interfaces, controllers, and other peripherals, such as keyboards and mice.

■ **Velocity**   MIDI message controls the loudness of a sound in a Software Instrument. It measures how hard a MIDI note is played.

■ **Volume**   (1) The loudness of an audio signal. (2) A section or partition on a hard drive.

■ **Waveform**   A visual display of an audio file.

■ **Waveform editor**   Software that can record, process, edit, and rewrite audio files—for example, BIAS Peak.

■ **Zero crossing**   The point at which an audio waveform crosses 0 dB.

B

Index

References to figures and illustrations are in italics.